Mao

# PROFILES IN **POWER**

*General Editor: Keith Robbins*

# Mao

## Shaun Breslin

Longman

An imprint of **Pearson Education**

Harlow, England · London · New York · Reading, Massachusetts · San Francisco
Toronto · Don Mills, Ontario · Sydney · Tokyo · Singapore · Hong Kong · Seoul
Taipei · Cape Town · Madrid · Mexico City · Amsterdam · Munich · Paris · Milan

**Pearson Education Limited**
Edinburgh Gate
Harlow
Essex CM20 2JE
England

and Associated Companies around the world

*Visit us on the World Wide Web at:*
*www.pearsoneduc.com*

First published 1998

ISBN 0 582 43748 2

*British Library Cataloguing-in-Publication Data*
A catalogue record for this book can be obtained from the British Library

*Library of Congress Cataloging-in-Publication Data*
A catalog record for this book can be obtained from the Library of
Congress

10 9 8 7 6 5 4 3 2
04 03 02

Produced by Pearson Education Asia Pte Ltd.,
Printed in Singapore

For Sarah, Patrick and Hannah

# CONTENTS

# LIST OF MAPS

# PREFACE

This book represents the culmination of ten years of lecturing on Chinese politics at the University of Newcastle upon Tyne. When I first started at Newcastle, I was fortunate to receive invaluable support and advice from Prof. David Goodman. This included copying David's lecture notes, which became the basis for my own lectures for a couple of years. As courses changed and evolved over the years, so my lectures changed. However, much of my understanding and knowledge of Chinese politics stems from David's teaching, and anybody who is acquainted with David's work will recognise his influence in this book.

While the majority of this book was written while I was at Newcastle, I completed it after I moved to Warwick to take up a research position in the Centre for the Study of Globalisation and Regionalisation. The Centre was established and supported by a grant from the Economic and Social Research Council, and I would like to thank the ESRC for their financial support. I would also like to thank Keith Robbins and Andrew MacLennan for their incredible patience while they waited for me to complete this book.

Finally, I would like to thank the students in the Department of Politics at Newcastle whom I taught between 1987 and 1997. Although they did not realise it, their comments, questions and discussions over the years went a long way to shaping the structure and content of this book.

# NOTE ON TRANSLITERATION

There are three systems of transliterating Chinese into English. For example, the city of 'Canton' (under the early system devised by the postal service) is written as Guandong using the *pinyin* system, and as Kuang-tung using the *wade–giles* system. Most books written before the 1980s, and works published in Taiwan, use a mixture of the *wade–giles* and postal service systems. This book primarily uses the *pinyin* system, which is now in common usage in China itself, and is the usual method of transliteration in recent work on China. However, in a few cases, the *pinyin* version of some names will not be familiar to non-Chinese readers. As such, the nationalist leaders Sun Yatsen and Chiang Kai-shek are referred to using the old styles of transliteration, rather than the less common Sun Zhongshan and Jiang Jieshi. To aid cross-referencing, the *wade–giles* spelling of place and personal names is provided in the glossary.

# INTRODUCTION

In December 1935 Mao Zedong's communist forces were in a very vulnerable position. They had spent the last year in an epic flight from the forces of the Guomindang leader, Chiang Kai-shek.[1] They had travelled for 368 days through 11 provinces, covering a total of roughly 12,500 kilometres. They had broken through four entrenched ranks of nationalist troops (losing half of their men in the process), crossed 18 mountain ranges and 24 major rivers. Of those men under Mao's control, only one in 20 of those who started the march made it through to the end.

Having first established a base in Wayabao in northern Shaanxi province, they moved to nearby Yanan in September 1936. This was one of the most desolate and barren areas of all China, and scraping a living from the land here was difficult at the best of times. With the influx of communists from the Long March stretching local resources to breaking point, this was far from the best of times. And with nationalist and warlord armies closing in on Mao and his men, then the future looked far from rosy.

Yet just 13 years and one month after moving into Yanan, Mao Zedong stood above Tiananmen Square in Beijing and announced the establishment of a new People's Republic of China (PRC). The party had gone from the verge of extinction in the winter of 1936 to national government in the autumn of 1949. It had defeated the nationalist Guomindang army that was vastly superior in terms of manpower, finances, military hardware, and supplies. It had also resisted the ferocity of the Japanese invasion between 1937 and 1945. And the victory had been largely achieved without significant support from external powers.[2]

1

From the jaws of defeat, the communists had fashioned an astonishing victory that ranks as one of the most dramatic stories in twentieth-century world history – a victory that owed much to the revolutionary skills of Mao Zedong. To be sure, he was not the only revolutionary leader – Zhu De, for example, stood alongside Mao during the revolution, having led his own group of men on the Long March. Other leaders like Peng Dehuai and Lin Biao were more directly involved in the conflict, leading troops on the ground while Mao concentrated on strategy from his base in Yanan. Nor should we just explain the revolution in terms of the genius of Mao. Lloyd Eastman, for example, points to the corruption and ineptitude of the Guomindang leadership.[3] Chalmers Johnson suggests that the Japanese invasion saved the communists – were it not for the new alliance to resist Japan in 1936, then Mao and the communists might have been finished off in Yanan.[4] While it is true that the inefficiencies of the Guomindang and the timing of the Japanese invasion clearly aided the Chinese Communist Party (CCP), it still needed to take political advantage of these opportunities. As the main strategist and party leader, the revolution was, more than anybody else's, Mao's revolution.

Certainly, the Chinese people were left in no doubt as to who was the main architect of the revolution and their saviour. Although other men took charge of key areas of government policy (for example, Premier Zhou Enlai's foreign policy initiatives), the CCP leadership promoted the vision of Mao as the 'Great Helmsman' – the man who was steering China through uncharted revolutionary waters towards a great future. For years, Mao's face, calligraphy, writings and image were everywhere in China. Statues of the great leader in various poses dominated numerous squares in schools and colleges, factories and city squares. His speeches were reproduced in newspapers and special collections to provide enlightenment for the people. Even Mao's less than wonderful poems were reproduced for the masses to devour, complete with a pasted-in monochrome plate of a seated Mao benignly surveying the countryside, and a fold-out facsimile of one of Mao's poems in his own calligraphy.[5]

During the Cultural Revolution, Mao was raised to almost godlike status. His image became ubiquitous, and the ability to recite his words, enshrined in the famous 'little red book', became a test of political correctness. Even the most mundane of conversations were prefaced by a eulogy to Mao – 'Long

Live Chairman Mao! Rice again for tea?'. At the end of the day, individuals were expected to enter into a ritual confession to the Chairman, informing him of their devotion to the revolution, and admitting to personal failings.

Some of the icons to Mao remain in place today. Mao himself is on display to the public in the 'Maosoleum' in the centre of Tiananmen Square. It is fitting that Mao should be at rest so close to the heart of many of his triumphs: the square where he proclaimed the establishment of the People's Republic on 1 October 1949; the site of the mass demonstrations in support of the Cultural Revolution; overlooked by the Great Hall of the People, the impressive government building constructed in only a few months during the heady days of the Great Leap Forward; and only a stone's throw from the party headquarters in Zhongnanhai. It is said that the 'Maosoleum' was constructed to withstand a nuclear strike, presumably so that the Chinese people could derive inspiration to continue the fight when they emerged from the labyrinthine nuclear bunker under Beijing. Although many Chinese still dutifully file into the hall to pay their respects, few would now gain much inspiration from Mao.

Although there is respect for Mao's revolutionary activities and for all that he did to bring the CCP to power, what he did with that power has left his image much tainted, and is the main focus of this book. For Mao, the seizure of power in 1949 was not the culmination of the revolution, but the start of a new phase. More important, there was no time to stabilise the new political system before pushing on with his revolutionary goals. Having aroused the revolutionary enthusiasm of the masses, it was important to use it before they reverted to a life of stability and certainty. It might be a very different stability and certainty than had existed before the revolution, but stability and certainty of any sort were the antidote to revolution. What was the point in struggling for so long if old power relationships were simply replaced by new ones (or indeed, if old ones were allowed to reappear)? In particular, what was the point in fighting to overthrow rule by the landlords and the Guomindang if the new communist leadership simply allowed itself to become a new ruling class or elite that placed their own interests above those of the masses? For Mao, the emergence of a new party class and the potential re-emergence of old classes in the countryside were inevitable if revolutionary zeal was sacrificed for the sake of consolidation and stability.

Mao looked to the Soviet Union and he saw what would happen in China if it chose to follow Moscow's revolutionary path. He saw a party that had abandoned the revolution in a search for stability; a party which had striven for economic gains irrespective of the impact on the masses and the long-term potential to establish a truly classless communist state. He saw a ruling party that had become isolated from the masses – the people on whose behalf it was meant to rule – and had become a complacent and self-serving ruling elite. For Mao, then, the Soviet model of development was a model of what not to do with the Chinese revolution. In order to make sure that the revolution was not wasted, Mao had to convince the people to follow him. As many in the CCP leadership were keen to learn from and follow the Soviet model, he also had to convince his colleagues that his way was best. If he couldn't convince them, then he would have to use other means.

Mao's revolutionary goals and his determination to implement them despite the scepticism of his colleagues left no area of Chinese society untouched or unscathed. For example, his desire to push ahead with revolution in the countryside meant that in just nine years, some rural families witnessed land reform and the elimination of landlords; the establishment of mutual aid teams; the creation of co-operatives; the move from co-operatives to collectives; and the move from collectives to communes. The last of these, the development of large rural communes during the Great Leap Forward, subsequently collapsed with the deaths of millions (30 million?) of Chinese from starvation (see Chapter 3). But Mao was now so convinced, or perhaps deluded, that he was right, that even mass starvation couldn't dent his confidence. From the ashes of the Great Leap he developed new, more radical initiatives which ultimately led to the chaos and terror of the Cultural Revolution (see Chapter 5).

For intellectuals, too, the Mao years were a period of great uncertainty and fear. After being asked to pass comment on the first seven years of communist control during the Hundred Flowers Movement, many subsequently found that their criticisms had gone too far, and faced the wrath of Mao and the party (see Chapter 3). During the Cultural Revolution, millions of intellectuals faced ritual public humiliation in front of mass rallies, and the destruction of their property and possessions. The number that died, either at their own hand or through the excesses of the Red Guards, can only be guessed at.

On the international front, Mao's impact was less obvious, but crucial nonetheless (see Chapter 6). Mao was never really at home with the business of diplomacy. He only ever left China twice (to visit Moscow) and much of the visible nature of China's foreign relations was left in the capable hands of Zhou Enlai. Zhou cultivated an image of a suave diplomat, talking to foreign leaders in a manner and language that they understood and expected. But behind the scenes, Mao's role in defining China's international relations should not be underestimated. The evidence suggests that Mao did play a pivotal role in deciding to enter the Korean War, and in the decision not to play a more active role in the Vietnamese War. But it is inconceivable that China would have broken ties with the Soviet Union, or forged a closer relation with America, or normalised relations with Japan without the Chairman's approval.

The role of Zhou Enlai as the figurehead of China's diplomatic relations demonstrates an important facet of Mao's rule. Although he was the most important of China's leaders, he was not the sole leader. It would be a fundamental mistake to view China from 1949 to 1976 as being under the sole rule of Mao Zedong. First, it is easy, but wrong, to fall into the trap of ascribing everything that happened to Mao's actions. For example, in the ideological sphere Mao was surrounded by 'thought minders' such as Chen Boda who helped formulate many of his ideas into coherent thought. Thus, what we refer to as 'Maoism' is often the product of more than one mind. Second, during certain periods from 1949 to 1976, Mao reigned without actually ruling. He took something of a hands-off approach and let others in the party leadership get on with running specific areas: Zhou Enlai in international relations, Li Xiannian and Bo Yibo in economic planning, Deng Xiaoping and Liu Shaoqi in party and state organisation and so on.

Third, Mao's power and influence did not remain static throughout the years. It waxed and waned in response to the efficacy of his policy preferences and those being pushed by colleagues in the party-state elites. For example, after the collapse of the Great Leap Forward, Mao took something of a back seat, whilst the policies of Chen Yun, Deng Xiaoping and Liu Shaoqi pulled China out of disaster. It was this political impotence that forced Mao into taking the radical step of launching the Cultural Revolution. The fact that he needed to initiate such an attack on the party-state administrative machinery displays his relative political weakness at the time. The fact that he managed to unleash the revolution also displays his immense latent power.

The Cultural Revolution was just one of a number of Mao's struggles with colleagues in the party. Indeed, perhaps the key to understanding Mao's impact on Chinese history is to analyse his conflicts with colleagues within the party. Almost from the foundation of the CCP in 1921, the party was split by disputes over tactics, policies and ideological interpretations, and Mao was at the centre of many of these disputes. The list of men who crossed Mao and fell from grace is an impressive array of communist leaders. In the 1920s and 1930s Mao fell out with Qu Qiubai, Chen Duxiu, Wang Ming, Li Lisan and Luo Zhanglong over the best ways forward for the Chinese revolution. Whilst Mao began to realise that the peasantry could provide the key to revolution in China, his colleagues insisted that the revolution lay in the hands of workers, much as it had in the Soviet Union.

On the Long March, Mao fell out with Zhang Guotao, who wanted to head off to the north-west to gain support from the Soviet Union, whereas Mao took his troops north to Shaanxi.[6] After 1949, Mao played a crucial role in the purge of Gao Gang and Rao Shushi; of Peng Dehuai, the then Minister of Defence, in 1959; of Liu Shaoqi, Deng Xiaoping, and countless others during the radicalism of the Cultural Revolution; and of his two former followers, Chen Boda and Lin Biao, in 1970 and 1971 respectively.

Although the sheer number of men that Mao played a leading role in purging is remarkable enough in itself, perhaps more remarkable still is the number of those purged leaders who had been closely associated with Mao. Of the men who crossed Mao before 1949, Mao admitted that Chen Duxiu had had a profound impact on his own development as a Marxist. According to Mao himself, Luo Zhanglong had only joined the party in response to an advert placed by Mao in Changsha.[7]

Of the men purged after 1949, the links with Mao were even stronger. Gao Gang had achieved the accolade of being named as Mao's close comrade in arms shortly before his dismissal. Peng Dehuai had worked closely with Mao from 1928, acting as one of the Red Army's key military strategists. Liu Shaoqi was Mao's first chosen successor and charged with many of the key functions of party-state leadership after 1949. Deng Xiaoping's rapid promotion through the CCP ranks was largely due to Mao's patronage, and he was highly thought of by the Chairman. Yet he was named as the number two person in authority taking the capitalist road in the Cultural Revolution, and, having been restored to power in 1973, was purged for a second time in the spring of 1976. Chen Boda was a faithful servant to Mao, and is even thought to have penned some of the works ascribed to Mao. Chen played an important role in initiating the Cultural Revolution, but was to become one of its victims. Lin Biao was Mao's representative in the PLA after taking over the Ministry of Defence from Peng Dehuai in 1959. He turned the military into a school for Mao's thought, producing the *Little Red Book* to disseminate Mao's ideas. Lin became Mao's 'closest comrade at arms' and chosen successor, but he too was to fall foul of the Chairman.

What explains the lengths to which Mao was prepared to go to purge people who, at least at times, appeared to be loyal followers? Mao and his followers always referred to the struggles as between two lines within the party. The purged men were following or pushing lines that at best were erroneous, at worst deliberately turning China towards capitalist restoration. Liu Shaoqi was accused of planning to turn China towards capitalism from the 1930s, and of having collaborated with America to usurp the revolution. This is a bizarre accusation against a man who for much of the time between 1947 and 1956 ardently supported Mao and worked hard to turn the Chairman's wishes into policies. The outlandish nature of these claims is explained by the need to justify in ideological terms the extent of the punishment meted out. By identifying them as counter-revolutionaries, the conflict between them and Mao became an 'antagonistic' contradiction – if these men were not defeated, then they would defeat the true and correct revolutionary path of Mao Zedong.

The analysis that follows in this book places a strong emphasis on the importance of Mao's ideas and ideological convictions in explaining the course of Chinese politics from 1949 to his death in 1976. Some would argue that this approach is misconceived, that Mao was simply motivated by a search for power and that he hid behind a smokescreen of ideological purity.[8] Whilst we should not ignore Mao's power considerations, we should also be wary of creating a false polarisation of contributory factors. Mao's desire to push ahead with his ideological programme and his desire for power went hand in hand. Put another way, without power, it would have been impossible for Mao to push through his policies – policies that he was convinced were the only 'correct' path to communism in China.

Mao was convinced that his ideas were the only way forward. In particular, he detested those who looked to the experience of the Soviet Union as a guide for the Chinese revolution. While the writings of Marx and Engels did have relevance for the Chinese revolution, they had to be adapted to fit the specific circumstances of China. There was no point in dogmatically adhering to a revolutionary doctrine that was built around an analysis of Europe in the nineteenth century. Nor was there any point in copying what Lenin and later Stalin had done in the Soviet Union. Just as they had adapted the basic ideas of Marxism to fit their own national circumstances, so Chinese communists should look to their own national circumstances. Marxism, in its abstract form, provided a guide to action, but the specific action itself must be based on Chinese conditions. As such, it is difficult to separate out Mao's ideological conflicts with his colleagues from foreign-policy conflicts. As those who disagreed with Mao over ideology to greater or lesser extents usually also favoured learning from the Soviet Union, the two issues became inextricably entwined.

This supreme self-confidence was at least in part a consequence of Mao's early successes. For example, before 1949 Mao was convinced that the peasantry could and should become the focus for the party's revolutionary activity. He saw no sense in relying solely on the urban workers to build a revolution when those urban workers constituted just 1 per cent of the population. The rural masses were dissatisfied and had a latent revolutionary potential that could be awoken with the correct action from the party. Despite the fact that almost all of the party's senior figures rejected Mao's strategy, he persevered and was eventually proved right.

From around 1935 to 1949, everything that Mao did, often in direct conflict with what Moscow wanted him to do, turned to gold. Yet once in power, other CCP leaders turned away from Mao's plans for the post-revolutionary state and looked elsewhere for their models. To make matters worse, Mao was aware of the political consequences of mortality. In the Soviet Union, Stalin's successor, Nikita Khrushchev, had been quick to denounce his predecessor, and to overturn many of his policies. Indeed, in some respects, the power struggles that Mao waged after 1949 were part of a pre-mortal succession crisis. It was not just a matter of getting his ideas in place, but ensuring that his opponents wouldn't be in a position to overturn them after his death. At the onset of the Cultural Revolution in 1966, Mao was 73 years old and suffering from ill health. His ideas and ideals had been largely ignored over the preceding five years as Liu Shaoqi, Deng Xiaoping and others tried to rebuild the economy that had been devastated by Mao's radical experiments during the Great Leap Forward. If he was going to return China to its correct revolutionary path – his revolutionary path – then he simply could not wait too long. If he was going to ensure that this correct revolutionary path would not be overturned, then he had to get rid of its (his) opponents once and for all.

Although Mao was a very powerful individual, even the most powerful autocratic dictator depends on the support of others to rule. In Mao's case, particularly after 1959, he was not in the kind of dominant position that Stalin held in the Soviet Union. In order to push through some of his policies, he had to build up alliances with other groups. For example, having failed to convince his colleagues in the central leadership to support his development plans in 1956, he built a new alliance with provincial leaders to ensure that he got his way. Similarly, when the party organisation seemed to be turning its collective back on Mao in the 1960s, he turned to the army under the leadership of Lin Biao as an alternative power base. And when he needed, or felt he needed, to overthrow those leaders who were taking the capitalist road, he exploited his reputation with China's young people to launch the Cultural Revolution.

Whilst Mao's tactical alliances did indeed allow him to relaunch his policies and strategies on more than one occasion, support was rarely given unconditionally. In particular, he was forced into adapting his policies when his allies thought that he had gone too far. For example, when the Cultural Revolution collapsed into chaos, the military units that restored order with the creation of revolutionary committees were extremely wary of the excesses of the Red Guards. Their desire to restore order helped force Mao to moderate his policies and shift his interpretation of radicalism.

Zhou Enlai's role is of particular note. Zhou had initially sided with forces that opposed Mao at the start of the Long March, but switched his loyalties at the historic Zunyi Conference. He was subsequently an important player in all the political twists and turns after 1949, surviving the numerous campaigns and purges unscathed. When Zhou died in 1976, a massive popular wave of sympathy swept China. Although the shock at the death of Mao later in the year was profound, Zhou was clearly highly respected by the Chinese people, and the emotion provoked by his death was essentially one of grief and respect rather than the more sombre mood after Mao's death.

Zhou was remembered as the man who had tempered many of Mao's excesses. In particular, he was credited with ensuring that Mao's supporters were kept in check in the 1970s. For example, his opposition to the growing power of Mao's one-time chosen successor, Lin Biao, was seen as an important factor in Lin losing Mao's approval in 1971. Similarly, Zhou's respect for the work of Deng Xiaoping and his desire to counterbalance the power of the hard left resulted in Deng's return to power in 1973.[9] Perhaps the question that remained unasked was if Zhou could exert such influence on Mao after the Cultural Revolution, could he have done more to prevent it, or at least moderate it, in the first place? Whilst the answer to this question probably went to the grave with Zhou and Mao in 1976, Mao relied heavily on Zhou's support within the central power framework from the Zunyi Conference onwards, and it is difficult to see how Mao could have initiated the Cultural Revolution had Zhou stood in his way.

What we see in Mao is a man who would use the formal structure of power to get his way if that worked, but who would use other means of control if the need arose. Wherever possible he would push through his own ideas, but he was aware of the need to compromise and adapt if that was what the situation demanded. He was willing to delegate control to others as long as they followed his commands, but would sacrifice even the closest of followers if they deviated from his line. He wanted to ensure that his ideas would live on beyond his death, but would purge his heirs apparent if they threatened his position or deviated from the truth. Ironically, in his commitment to ensuring that his ideas were dominant in Chinese politics, he all but ensured that they would be abandoned after his death.

. . .

## NOTES

1. The Guomindang is the name of the nationalist party which ruled China from 1927. After their defeat at the hands of the communists, the Guomindang escaped to Taiwan, where they remain in power to this day.
2. Whilst the Soviet Union did play a role in the civil war, it remained committed to restoring the nationalists to power, and maintained diplomatic links with the Guomindang until 1949.
3. Eastman, L. (1984) *Seeds of Destruction: Nationalist China in War and Revolution 1937–1949* (Stanford: Stanford University Press).
4. Johnson, C. (1962) *Peasant Nationalism and Communist Power: The Emergence of Revolutionary China, 1937–1945* (Stanford: Stanford University Press).
5. Mao Tsetung (1976) *Poems* (Beijing: Foreign Languages Press).
6. Zhang's later collaboration with the Guomindang during the war against Japan led Mao to denounce him as attempting to betray the party.
7. Although this claim has been rejected by others. Snow, E. (1937) *Red Star Over China* (Gollancz: London).
8. See, for example, Simon Leys's explanation of the causes of the Cultural Revolution in Leys, S. (1977) *The Chairman's New Clothes: Mao and the Cultural Revolution* (London: Allison and Busby).
9. And Deng's own popularity after 1976 owed much to his previous relationship with Zhou.

# Chapter 1

# FROM PEASANT TO POWER

. . .

## THE MAKING OF THE REVOLUTIONARY

Mao Zedong was born in Shaoshan in Hunan province on 26 December 1893. In later life, Mao was to make much of his peasant background – he came from the peasantry and instinctively knew what the Chinese masses felt. In reality, however, Mao had a rather privileged and atypical upbringing (at least in the context of the day). For example, alongside his two younger brothers and his adopted sister, his mother brought him up in a Buddhist environment.[1] Furthermore, while his father had once been a peasant (albeit a relatively wealthy one), by the time Mao Zedong was born he had developed a prosperous business as a grain merchant. In short, as Hollingworth notes, he was born into a family that in many ways represented the antithesis of everything that the atheist egalitarian Mao was later to believe in.[2]

Hollingworth's portrayal of Mao's early life paints a picture of a man who was a natural born rebel. He ran away from home at the age of ten to escape the beatings that were part and parcel of family discipline; he refused to accept the betrothal that his father had arranged to a local girl in what was essentially a business deal to gain more labour for the Mao family's land; and he preferred to spend his school holidays travelling around the countryside of Hunan staying with peasant families rather than returning home to his secure middle-class family.

Although these early acts of defiance were very personal actions against his family, they nevertheless were political actions – albeit unintentional political actions. By rebelling against his family, Mao was rejecting the basic principles of the Confucian social order which had not only dominated China for thousands of years, but which also underpinned the political order.

Confucianism placed a heavy emphasis on understanding your position in the social hierarchy, and conducting yourself accordingly in the 'correct' manner towards people of different social status. For example, within the family, women were considered inferior to men and younger males inferior to older males.[3] Each person's position within this hierarchy of worth in the family carried with it specific duties and responsibilities, both to other individuals within the family and to the family itself. Thus, had Mao been a good Confucian son, he would have accepted his father's authority with a sense of filial piety. His father was older and wiser; for example, by arranging a marriage for his son, he was acting out of consideration for the greater good of the family that Mao too should have accepted with equanimity. But whilst Mao's acts of personal rebellion would have been extraordinarily radical in earlier times, they were not quite so extraordinary in the context of turn of the century China.

*got some social capital?*

. . .

## CHINA AT THE TIME OF MAO'S CHILDHOOD: A REVOLUTIONARY ENVIRONMENT

The Chinese imperial system can be traced as far back as the establishment of the Xia dynasty in c.2205 BC.[4] Perhaps more meaningfully, when Qin Shi Huangdi unified China in 221 BC, he set in place a political structure which survived more or less intact until 1911. By the time of Mao's birth, however, the strains and pressures that were eventually to lead to its demise were already clearly evident. Population growth and urbanisation had begun to alter the social fabric of China in the late eighteenth century, but the watershed for the imperial system came in 1839 in the form of military conflict with Britain.

When King George III sent an embassy to China to negotiate a new trade relationship in 1793, the Emperor Qian Long responded that: 'The Celestial Empire possesses all things in prolific abundance, and lacks no product within its borders. There is therefore no need to import the manufactures of outside barbarians in exchange for our own products.' The Emperor's words here are an expression of the sinocentric world-view that dominated the imperial system. China was seen as the centre of civilisation – indeed, the Chinese word for China is *zhongguo* or 'central kingdom'.[5] Those states which accepted Chinese supremacy – most clearly Korea, but to different extents the Japanese and the people of what became Vietnam – were considered to be part of the 'sinitic' world, and therefore worth dealing with. Those who rejected these ideas were simply barbarians who had nothing whatsoever to teach China, and were not worth dealing with unless they too accepted the sinocentric view.

Despite the official response, the British were undeterred in their commitment to gaining access to Chinese silk, tea and spices. The solution was opium. Grown in northern India and exported to China under the auspices of the British East India Company, the opium was distributed around southern China with the help of enterprising local officials. And even though the Chinese authorities declared opium contraband in 1800, and banned its smoking outright in 1821, the trade flourished. In the century from 1736, opium imports into China increased a thousandfold, and on the eve of the war with Britain in 1838, opium accounted for over half of all imports into China (and doubled again between 1838 and 1853).

War between Britain and China broke out in 1839 when the Chinese authorities seized and burnt opium being stored in warehouses in Canton. Having revoked the British East India Company's monopoly on exporting opium to China, the British sent a fleet to China in the name of defending 'free trade'. Faced with this vastly superior fleet – in terms of the boats themselves and the armaments and fire-power that they carried – the Chinese authorities agreed to sign a treaty accepting the British demands; but then vacillated and simply waited for the British to return home. When the gun-boats returned, the Chinese finally ratified the Treaty of Nanjing, which now included extra protocols granting even greater concessions to the British.

Defeat in the Opium Wars[6] had profound and far-reaching consequences for China. On one level, China's national pride was severely wounded, not only by losing to the barbarians, but also by being forced to cede Chinese territory to Britain in the shape of Kowloon and Hong Kong. Furthermore, the British were granted rights to trade in China's coastal cities and also granted extra-territorial rights, which made British citizens immune from Chinese law. While the psychological impact of the Opium Wars might be difficult to calculate, the massive indemnity the Chinese were forced to pay to cover Britain's expenses in the war provided a more concrete legacy.

Once the British had established the weakness of China's military (particularly naval) defences, many other states followed the example. Of all the military humiliations in the second half of the nineteenth century, the most humiliating of all was China's defeat at the hands of Japan in Korea. Not only did China lose her traditional influence over the Korean peninsula, but also lost to a nation that she traditionally perceived to be a vassal state. With each defeat, more and more territory was opened to the western powers, and more and more treaties forced the Chinese to pay out indemnities to them. In financial terms, the final straw came when the Boxer rebels began a campaign of terror against westerners in China. Western powers allied to invade Beijing and put down the rebellion, and the subsequent 1901 Boxer Protocol imposed an indemnity of US$334 million (with a 4 per cent interest rate) which all but bankrupted the Chinese state.

The imperial system responded to each new indemnity by increasing the tax burden on the peasantry. Unable to meet the state's fiscal demands, many peasants turned to money-lenders to fill the gap. Interest rates were exorbitant: money lent in the spring had to be repaid with a 100 per cent interest rate in the autumn. Slowly, but surely, the already fragile existence of many peasants was eroded.

These pressures resulted in a number of rebellions against imperial rule in the period preceding Mao's birth.[7] The largest and most important of these, the Taiping Rebellion of 1851–64,[8] defeated imperial armies across the southern half of China, and even established a new rival national government in Nanjing before collapsing through a combination of internal divisions and renewed imperial attacks.[9]

Faced with these external and internal challenges to its authority, the imperial system twice tried to reform itself in the second half of the nineteenth century. But rather than strengthening the imperial system, both attempts at reform did much to hasten imperial decline. The first attempt at reform, the Tongzhi Restoration[10] in the 1860s, was built on the concept of *ziqiang* or self-strengthening. There was no notion here that the imperial system needed fundamentally to re-assess its underlying principles and practices, but just that it needed to change some specific policies in order to ward off the immediate threats and challenges, and return to the golden days of the past. Thus, a new foreign office was established in order to deal with the western powers, with the hope of dealing with any future conflict between China and western powers in keeping with western diplomatic procedures, and thus reduce the possibility of military conflict. China's military forces were also developed to deal more effectively with both external military challenges and internal rebels like the Taipings.

In many ways, the Tongzhi Restoration missed the point entirely. As Mary Wright put it in her excellent interpretation of nineteenth-century China: 'What was required was not merely a restoration at the eleventh hour of effective government along traditional lines but the creation of new policies that could ward off modern domestic and foreign threats'.[11] The irony here is that although from the vantage point of history we can assess the reforms as being far too conservative, for many within China itself at the time, the reforms were too radical. Many within the imperial system itself feared that any change would undermine their own position and status, and the Tongzhi Restoration eventually simply petered out in the face of obstruction from sceptics both in the imperial court itself and throughout the imperial bureaucracy across the country.

The Tongzhi Restoration nevertheless had three important consequences for imperial rule. First, military modernisation entailed the devolution of considerable operational autonomy to the military leaders in the regions. Military leaders like Yuan Shikai, who headed the Northern or *Beiyang* Army, became important power-brokers, and continued imperial rule eventually became contingent on their support. Second, for some of the younger generation within the Chinese imperial bureaucracy, the failure of the Tongzhi reforms to bring about real change was a great disappointment. If the entrenched conservatism of the imperial bureaucracy would not accept even these limited changes, then perhaps the imperial bureaucracy itself would have to be reformed by compulsion if China was to survive.

Third, the Tongzhi reforms introduced an element of western learning to improve Chinese understanding of the attitudes and actions of the western powers. Whilst access to western learning was strictly limited, it did give some younger educated Chinese their first experience of western history and ideas. For those who were disillusioned with the imperial system and its inability to accept limited reform, western history provided both positive and negative examples of what happened to entrenched political systems that refused to change.

For Kang Youwei, a young scholar who had progressed with flying colours through the Confucian examination system into the imperial bureaucracy, the negative example came from the partition of Poland by the great powers – a situation that he saw had much in common with the way in which the contemporary powers were dealing with China. If China (and not just the imperial system) was to survive, then it must learn from the reforms of Peter the Great in Russia, or even of the Meiji Reformers in Japan, and undertake a root and branch modernisation of the Chinese political and social structure.

Kang's constant petitions to the Emperor to learn the lessons of history eventually bore fruit, and in 1898 Kang Youwei and another young reformer, Liang Qichao, instituted a number of radical reforms aimed at rapidly modernising China. The Confucian examination system was to be abandoned, and western learning was to become dominant at all levels; radical bureaucratic reform would be introduced to support new 'western' style economic development; and freedom and liberalism would become the new basis of politics and society. Not surprisingly, these reforms provoked intense anger from all those who stood to lose from the changes – which included virtually everybody within the imperial court and the imperial bureaucracy. Crucially, the military forces of Yuan Shikai, brought to Beijing to force through the reforms in the face of this opposition, abandoned the Emperor and sided instead with the conservatives under the leadership of the Empress Dowager, Cixi. Although Kang and Liang escaped from Beijing, the Emperor himself was arrested and after a Hundred Days of Reform the old imperial system was restored – but without a real Emperor at its head.

The failure of the Hundred Days of Reform marked the last real attempt to reform the imperial system from within. For those who believed that China had to change to survive, any chance of reforming the existing structure seemed much less likely than overthrowing the basic structure itself. This was particularly true of those young men who had been sent to Japan to study and learn how the Japanese themselves had responded (much more successfully) to the arrival of the west, and to gain a second-hand understanding of western ideas.[12] Rather than becoming the saviours of the empire, many of these students instead took the lead in looking to the non-Chinese world for solutions to China's ills. Indeed, it was Chinese students in Japan who established the Chinese Revolutionary Alliance in 1905 under the leadership of Sun Yatsen – the first national political organisation committed to overthrowing the empire. As these students sent books and texts back to their friends in China, and then returned to take up positions within the imperial bureaucracies and armies, a revolutionary movement began to take shape within China.

Imperial rule continued until 1912, but with the imperial court consumed by its own factional in-fighting, the political vacuum in Beijing all but necessitated local leaders taking more and more power onto themselves. When they lobbied for a greater say in national politics with the creation of a new national assembly, they were frustrated by proposals that would have packed the assembly with the kinsmen of the courtesans, essentially maintaining a veto for the central imperial court.

These frustrations came to a head in October 1911 when troops in Wuhan in central China rebelled, fearing that an investigation into an accidental bomb explosion would reveal the extent of support for the Revolutionary Alliance within their ranks. Wuhan fell in just three days, and its declaration of independence from the empire was swiftly followed by similar declarations from other provinces as the revolution proceeded more by provincial decrees than by violence. The final straw for the empire came when Yuan Shikai took his troops south to defeat the rebels in Wuhan. Rather than engaging in conflict, Yuan engaged in discussions, and having secured the promise that he would become President of the new republic, the military joined the revolution and the empire's fate was sealed.

On 12 February 1912 the last Emperor, Puyi, formally abdicated, but rather than marking the end of uncertainty and turmoil in Chinese government, it merely marked the start of a new period of uncertainty. The Revolutionary Alliance reformed itself as the Nationalist Party – the Guomindang – to fight China's first (and to date only) national parliamentary elections. Although they won the vote, the new President Yuan Shikai simply declared the elections invalid and attempted to reconstitute power around himself. Indeed, in November 1915 Yuan went as far as restoring the empire and, unsurprisingly, choosing himself as the new Emperor. By this stage, however, the new regime had lost the support of those same local leaders who had brought it into existence, and by the time that Yuan died in June 1916 China had no effective national leadership as different groups claimed national leadership from different power centres (the Guomindang in Canton, the residual supporters of Yuan Shikai in Tianjin, and Li Yuanhong as Republican President in Nanjing).

.   .   .

## MAO'S EARLY POLITICAL INFLUENCES AND ACTIONS

Mao's early acts of defiance against his family are more understandable when viewed in light of this political environment. He was born into an environment in which all the old certainties were being questioned, and increasingly being rejected. It was a time when all Chinese were being forced to think about the basic principles that had underpinned the Chinese state and society for centuries, and Mao was far from alone in thinking that things had to change, and change radically.

But like many of his generation, Mao did not reject everything from China's past. The national humiliation of defeat in the Opium Wars and in other subsequent conflicts left deep and long-lasting scars on the entire nation. Mao and many of his generation felt that China had been betrayed by its leaders, who had failed to respond to the new challenges provided by the arrival of the western powers. Whilst they rejected the policies and many of the principles of China's Confucian leaders, they were inspired by the goal of restoring China to its past glory and position of pre-eminence in the world. It was not that they accepted the supremacy of the west *per se*, but that China had to learn from the west's temporary dominance, and use elements of western thinking and practice to put China back where it belonged.

A strong nationalist sentiment became one of the key features of Mao's political thought. If there is one constant element that stayed with Mao throughout his entire political life, it was the desire to see China returned to its rightful place as a powerful nation. Mao's belief that China should not have to kowtow to anybody became manifest in a brand of Marxism that had deep roots in Chinese nationalism – in many ways a form of national socialism that was often far removed from the teachings of Marx and Engels.

It is important to reiterate that Mao was not alone in reject-ing elements of the past and looking outside China for new solutions. But it is also important to recognise that this was by no means a mass movement. Those young Chinese searching for new foreign solutions were predominantly young men in the towns and cities who were able to gain more than a rudi-mentary education. Thanks to the wealth of his family, Mao was one of these young men, attending the normal school in Changsha,[13] the provincial capital of his native Hunan prov-ince, at the time of the 1911 revolution. Here, Mao read more about recent Chinese history, and first came into contact with the new ideas flooding into China at the time, usually via those Chinese students in Japan.

At this stage, liberalism and not Marxism attracted most attention from young Chinese.[14] This was partly due to the pol-itical messages that liberalism carried. In particular, the French Revolution was taken as a shining example of how to construct a new state-system after the overthrow of an entrenched royal family. But if anything, the social implications of liberalism had more resonance for the young Chinese of the time. Although Mao himself interrupted his studies for six months to serve in the revolutionary army in Changsha, he was initially more con-cerned with social rather than political revolution. In addition to reading translations of western liberal thinkers such as Montes-quieu, Carlyle and Mill, and the newsletters of the Revolutionary Alliance, Mao and his contemporaries became fascinated by the lessons that could be found in western literature. Of all the foreign books being read in China at the time, few had more of an impact than Ibsen's *A Doll's House*. This story of a woman who refused to accept the oppression and tyranny of the tradi-tional family structure, and instead took her future in her own hands, deeply impressed Mao and many others. Indeed, much of Mao's earliest writing echoed Ibsen's sentiments, dealing with the role of women in society and attacking the traditional Confucian family structure.

Mao became involved with what we now call the May Fourth or New Culture Movement by contributing to *New Youth*, the magazine that was at the vanguard of distributing these new ideas. The May Fourth Movement was a movement by a small group of young urban intellectuals for young urban intellec-tuals. Its impact beyond the confines of this small group was strictly limited. But for people like Mao, it was the spark that politicised a generation into political activity,[15] and helped formulate and shape the ideas of many of China's later generation of political leaders.

.   .   .

## FROM MAY FOURTH TO MARXISM

The May Fourth period was an important turning point in China's history. It is named after the mass demonstration that occurred in Tiananmen Square in Beijing on 4 May 1919, but is now used to refer to an indeterminate period before and after the demonstration in which young urban educated Chinese became increasingly interested in western ideas. By 1919, any hope that the 1911 revolution had marked the start of a new beginning for China had disappeared. The new republican system had collapsed into armed conflict between different groups, and even within the groups themselves. Within this power vacuum, strong regional leaders assumed more and more control, leading to the *de facto* division of China into different spheres of influence dominated by military might.

The demonstration of 4 May was a direct response to China's treatment at the hands of the great powers at the end of the First World War. Thousands of Chinese had fought with the allies during the war and many others had worked in armaments factories in France. And if this was not enough to gain a reward from the allies, Woodrow Wilson's stated principle of allowing self-determination for all peoples seemed to imply that the western powers would hand back to China all those territories that had been taken as a result of China's military defeats from the Opium Wars onwards. In the event, German control of land in Shandong province in north China was revoked, but rather than returning it to China, the land was instead transferred to Japanese control.

For those Chinese searching for a new model for Chinese society, the failure of the western nations to treat China fairly undermined the validity of the western liberal approach. Although the Bolshevik revolution in the Soviet Union provided a concrete example of how a nation could reassert itself in the face of foreign imperialism and arrogance, Marxism was far from the only new idea that provided an alternative to both the traditional Chinese view and the western liberal view. The anarchist ideas of Bakunin and Kropotkin were much more popular than Marxism in the first decade of the twentieth century. Indeed, Dirlik refers to anarchism as the 'midwife' to Marxism, in that many of those who formed and joined the Communist Party in the 1920s became interested in revolutionary politics by reading about anarchism in the first instance.[16]

Mao's own introduction to Marxism appears to have occurred during his time in Beijing and Shanghai in 1918–20. On arriving in Beijing in 1918, Mao found a job as an assistant librarian at Beijing University[17] under the head librarian, Li Dazhao. Inspired by the October revolution, Li was one of the first men to embrace Marxism, and established a study group in Beijing to discuss its applicability to China. Crucially, Li argued that the sheer size of the Chinese peasantry meant that any successful revolutionary movement must contain revolutionary activity by the peasantry, and not just rely on the urban proletariat. It is notable that Mao's own brand of Marxism was also built on an understanding of the revolutionary potential of the peasantry.

Although Mao was inducted into the Chinese Communist Party at its inception in Shanghai in 1921, his Marxist credentials at the time were (and some would argue remained) somewhat weak. While he had read some of the works of Marx and Engels, his political ideas were shaped more by his first-hand experiences and analyses of what was wrong with China than by any abstract theoretical works. In this respect, Mao's views of revolution and Chinese Marxism were very much in the minority at this time. Unlike Mao, most other party members were heavily influenced by Marxist ideology, and particularly by Leninist interpretations of revolution. The influence of the Communist International (Comintern) was particularly important here. Charged with exporting revolutionary ideas, Comintern agents like Voitinsky, Maring and Otto Braun played an important role in educating and organising Marxists within China. Promising students were also taken to Moscow for training in ideological and organisational affairs at the Sun Yatsen University. On their return to China these 'returned students' (also known as the 28 Bolsheviks) remained very close to their Comintern masters, and were fierce proponents of the Leninist view.

In addition to these Moscow-trained communists, a small but significant number of Chinese communists travelled to Europe on work-study programmes. For example, Zhou Enlai, China's Premier after the revolution, went to France in 1920, where he organised Marxist discussion groups and political cells amongst Chinese workers which were then incorporated into the French Communist Party. The youngest member of the group accompanying Zhou Enlai and a prominent political activist in Lyon was a young man from Sichuan province called Deng Xiaoping – the man who led China away from Maoism and towards economic reform after 1978.[18]

Mao's main area of disagreement with these Comintern-influenced communists was over which groups in society represented the true revolutionary force. The Comintern 'orthodoxy' was that when the revolution occurred, it would be through the actions of the urban working class. Although the urban proletariat numbered less than 2 per cent of the total population, the party should nevertheless concentrate on promoting trade union activism and building an urban movement. Mao, however, like Li Dazhao before him, felt that this emphasis on building an urban revolutionary movement ignored the reality of Chinese circumstances. Not only were the peasantry by far the biggest class numerically, but there was also deep suffering and discontent in the countryside that could, if correctly handled, be transformed into revolutionary activity.

With the CCP dominated by pro-Comintern members, Mao's ideas remained very much in the minority. And despite his growing interest in the peasantry, Mao himself played an important role in developing an urban-based movement in the 1920s. This was partly because Mao was firmly committed to building an urban party *alongside* the politicisation of the peasantry, but it was also because Mao accepted party discipline. Thus, one of his earliest party duties was to organise trade union activities in Hunan and western Jiangxi provinces, a task he performed with his customary zeal. Similarly, although Mao appears to have opposed alliance with the Guomindang, he expended enormous energy working within the Guomindang power structure once the decision was made in 1923.

. . .

## THE COMINTERN, THE GUOMINDANG AND THE CCP

The Guomindang–CCP alliance of 1923–27 was an uneasy marriage from the beginning, and owed more to the Comintern's vision of China's future than it did to a desire to collaborate from the Chinese partners. Whilst doing much to help establish the CCP, the Comintern did not expect an imminent communist revolution in China. The development of the communist movement was part of a longer-term strategy for China; in the short run Moscow placed its emphasis on promoting the Guomindang as the next government of a unified China.

When the new republic collapsed into turmoil with Yuan Shikai's annulment of the 1911–12 elections, Sun Yatsen and the Guomindang established their own rival provisional government in Guangdong. From 1913 to his death in 1925, Sun spent the remainder of his life coping with the fragmentation of the party into bitter factional conflict. Nevertheless, a Guomindang that was responsive to the Comintern's wishes remained the best option for the Soviets keen to see friendly regimes on the other side of their enormous Asian borders.

Although initially sceptical of the alliance, Mao's period working within the Guomindang stood him in good stead in later years. After a brief period in the propaganda department, Mao became head of the Peasant Training Centre. In one of the great ironies of the Chinese revolution, the Guomindang provided Mao with the opportunity to develop a revolutionary strategy that was ultimately to contribute to their defeat at the hands of Mao's communists. In his formal report on his research, 'On an Investigation into the Peasant Movement in Hunan', Mao reiterated his belief that the peasantry was a potential revolutionary force. And perhaps for the first time, we see Mao advocating a specific policy – the redistribution of land – which he believed could harness this revolutionary potential.

Despite his research in and on Hunan, Mao's colleagues remained unconvinced, and rejected his proposals to promote rural land reform at the 5th Party Congress held in Wuhan during April and May 1927. Mao was heavily criticised at this time by Comintern agents working in China, and by a number of top party figures. For example, Chen Duxiu, the man who established the first communist cells in China, is said to have opposed even discussing Mao's plans in 1927. Qu Qiubai, a trade union activist from Shanghai, also opposed Mao on the grounds that the revolution lay in the hands of the workers alone. So too did Li Lisan, who had been trained in labour organisation in Lyon and Moscow; Luo Zhanglong, a founder member of the party, and a man whom Mao claimed to have personally recruited into the party; and Wang Ming, the man who spent the period of the Long March claiming to be the CCP leader whilst safely ensconced in Moscow. Mao did not forget the way he was treated and the party formally vilified all of these men after 1949 for supporting the erroneous Moscow line against Mao.

The wisdom of the emphasis on building an urban-based revolution was put to a premature test in 1927 when the Guomindang–CCP alliance collapsed into outright hostility. With Sun Yatsen's death in 1925, the Guomindang entered a phase of further factional infighting in the search to find a successor. The man who emerged victorious was Chiang Kai-shek,[19] who had originally joined Sun Yatsen's Revolutionary Alliance whilst studying in Japan. However, on his return to China in 1910, Chiang spent a number of years on the fringes of the Shanghai underworld, and many in the party were intensely wary of his close connections with a number of secret societies operating on the fringes of Chinese society. Indeed, two of the Guomindang's most powerful leaders, Hu Hanming and Wang Jingwei, refused to accept Chiang's leadership, and established their own rival power bases.[20]

Chiang's rise to power owed much to the fact that he had won the patronage of Sun Yatsen whilst serving in the Guomindang armed forces in Canton in the early 1920s. Chiang was sent for military training in the Soviet Union in 1923, returning to lead the important Whampoa military academy where he became the most powerful military force within the party and surrounded himself with a clique of Whampoa graduates. Despite (or perhaps because of) his close connections and political debt to Moscow, Chiang was sceptical about the alliance with the CCP. And once the political environment proved favourable, Chiang moved to bring the alliance to an abrupt end.

With support from Moscow, the new Guomindang armies under Chiang's leadership embarked on the Northern Expedition, a campaign aimed at reunifying China through military might. Chiang established a new national government first in Wuhan and then Nanjing in 1927. However, rather than defeating the warlord armies in battle, the Guomindang rather unified the country by entering into alliance with the key warlords whereby the warlords retained their local power in return for accepting the national authority of the Guomindang. What this meant in practice was that when the Guomindang established a new national capital in Nanjing in 1927, they only had effective direct control over the surrounding two or three provinces.

Despite of (or perhaps because of) his relationship with Moscow, Chiang was intensely suspicious of the long-term wisdom of allowing the communists to flourish within the Guomindang party organisation. With his position as national leader underpinned by his new-found alliance with the allied warlords, he no longer needed to retain his old alliance with the communists, and in 1927 acted to rid the party of not only CCP members but also left-leaning Guomindang members. Faced with an apparent threat to its very existence, and spurred on by Comintern agents, the CCP instigated an urban uprising in Nanchang in August 1927 in an attempt to jump-start the proletarian revolution. The uprising was an abject failure, but in the retreat Mao was impressed by what he perceived to be a more revolutionary attitude displayed by the peasantry than by the urban population. Taking affairs largely into his own hands, Mao planned an attack on Changsha in what became known as the Autumn Harvest Uprising. The uprising was nearly aborted when Guomindang troops arrested Mao and prepared to execute him. Miraculously, Mao escaped and hid in grass while a detailed search failed to find him. A cynic might conclude that the bribe that Mao said the guards refused to accept did, in fact, find its way into the captors' hands.

Convinced that the countryside was on the verge of revolution, Mao co-opted local coal-miners into an attempt to harness the revolutionary potential of the peasantry. Not for the last time in his political career, Mao had overestimated the revolutionary stirrings of the peasantry, and when the rebellion failed to materialise, the rebels turned tail and fled. Mao was subsequently criticised by the party for embarking on an unplanned rebellion that was more a military campaign than a proper political campaign based on an objective understanding of local conditions. Mao was suspended from the Politburo, and according to him, even dismissed from the party. More pressing than this official censure, Mao and the remnant of his forces faced capture by the Guomindang, and fled to the Jinggangshan in the relatively remote, barren, but safe mountains of western Jiangxi province. But out of this defeat came the seeds of later victory.

·   ·   ·

## THE JIANGXI SOVIET

Mao's small group of rebels were slowly but surely swelled by the arrival of communists escaping from similar botched urban rebellions in Nanchang and Canton. Crucially, Mao's forces were to be joined at Jinggangshan by those led by Zhu De in April or May 1928, retreating from the south. The combination of the political ideologue, Mao Zedong, with the military commander, Zhu De, was to become a potent and ultimately successful force. Indeed, Wilson goes as far as to argue that 'if this union had not come off, Mao would have remained at best a discredited provincial leader'.[21] These forces were to be further enhanced in the autumn with the arrival of a small force led by Peng Dehuai. This event was not that significant in itself, but does tell us something about Mao's loyalty to his comrades, and his commitment to his own ideological convictions. Peng stood alongside Mao for much of the rest of the period of the revolutionary struggle. He was a key military commander before 1949, and after the revolution he was charged with overseeing China's involvement in the Korean War. Yet when he crossed Mao in 1959, when he criticised Mao's Great Leap Forward and called for stronger ties with the Soviet Union, Mao did not hesitate to dismiss and vilify Peng.

It was at Jiangxi that Mao began to turn his notions of revolution into a concrete revolutionary strategy. Stuck in the mountains of Jiangxi, Zhu De, Tan Zhenlin (the party leader) and Mao built their capital at Ruijin. They initially had only around 10,000 men, and perhaps as few as 2,000 rifles between them. While Mao was already confident of the revolutionary credentials of the peasantry, this on its own was not sufficient to win the revolution. A spontaneous uprising to overthrow the twin evils of feudalism and colonial exploitation would not happen overnight. Indeed, in order to save the party in the short run, it needed to build a strong politicised army. The revolutionary victory, then, would be a result of military conquest.

At the Kutian Conference of December 1929 – January 1930, Mao took control of the Red Army. He developed four key ideas and policies during this time – ideas and policies that were ultimately to go a very long way to bringing the communists to power. The first was the importance of political indoctrination within the Red Army to form a cohesive unit. The loyalty of the army must be to ideas, not just to their leader, as Mao thought was the case within the Guomindang forces. Through political indoctrination, the troops' commitment to the fight would be underpinned by their commitment to the cause.

The second idea was to create unity between the people and the party: to spend time talking to the people to find out what their interests and ideas really were and to turn these ideas into practical policies that the people would accept and embrace. Whereas the Guomindang was aloof from society and never really tried to build a mass base of support, Mao saw the CCP's survival and ultimate victory as being predicated in the will of the people. In many ways, this approach not only distanced the CCP from the Guomindang, but also distanced Mao from those in the party who remained faithful to Moscow's revolutionary prescriptions. The party must not place its faith in ideas and policies designed in Moscow, or even designed by an elite group of professional revolutionaries who thought that they knew best. The party must place its faith in the ideas and wishes of the people whom it was supposed to represent.

The third idea, related to this, was to create unity between the army and the people. Again, this idea was based on learning from the mistakes of the Guomindang and presenting the communists as the antithesis of the nationalists. The arrival of armed forces into a village in China was typically the onset of a period of terror. Particularly, but not uniquely, the Guomindang armies had a reputation for brutality, conflict and ill discipline. Mao knew that if the people were to be persuaded not to inform on the communists, and even to join them in their struggle, then the correct conduct of the army was going to be crucial. The army was going to be the communists' first point of contact with most peasants, and their trust and support might not be immediately won, but could easily be immediately lost.

Thus Mao developed the Three Rules and Eight Points of Behaviour to guide the conduct of the army in their relations with the people. These were:

The Three Rules:
   Obey orders in all your actions
   Do not take a single needle or thread from the masses
   Turn in everything captured

The Eight Points of Behaviour:
　　Speak politely
　　Pay for everything
　　Return everything you borrow
　　Pay for anything you damage
　　Do not hit or swear at people
　　Do not damage crops
　　Do not take liberties with women
　　Do not ill-treat captives

From the perspective of history, these 11 points may not seem particularly radical (if at all). But it is worth re-emphasising that this was the total antithesis of the approach and attitude of the Guomindang troops. Indeed, it became the source of popular inspiration and support for the party throughout the revolutionary struggle, and helped swell the ranks of the Red Army – not just from the people themselves, but also in large numbers from disaffected Guomindang forces.

The fourth, and last, idea was the development of a mobile warfare strategy. Again, this might not seem radical from the perspective of history, but it was a bold and radical move at the time. Mao recognised that the CCP simply did not have the manpower or the supplies to fight the nationalists in a traditional conflict. The Guomindang, much influenced by the development of the Prussian army, put their faith in static trench warfare – dig in and fight for the land. For Mao, land could be retaken at a later date, men could not be brought back to life. Aided by the mountainous terrain of the Jiangxi Soviet area, Mao argued that it was far better to develop a mobile guerrilla strategy, and if this meant running away to fight another day, then this was much better than standing, fighting and losing. The new military tactics for the Red Army were encapsulated as: when the enemy advances, we retreat; when the enemy camps, we harass; when the enemy tires, we attack; when the enemy retreats, we pursue.

The experiments in building a new revolutionary strategy in Jiangxi were largely very successful. But despite the steps taken by Mao, Tan Zhenlin and Zhu De to build a new approach in Jiangxi, the voice of orthodox Comintern-inspired communism still held sway in the Chinese communist world. For example, while Mao and the others were doing their best to establish a new movement from Jiangxi, the CCP held its 6th Party

Congress in Moscow, with no representatives present from Jiangxi. Under the leadership of Li Lisan, the party reaffirmed its commitment to revolution in the cities, even though only around 3 per cent of party members were now in the cities.

Events came to a head in 1930 when the nationalists organised a period known as the 'White Terror' in the cities to flush out communists and anybody with left-wing sympathies. With their remaining urban movement under threat of extinction, the communists instigated uprisings in Changsha (defeated by gunboats from the US, UK, France and Italy), Nanchang and Wuhan in July 1930. When these uprisings were crushed, the defeated troops fled to the countryside. Worse was to come in January 1931 when the British Settlement Police arrested the remnants of the Shanghai party membership. In April the head of the CCP security organisations, Gu Shunzhang, defected to the Guomindang with a full CCP membership list – and the White Terror really began in earnest.

.   .   .

## THE COLLAPSE OF THE JIANGXI SOVIET AND THE LONG MARCH

The collapse of the urban-based party might in theory have played into the hands of Mao and the Jiangxi Soviet leadership. Certainly, by the end of 1931, there were around 2–4 million people in the Jiangxi Soviet, including 100,000 troops. Yet in many ways, this created more problems than solutions. As more communist forces made their way to Ruijin, and Guomindang troops defected to the communists (20,000 troops in one go in December 1931), it became increasingly difficult to sustain the soviet with more people to feed but only limited land and resources available.

Furthermore, notwithstanding the failure of the attempts to instigate urban uprisings in 1927 and 1930, many of the proletarian leadership remained welded to their ideas. Indeed, rather than accepting the wisdom of Mao's views, Mao was actually sidelined by the arrival of proletarian communists escaping the fiascos of 1930 and 1931. Power in the Jiangxi Soviet passed into the hands of the newly arrived Comintern agent Otto Braun, and his key supporters, Bo Gu and Zhou Enlai. According to some sources, Mao was actually placed under house arrest by the newly arrived leaders; others suggest that they tried to encourage Mao to travel to Moscow for 'medical treatment'. Whatever the case, Mao was clearly manoeuvred out of power and had no say in the decision to leave the Jiangxi Soviet and set out on the Long March.

The decision to leave was in many ways forced by the Guomindang. Four previous military campaigns to destroy the Jiangxi Soviet had failed, partly because of the new guerrilla tactics of the Red Army, and partly because of the lack of enthusiasm that many Guomindang military leaders had for the campaign. For the fifth campaign, Chiang Kai-shek himself took personal control, and devoted around 800,000–1,000,000 men, 200–400 planes, and modern German armaments to the campaign. As they enclosed the Jiangxi Soviet, bit by bit cutting down the land under communist control, the new Jiangxi Soviet leadership took the decision to shut up shop and leave.

On 16 October 1934 the communists began to abandon Jiangxi in five columns. The nationalists had dug four concentric circles surrounding the Soviet, and in breaking through the trenches the communists lost something like half of their army by December. They were also forced to leave behind most of their equipment, not to mention all the political and economic successes of the previous years. The communists moved out heading west with little clear idea of where they were going, and over the New Year of 1935 they found themselves in Zunyi. At a conference that became a post-mortem on the wisdom of leaving Jiangxi, Zhou Enlai crucially lent his support to Mao and Mao's strategies. Although Mao did not become the formal leader of the Chinese communists at this stage, he was henceforth the *de facto* head of the Chinese communist revolution.

The Long March was in many ways an unmitigated disaster. The troops finally arrived in the relatively safe haven of Wayabao in December 1935, before being forced out to a new soviet at Yanan in northern Shaanxi in September 1936. Of the men under Mao's control in the First Front Army, only around one in 20 made it to Yanan. When He Long arrived with the Second Front Army, only around half of the original troops had survived. The communists had been on the march for 368 days. They had travelled 12,500 kilometres across 11 provinces, crossing 18 mountain ranges and 24 major rivers. And at the end of this, they were left in one of the most desolate areas of China – yet in the space of 13 years they were in power!

But bad as things may have been, the most important fact was that the party had survived. And in the process of surviving, the party and the Red Army had come into face-to-face contact with ordinary Chinese peasants across the country, and in many cases had vastly impressed them. As Mao declared, the Long March had sowed the seeds of the revolution:

it is a manifesto, a propaganda force, a seeding machine

it has proclaimed to the world that the Red Army is an army of heroes

it has announced to some 200 million people in eleven provinces that the road of the Red Army is their only road to liberation.

In many ways, then, the Long March was the communists' recruitment sergeant.

Once in Yanan, the party set about laying the foundations of the strategies that were to epitomise its approach throughout the remaining revolutionary period. Attempts to build the support of the peasantry were conditioned by the desire – in many ways the absolute necessity – of not alienating the existing power-holders. Thus, there was an immediate policy of moderate land reform – no collectivisation of land, or overthrowing the landlords, but a reduction of rents by 25–40 per cent. The party also took steps to include existing power-holders in new forms of organisation and government, whilst at the same time bringing the peasants into power in an alliance of party, peasants and local leaders.

There can be no doubt that the communists were aided in the establishment of the new Yanan Soviet by the growing threat from Japan. Having annexed Manchuria in 1931, the Japanese had steadily spread their influence into northern China, and had met little resistance from the Guomindang on their way. Indeed, student protests against Japanese expansionism had actually been met by force by the Guomindang authorities. Wherever they went, the communists took the opportunity to put forward their own nationalist credentials. Overthrowing colonialism in general, and defeating the Japanese in particular, became the main priority for the party, and in their rhetoric at least, they stood in stark contrast to the apparently capitulationist Guomindang, who had devoted their energies to trying to destroy the communists and ignored the Japanese threat.

In fact, had it not been for the Japanese threat then the communists might not have survived long in Yanan. Having forced the communists into Yanan, Chiang was keen to wipe them out once and for all. However, the warlord armies under the control of Zhang Xueliang (whose own father had been overthrown and killed by the Japanese) refused to attack, arguing that the Japanese were the main threat and they should be dealt with first. Irritated by this challenge to his authority, Chiang Kai-shek flew to nearby Xian to oversee the final defeat of the CCP in December 1936 – where Zhang Xueliang promptly kidnapped him.

Chiang was only released after he agreed to turn the focus of attention to the Japanese and form a united front with all patriotic forces. This event was perhaps the crucial turning point for the CCP. In the first instance, it saved the communists from possible annihilation and gave them a breathing space to establish their policies and ideas in Yanan. In the longer term, the new united front against Japan saw the creation of the Eighth Route Army to resist the Japanese under Lin Biao, He Long and Liu Bocheng paid for and equipped by the nationalists.

Indeed, for Chalmers Johnson, the Japanese invasion was the key to the CCP's victory. In addition to the short-term gains, it gave the communists the opportunity to forge their nationalist credentials, and as noted above, made people of whatever complexion more likely to accede to communist control. Although the revolution was won by the CCP, the 1949 revolution was a victory for nationalism as an ideology and not communism.[22]

There can be no doubt that there is much truth in Johnson's analysis. Mao's brand of Marxism from the beginning was heavily influenced by China's humiliation at the hands of the western powers, and later Japan. The revolution, in Mao's eyes, was as much to liberate China from colonialism as it was to liberate the Chinese people from the shackles of feudalism. It is also true that the communists utilised the nationalists' own apparent failings in defending China's national sovereignty to push their own nationalist credentials. And to this end they were remarkably successful. When the Japanese launched a full-scale invasion in 1937, the nationalists abandoned their capital at Nanjing, moving westwards down the Yangtze, first to Wuhan, and then deep into the south-west of China at Ch          in Sichuan province.

While the nationalists were relatively safe from ʲ ese aggression in the south-west, Yanan and the were much closer to the front line of Japan's scorched earth policy in northern China. They naturally became the first safe haven for those forced off the land – they were simply closer to the action. But they also became the focus for wider opposition to the Japanese occupation. Particularly after the Americans joined the Pacific War after Pearl Harbor, the nationalists appeared more concerned with building up their power for the resumption of the civil war than they did in beating off the Japanese. If the Americans were going to defeat the Japanese, then why bother losing troops, expending money, resources and men in simply speeding up the inevitable?

Thus, the nationalists traded with the Japanese occupiers, stored up weapons and finances from the Americans intended for the anti-Japanese struggle, and waited for the more important battle to come. Nationalist troops also defected in large numbers to the Nanjing government established by the Japanese to rule occupied China under the cloak of Chinese rule. The communists suggested that this was nothing more than a cynical ploy to keep their forces out of harm's way, and fed and funded by the Japanese, until the civil war resumed as it inevitably would.

The sin was compounded by the nationalists' continued aggression against their supposed allies. In January 1941 they all but destroyed the communists' New Fourth Army in what became known as the South Anhui Incident. The attack on the communists when they were trying to fight the Japanese only served to enhance the nationalist credentials of the communists. Over the remaining years of the anti-Japanese conflict, many overseas Chinese returned to fulfil their patriotic duty. Whilst some did indeed make their way to Chongqing, Yanan and the communists became the focus for resistance for many non-communists. Indeed, Eastman puts the communists' victory down to the ineptitude, corruption and inefficiency of the Guomindang – the communists didn't so much win the revolution as the nationalists handed it to them on a plate.[23]

. . .

## NATIONALISM AND COMMUNISM IN YANAN

While nationalism was a considerable force in gaining popular support for the communists, it was not the only tactic pursued. Gillin,[24] for example, places the emphasis on the radical land

reform programme in Shanxi province as a catalyst for winning the peasants' support. Thaxton's study of the Taihang
guerrilla base area supports this view, noting that, if anything,
nationalist appeals only detracted from the campaign against
the landlords.[25] Selden similarly argues that whilst the party
adopted anti-Japanese slogans after 1935, the campaign against
exploitation and the landlords was the key to building the
rural support base that brought them to power.[26]

A number of authors have tried to find a once-and-for-all
explanation for why the communists won power. Was it the
failings of the nationalists, the nationalist appeal of the communists, the communists' radical land reform programme, or
the fact that the communists deployed a broad and moderate
united front policy to win over non-communists? But one of
the major successes of Mao's revolutionary strategy was his
flexibility. The key thing was identifying what worked in any
specific place at any specific time. Mao placed great emphasis
on identifying what the major contradiction was at the time,
and then building an alliance of forces to defeat that contradiction. Thus, on a general level, when the Japanese occupation was seen as the major contradiction, then the alliance to
defeat the Japanese might include the national bourgeoisie
(rich peasants, small landlords) and the petty bourgeoisie (pro-
fessionals, intellectuals, small traders etc). If the Guomindang
was seen as the major contradiction, then these groups might
again form part of the communists' allied forces, as the nationalists had done so much to alienate them. But when feudalism
and capitalism were seen as the major contradiction, then this
meant a tighter revolutionary alliance, and revolution against
the bourgeoisie.

Clearly, perceptions of what constituted the major threat
changed over time depending on circumstances. But the major
threat might also vary over place, and not just over time. In areas
where the communists were strongest, the campaign against
the landlords could be implemented. Where they were under
greater threat, either from the Japanese, the Guomindang, or
where the local population were unconvinced, then nationalism
and/or a moderate united front were more applicable. Perhaps
crucially, Mao pushed for a united front with rural and urban
elites, as a renewed civil war with the nationalists became inevitable.[27] Recognising that nationalist aspirations alone were not
going to win the revolution once the main force of colonialism

had been defeated, Mao argued that the acquiescence, if not support, of the middle classes was essential if the nationalists were to be defeated.

This is not to say that Mao simply abandoned his political convictions in order to seize power. While a broad united front was necessary to win the revolution, Mao was committed to ensuring that the party itself was a coherent and cohesive organisation following a specific political line. It perhaps goes without saying that the political line in question was Mao's own. Despite Mao's ascension to power at Zunyi, he still did not have a free rein in policy-making. Amongst the party leadership at Yanan, there were a number of leaders – indeed, the majority of leaders – who held on to notions of revolution and politics that owed much to Moscow and the Comintern. Some of these proletarian communists went along with Mao – particularly if he could deliver the revolution – but had very different visions of how any post-revolutionary society might work. Others, notably the group of '28 Bolsheviks' who were closest to the Comintern line, were even critical of strategy and policy in Yanan and other communist base areas, pointing to the contradiction between Chinese practice and Marxist-Leninist ideology. In combination, these provided a considerable obstacle to Mao and his ideas. If the revolution was won, then these men seemed likely to revert to type – to return to the Moscow-inspired Leninist model that had proved so unsuccessful in the revolution to date. As Steven Levine puts it, they were 'an urban party sojourning in the countryside'.[28]

So while the party was adopting a united front to convince the waverers in society, Mao was instigating a campaign within the party in Yanan to enforce his own ideas and strategies. Had they known at the time that the rectification campaign implemented in Yanan was a foretaste of what was to come after the revolution, some of China's leaders might have tried to dispense with Mao there and then. The main point of the rectification campaign was to establish the differences between orthodox Marxism – the writings of Marx and Engels and the experiences of the Soviet revolution – and Chinese Marxism. Whilst the latter was indebted to the former, the practical and unique experiences of the Chinese revolution must take precedence over dogma. Mao wanted to 'sinify' Marxism, or to develop a distinct brand of Marxism that reflected the realities and experiences of his revolution.

As part of this process of 'sinification', Mao railed against commandism – the process whereby party cadres told the people what to do because they, the party cadres, the revolutionary elite, knew what was best. Mao argued that the revolution should be embedded in the will of the people. The party must accept that it could learn from the people, and indeed it would only succeed if it actually listened to the people. In short, the Chinese proletariat[29] should be the source of wisdom and policy, and not dogmatic adherence to the works and ideas of Marx, Engels and Lenin.

The rectification campaign entailed party members getting together in small groups to discuss a number of documents which were provided by the party leadership. Although the works of other leaders were included in the compulsory texts, the vast majority were either written by Mao himself, or by writers sympathetic to Mao's line. The aim, originally at least, was not to flush out Mao's opponents and banish them from the party, but to give them a chance to rectify their failings by re-appraising their ideas. In practice, those who claimed to have seen the errors of their ways were rewarded by being brought back into the fold. Those who resisted intense peer pressure to conform became subject to investigations into their past by the communists' secret police force, headed by Mao's close ally Kang Sheng. Forced confessions, torture and execution were not unknown, and there is evidence that even Mao may have thought that it had gone too far. In the short term, the rectification campaign helped Mao to reassert his vision of revolution over those of the 28 Bolsheviks. But if they thought that they could ignore Mao once in power, they were very much mistaken. Not only did Mao's convictions return to haunt them on a number of occasions after 1949, but many also suffered at the hands of Kang Sheng during the Cultural Revolution.

. . .

## THE ASSUMPTION OF POWER

The war against Japan was a godsend for the communists. It first saved them from annihilation, and then gave them an opportunity to build support from a number of key groups. Nevertheless, when the Japanese capitulated after the American nuclear strikes on Hiroshima and Nagasaki, there was still much to be done to prevent the nationalists from re-taking the reins of power. The nationalists held a massive superiority in terms of manpower and supplies. They also, initially at least, had the support of both the United States and the Soviet Union. But in the space of three and a quarter years, they were ousted from power, and forced out of China to the safe haven of Taiwan.

Despite the attempt by the American Marshall Mission to mediate a new coalition government between the communists and the nationalists, the civil war was essentially resumed by July 1946. The war can be roughly divided into three periods.[30] In the first year of the conflict, the Guomindang were on the offensive, gaining considerable territory in northern China, including the important capture of Yanan itself in March 1947. But while the communists recognised that losing Yanan was a big psychological blow, Mao was not prepared to fight to the death to keep it. As he had done in the Jiangxi Soviet period, Mao deployed guerrilla tactics, and was prepared (if not happy) to retreat and preserve manpower rather than fight a battle that he could not win.

Despite the territorial gains for the nationalists, the war was beginning to slide away from them even in this early period. During the first year of the war, they lost a million men, either by death or by defection to the communists. In comparison, the communist troops increased from around 800,000 to two million as troops defected, and the seeds of the Yanan period bore fruit with new recruits to defend the gains made under communist control. In the second phase from July 1947 to June 1948, the communists returned to the offensive, 'liberating' 146 cities and re-taking Yanan. During this period, the divisions within the Guomindang troops became ever sharper, and victory was frequently won as the poorly treated and ill-fed nationalist troops defected or simply gave up the fight.

The final phase of the war ran from June 1948 to October 1949, and the main battleground switched to north-east China. It is somewhat ironic that Mao's revolution, which was built on the revolutionary enthusiasm of the peasantry, was finally delivered in the one area of the country where the communists had considerable support in the cities. When the Japanese surrendered, the communists were in the best geographic position to move into the former occupied lands of north-east China. The Americans tried to transport nationalist troops into the north-east, but were refused permission to land troops in

Soviet-occupied Port Arthur, which had previously been designated a 'civilian city'. This action gave the communists the breathing space they needed to establish themselves in the north-east, and for Levine it meant that the Chinese revolution, in its final stages at least, actually owed more to the 'orthodox' Leninist concept of taking the cities first.[31]

As morale and cohesion collapsed in the nationalist forces, the communists won three key battles: Liaoxi-Shenyang, Huai-Hai and Tianjin. Chiang Kai-shek later put the blame on his commanders – their spirit was already broken and 'their morality is base'. He baled out on 21 January 1949, handing leadership over to Li Zongren. But the tide of the revolution was now inexorable. Ten days later, Beijing fell to the communists, followed by a string of other cities as the nationalists went on full retreat. On 30 September 1949 the party Central Committee elected Mao Zedong as the Chairman of the new People's Republic, which was formally established the following day at a mass rally in Tiananmen Square.

That the Chinese Communist Party survived the disasters of 1927 and 1930 is remarkable enough in itself. The fact that it survived the Long March, Japanese aggression, and Guomindang attacks in 1937–45 is equally remarkable. That it then went on to establish a new government by defeating a bigger, better-equipped army is nothing short of staggering. But winning the revolution was only the start. For Mao, it signalled the start of a new period of revolution that would bring forth more glorious advances. For many of his colleagues, it signalled the start of a period in which few of them were to survive unscathed by Mao's ambitions.

. . .

## NOTES

1. Buddhism was not a major religious force in China at the time, so Mao's religious background was rather atypical.
2. Hollingworth, C. (1987) *Mao* (London: Triad) p. 15.
3. Indeed, the relationship between father and son was considered much more important than the relationship between husband and wife, with the wife only achieving any social status once she had provided the family with a male heir.
4. Although its successor, the Shang dynasty of 1765–1123 BC, is the earliest dynasty proven to exist by archaeological findings.

5.   I think this is a better translation than the more often used 'Middle Kingdom', which can be taken to mean in the middle of two places rather than the idea of centrality or 'core'.

6.   Wars in plural here as the Arrow War of 1856–60 is often referred to as the Second Opium War. When the Chinese arrested the Chinese crew of a British flagged ship for piracy, the British authorities sent another military expedition to China. The Chinese again agreed to a treaty and again vacillated until a British force entered Beijing and burnt the Emperor's Summer Palace to the ground.

7.   For example, the Nian Rebellion of 1853–68, the Northwest Moslem Rebellion of 1862, and the Yunnan Moslem Rebellion of 1858–73.

8.   See Shih, V. (1967) *The Taiping Ideology: Its Sources, Interpretations, and Influences* (Seattle: University of Washington Press).

9.   The imperial forces were also supported by the western powers who feared that the rebellion was damaging their economic interests in China. One of the key western adventurers was Charles George Gordon, who earned the nick-name of 'Chinese Gordon' before later finding more fame through his actions at Khartoum.

10.  Named after the honorific title of the Emperor.

11.  Wright, M. (1957) *The Last Stand of Chinese Conservatism* (Stanford: Stanford University Press).

12.  Japan was a much safer option than sending students directly to the west. Furthermore, they had already translated many western texts, and Chinese students could more easily understand the characters than the western languages themselves.

13.  The Chinese educational system has separate schools and universities to train teachers. These are known as 'shifan' schools and universities, which are usually translated into English as 'normal' schools etc.

14.  Indeed, Schram refers to this period as Mao's liberal phase. Schram, S. (1988) *The Thought of Mao Tse-tung* (Cambridge: Cambridge University Press).

15.  See Chow T. (1960) *The May Fourth Movement: Intellectual Revolution in Modern China* (Cambridge, Mass.: Harvard University Press).

16.  Dirlik, A. (1989) *The Origins of Chinese Communism* (New York and Oxford: Oxford University Press) p. 3.

17.  A rather grand title for a position which entailed a considerable degree of cleaning and tidying.

18.  In addition, Li Fuchun (arguably China's main economic planner in the 1950s) and Zhu De (one of the architects of the party's military strategy before 1949 and Politburo member until his death in 1976) also spent time in Chinese communist cells within Europe. See Gray, J. (1990) *Rebellions and Revolutions: China from*

the 1800s to the 1980s (Oxford and New York: Oxford University Press) p. 207.

19. Chiang Kai-shek is also known as Jiang Jieshi in the mandarin-speaking world. However, the more common usage of his name will be used throughout this book.

20. Wang Jingwei actually sided with the Japanese after the 1937 invasion of China and became leader of a Japanese puppet regime in Nanjing.

21. Wilson, R. (1979) Mao, the People's Emperor (London: Hutchinson) p. 131.

22. Johnson, C. (1962) Peasant Nationalism and Communist Power: The Emergence of Revolutionary China, 1937–1945 (Stanford: Stanford University Press).

23. Eastman, L. (1984) Seeds of Destruction: Nationalist China in War and Revolution 1937–1949 (Stanford: Stanford University Press).

24. Gillin, D. (1964) 'Peasant Nationalism in the History of Chinese Communism', Journal of Asian Studies 23 (2).

25. Thaxton, R. (1983) China Turned Rightside Up: Revolutionary Legitimacy in the Peasant World (New Haven: Yale University Press).

26. Selden, M. (1971) The Yenan Way in Revolutionary China (Cambridge, Mass.: Harvard University Press).

27. Shum, K.K. (1988) The Chinese Communists' Road to Power: The Anti-Japanese National United Front, 1935–1945 (Hong Kong and New York: Oxford University Press) p. 4.

28. Levine, S. (1987) Anvil of Victory: The Communist Revolution in Manchuria (New York: Columbia University Press).

29. The Chinese word for proletariat is 'wuchanjieji'. Literally translated, this means 'classes without property'. As such, when the Chinese communists used the term proletariat, they were referring to the property-less peasantry as well as the urban working classes.

30. See Rodzinski, W. (1979) A History of China: Volume II (Oxford and New York: Pergamon Press).

31. Levine, Anvil of Victory.

# Chapter 2

# ESTABLISHING THE NEW POLITICAL ORDER: MAOISM AND ITS CRITICS

*is this Breslin's answer to this Q?*

*answering Q.5*

In many ways, winning the revolutionary struggle was much easier than establishing a new revolutionary state. The CCP had benefited greatly from popular hostility to both the Japanese (and previously western) colonisation, and to Guomindang rule. The rise to power in 1949 was only possible due to the elimination of both of these threats. In the very process of victory, the glue that held the broad revolutionary movement together might simply disappear – the victory had eliminated the common threats and enemies.

To make matters worse, CCP rule in 1949 faced considerable internal and external challenges. Externally, the Guomindang remained an important threat. Not only were the remnants of the Guomindang safely ensconced on Taiwan, but pockets of Guomindang forces also continued fighting in the south-west for a number of years. Furthermore, the American-led diplomatic and trade embargo on China isolated the new leadership and forced them into a closer alliance with Moscow than some in Beijing thought wise (see Chapter 6). When the onset of the Korean War pushed Taipei and Washington closer together, the threat of an attack on two fronts could not be discounted. Combined with the American presence in Japan, and the return of the southern half of Vietnam to first French and later American influence, the CCP found itself facing hostile neighbours from its Korean border in the north-east right round to the Indian border in the west.

This fear of foreign intervention and a counter-revolution should not be underestimated. Mao's threat perceptions remained high throughout the 1950s, 1960s and much of the 1970s, and were a major determinant of both foreign and domestic policy-making. Indeed, Mao's fear of both the evil capitalist west, epitomised by America, and of undue influence from the Soviet 'socialist imperialists' was a key consideration in the evolution of an independent Chinese revolution. In addition, the real fear of invasion from either the Americans or the Soviets, or, worse still, both in alliance, was a significant factor in the development of the specifics of many of Mao's domestic political and economic reforms.

*[margin note: AMS + soviet threat]*

Internally, we must consider the extent of devastation the country had suffered for much of the preceding century. China had been ravaged by the ferocious Japanese invasion; by civil war between the communists and the nationalists from (on and off) the 1930s; by inept Guomindang rule; by the virtual collapse of national government from 1911; and by the requirements of western imperial powers since the 1840s.

*[margin note: devastated China]*

In addition, the speed of the Guomindang capitulation in 1948 and 1949 left the CCP with a number of problems. The heartland of the revolution had been the guerrilla base areas of northern China and, after the Japanese surrender in 1945, the north-east. When they established the new People's Republic in 1949, the communists lacked any real substantial support and power base in vast swathes of the country, particularly south of the Yangtze River. Furthermore, their power base in the major cities was also very weak, the urban CCP movement having been largely wiped out by the Guomindang 'White Terror' in the early 1930s. Governing revolutionary base areas was one thing, governing the entire country with all its complexities was another matter altogether.

Overcoming these problems would be a significant challenge for any new regime. Simply restoring political control over a fragmented and impoverished nation, and rebuilding the economy from a century of neglect and devastation, would be enough to keep most leaders occupied for quite some time. But simple restoration of order was not enough for Mao. The revolution was not completed in 1949. For Mao at least, the seizure of power was only the beginning.

· · ·

## RULING CHINA: LIMITS TO MAO'S POWER

In many of the books and articles written about China in the 1950s and 1960s, there was a tendency to depict everything that happened as a result of Mao's own initiatives. Such a 'Mao-centric' view of Chinese politics made things easier to understand. It was also excusable given the limited amount of reliable information that came out of China at the time. The CCP kept its internal disputes firmly behind closed doors, and presented an image of unity to the outside world, with Mao as the Great Helmsman and the supreme power. Furthermore, perceptions of how Stalin managed a totalitarian system in the Soviet Union provided an established framework that some scholars assumed could simply be transferred to analyses of other communist party states.

We are in many ways entirely correct to talk in terms of 'Mao's China' (he was the single most important figure in the country's evolution after 1949) and to take a Mao-centric approach (he was the central figure to whom all other political actors referred in defining their own approaches and strategies). But China never was a totally totalitarian state, and Mao was never an all-powerful figure who could single-handedly shape the entire country and its destiny. There were considerable limits to Mao's power, and the way that he tried to overcome these limits was an important determinant of the evolution of Chinese politics while he was alive.

*Controlling the Provinces*

Ever since the Emperor Qin Shi Huang Di unified China in the second century BC, Chinese rulers have grappled with the complex task of maintaining control over the nation. Indeed, the communists' own rise to power was in no small part facilitated by previous regimes' failures to maintain control over disparate regions. For example, the final collapse of the Qing dynasty in 1911 was in many ways a multi-level *coup d'état* by regional power-holders who had wielded *de facto* local authority since the start of the century. Neither did the Guomindang's failure to establish control over all China's provinces after 1927 exactly help them to become an effective national government during the Nanjing era.

So when the CCP came to power in 1949, the lessons of the importance of ensuring effective national control were evident. The CCP's rise to power had been facilitated by the collapse of central authority, and its future could not be assured if it did not move to establish control over the provinces. But establishing

CCP officials in charge of provincial affairs was only the first step. The Qing dynasty finally lost power in 1911 because it had allowed too much power to slide into the hands of powerful local figures at the end of the nineteenth century. China's new leaders must have been aware of one crucial fact: the growth of provincialism and 'warlordism' was a result of inefficient central government, and not its cause. Thus, although restoring central control was a relatively simple feat, maintaining it would be an entirely different matter.

The revolution was, in many ways, a revolution of the peripheries. The revolution had been fought and won away from Beijing, led by men from the provinces. For these leaders the evidence of the period of the revolutionary struggle was all too clear. If effective central control was not built by the CCP, then their tenure in power could not be guaranteed. But as became equally as clear in the early 1950s, over-centralised control produced almost as many problems as too lax central control. With the newly created central planning organisations charged with establishing detailed plans for the entire country, they rapidly became swamped with work, leading to inefficiency, inflexibility and bad planning. Furthermore, the emphasis on centralised control meant that local conditions were often ignored as the planners attempted to devise national policy. Local authorities simply did not have sufficient leeway to interpret policy in a way that actually worked in their area.

The problem then (or contradiction as Mao put it in his 1956 speech[1]) was not simply building central control, but building a system that allowed for local flexibility and initiative within an overall framework of central guidance, control and goal-setting. This has proved to be an extremely difficult feat to accomplish. The priorities of central guidance and control have frequently conflicted with the priorities of local initiative and flexibility, and the period 1949–76 was punctuated by a number of major policy changes as the central leadership tried to find the correct balance between centre and province. Part of the problem here was deciding where (or who) to devolve power to – to multi-provincial large regions, to the provinces themselves, or even to lower levels?

After seizing power in China in 1949, the CCP's initial choice was to group provinces together in large regions that formed the unit of organisation for party, state and military administration. The division of China into these regions was largely a matter of expediency in order to consolidate national power as they roughly corresponded to the areas under the control of the various field armies that liberated China at the end of the civil war.[2] The large regions were disbanded between August 1954 and July 1955 and replaced by the provinces as the immediate sub-national level of administration. The provinces remained the immediate sub-national level of organisation for party and state affairs until January 1961, when large regions were re-introduced for party affairs only. These were again disbanded during 1967 and 1968 at the height of the Cultural Revolution, and provincial-level units have retained their position as the immediate sub-national level of organisation ever since.[3]

To compound this problem, there was also the question of how much power the centre should devolve to lower-level organisations. Thus, during 1956 and 1957 the CCP devolved considerable economic decision-making powers to lower-level authorities, only to restore many of these powers to the central planners after the Great Leap Forward. But by 1964, the balance had switched back to over-centralisation being the major problem, and another decentralisation campaign was initiated. These decentralisation tendencies were increased during the Cultural Revolution with the emphasis on building self-reliant economic regions.

Even during periods of relative provincial autonomy, the extent to which local leaders were allowed to deviate from central policy was always somewhat ambiguous. Leaders were expected to adhere to central directives, while at the same time suiting measures to local conditions (*yin di zhi yi*). But the division between what was permissible flexibility and what was illegitimate 'localism' was never clearly established. Furthermore, if local leaders decided to play safe and stick closely to central guidelines, then they could be accused of neglecting their duties and responsibilities. To make matters worse, if policy initiatives changed at the centre, as they often did, local leaders could find themselves being judged retrospectively. Actions that had been permissible at the time were often subsequently deemed to have been illegitimate.

Perhaps not surprisingly, then, being a provincial leader was a very precarious occupation at the best of times. During periods of political uncertainty and conflict in Beijing, it became almost impossible for local leaders to know which way to jump. An analysis of the conflicts that accompanied the Great Leap Forward provides a particularly good example. Teiwes notes that from late 1957 to 1959, purges affected leading personnel in 12 provinces.[4] In eight cases, charges of localism or local nationalism were made against provincial leaders – they were over-emphasising the importance of local interests and ignoring central directives. In most cases leaders were charged with practising 'rightist deviationism', which meant that they had been too cautious in accepting Mao's communisation policy and had tried to defend the status quo.

However, when the folly of the Great Leap became clear with the human suffering of the great famine in 1960–61, a backlash emerged against those who had taken the lead in pushing for communisation. Thus, provincial leaders were purged in six provinces for showing excessive enthusiasm in the implementation of Great Leap policies – they had failed to consider the local situation and had stuck too firmly to an inappropriate central directive. What they had done was entirely correct in the fevered environment of the Great Leap, but was now retrospectively deemed to have been wrong. As Teiwes comments: 'The men in charge of China's provinces had to cope with shifting national policy, and some were unable to navigate successfully in the rapidly changing situation'.[5]

The importance of regional-level politics in Mao's China cannot be ignored. Not only Mao, but the central leadership as a whole were in many ways dependent on the loyalty (or otherwise) of provincial leaders for the success (or failure) of their policy initiatives. David Goodman, for example, presents us with examples from his study of Sichuan province where the local leadership implemented what they thought was best for themselves and their province irrespective of what the central government was telling them to do.[6] Vogel similarly paints a picture of 'Maoism' in Canton that at times varied significantly from Maoism as Mao intended it in Beijing.[7] Indeed, for some writers on post-revolutionary China, attempts to unravel the mystery of China by analysing central-level politics is a misguided and futile project. Donnithorne, for example, portrays China in the 1960s (a period when the provinces had considerable formal control over their own economic affairs) as 'a cellular economy'[8] – a form of mutual dependency between the central authorities and powerful local interests. Whitney[9] takes an even more extreme view, arguing that the real locus of power in China lay in the provinces, with the centre acting merely as a judge or an arbitrator attempting to balance the competing and usually conflicting demands of different local interests.

An understanding of the importance of local-level politics is important here for two main reasons. First, Mao was very much aware of the role of local-level leaders in the balance of power in China, and as we shall see in later chapters, defined his political strategies accordingly. When central leaders proved sceptical of Mao's developmental strategies in the 1950s, Mao sought a new constituency from those provincial leaders who were more sympathetic to his views. When he wanted to promote the idea of communisation, he went back to his home province of Hunan which provided him with a shining example of a perfect commune that he held up for everybody else to follow. When Mao was forced to take more of a back seat in Chinese politics after the Great Leap, loyal leaders in the provinces continued to keep his ideas alive. Indeed, the radical Maoist leadership in Shanghai – the people who were to become known as the Gang of Four – provided crucial support for Mao and did more than most to help initiate the Cultural Revolution.

Second, policy could be and was distorted as it passed through the system from central planners down to provincial leaders, and then down to lower-level leaders in counties, towns and communes. As this book is a study of Mao the leader, it obviously concentrates on what he said and did in Beijing – it is a study of the exercise of power at the political centre. But this is not intended to suggest that what Mao said in Beijing was always done in Sichuan or Guizhou or anywhere else.

*Controlling the Gun*

Mao's understanding of the importance of the military in the political process is perhaps best summed up by his famous dictum that 'political power grows out of the barrel of a gun'. During the revolution, the party and the army were virtually indistinguishable from each other, and Mao himself did more than most to develop the military strategy of the Red Army and to cement the party and army together fighting a common cause. That symbiotic relationship did not simply die overnight, and while the military was officially under party control after

1949, the key question that remained was which parts of the military were loyal to which parts of the party?

With the establishment of the new People's Republic, the Red Army was renamed the People's Liberation Army (PLA) – a generic term that covered the air-force and the navy as well as the standing army. It also included special units such as the 8341 unit which was charged with protecting the party leadership in Beijing. The 8341 unit was under the command of Wang Dongxing, the man who had served as Mao's bodyguard during the Yanan period, and a man who remained more loyal to Mao than to the party leadership as a whole. Indeed, during the early days of the Cultural Revolution, the 8341 unit acted to support Mao in his struggle against the rest of the party-state leadership in Beijing – by expressing their loyalty to Mao, they necessarily acted against the rest of the party.

The military maintained their interaction with the party in two main ways. First, the new party and state organisations created after 1949 were often staffed by men and women who transferred from the military into civilian positions. They carried with them feelings of loyalty and responsibility to the military as a whole, and often to the specific military units in which they had served. Indeed, for Whitson, these personal loyalties were much more important than loyalty to the army as a whole, and these localised loyalties spilt over into political conflict.[10] The key to understanding Chinese politics for Whitson is understanding conflict between representatives of the different field armies that liberated China in 1948–49. Once installed in civilian jobs, the representatives of these field armies fought to protect the interests of their former comrades in competition with representatives from the other field armies. As such, Whitson's approach downplays the importance of Mao's ideological and political conflicts with his colleagues in the party-state elites, and instead depicts a situation which somewhat resembles the conflicts between different warlords in China in the first half of the twentieth century.

Second, leading military figures were given formal positions of power and responsibility within the civilian political structure itself. Perhaps the central military-political position in China was the position of Minister of Defence, a position within the state sector which also saw the incumbent holding a position in the party's leading decision-making bodies. It was also a position that was always filled by a serving military leader. Formal control over military affairs lay with the party's own military affairs commission. But as the Minister of Defence was not only a member of this commission, but also charged with overall control of the military structure in order to best secure the defence of the nation, the military was essentially controlled by one of its own.

Party–army relations during the Mao period were dominated by the debate between those who wanted to maintain the army's political role as a bastion of revolutionary zeal, and those who wanted to establish a professional, more apolitical fighting unit based on the model of the Soviet Red Army. China's first Minister of Defence, Peng Dehaui, was very much a proponent of the latter approach. Despite having impressive revolutionary credentials in the struggle before 1949, Peng's view of the military's position and basic philosophy was very much shaped by his experiences in leading the Chinese forces during the Korean War. The guerrilla tactics that had proved so successful in the civil war found wanting when faced with the technological and organisational superiority of the US-dominated UN forces. For Peng, if China wanted to defend its national integrity in any future conflict with the US, the lesson was clear – 'people's war' was no longer the answer, and what China needed was a modern professional fighting force.

The de-politicisation of the military that would accompany this transition placed the debate very much in the political context, and was anathema to Mao. Furthermore, Peng's proposals entailed both learning from the experience of the Soviet Red Army and relying on the Soviets for technical and tactical advice and support. Peng believed that whilst the military was undergoing this transition, China would be vulnerable to foreign aggression. It was thus essential that China maintained its close relationship with the Soviet Union and remained under the Soviet military and nuclear umbrella for the foreseeable future.

Peng's leadership of the Ministry of National Defence provided an important constraint on Mao's power. First, Peng's views on the military's own role and its reconstitution into a professional fighting force conflicted sharply with Mao's own views regarding the maintenance of the revolutionary zeal and political role of the army. Second, Peng's position impinged on issues of foreign relations, promoting a much closer alliance with the Soviet Union (and the importance of learning from the Soviet model) than Mao believed wise even in the early 1950s. Third, Peng was not content to confine himself to discussing military affairs. Like other military leaders, Peng believed that he not only had a right (he was, after all, a member of the party's leading bodies) but perhaps even a duty to speak up on political issues. Peng was virulently opposed to Mao's strategy for developing China, preferring instead an approach that owed much to the experiences and practices of the Soviet Union. While other leaders shared this approach and its criticisms of Mao, few were as loud or as critical as Peng. And indeed, it was the loudness and extent of his criticisms that were to lead to Peng's own political downfall after launching an all-out attack on Mao during a party meeting in Lushan in 1959.

Peng's replacement as Minister of National Defence was Lin Biao. Lin was also a man with great military credentials. Like Peng, Lin also had strong connections with the Soviet Union, and may even have fought with the Soviet Red Army against the Nazis at the battle of Leningrad.[11] Lin Biao, however, was very much Mao's man. He not only maintained the PLA's political role, but also intensified political education in the ranks and promoted Mao's ideas and authority wherever possible. But even with Lin as Minister of National Defence, Mao could not count on the total support of the entire military due to the structural divisions within the PLA itself.

Important as the Minister of Defence was, he did not have day-to-day operational control over the troops. The PLA was divided into a number of Military Regions, each of which consisted of at least two provinces,[12] and the Military Region commanders had considerable autonomy over the troops under their command. Thus, even though the Minister of Defence might be advocating Mao's views, this was no guarantee that all regional commanders would follow the same line. The best example here comes from the Cultural Revolution. Although the PLA was ordered to 'support the left' by the party, the state and the PLA leadership, many local level commanders refused; indeed, some stepped in to support party leaders who were being attacked by the radical Maoists.

The military, then, at various levels, was an important constituent of power politics in Mao's China. At times, it provided a brake on Mao's ideas and initiatives, most notably while Peng Dehuai was Minister of Defence before 1959. At other times, it provided an alternative support structure for Mao in his struggle

51

with his colleagues in the party-state hierarchy, particularly when Lin Biao ran the Ministry of Defence in the prelude to the Cultural Revolution. And when the Cultural Revolution collapsed into chaos, it was the military across the country that restored order on China's streets, and exerted considerable pressure on Mao to de-radicalise the movement and rein in the radical Red Guards. With the party structure ripped apart by the bitter conflict of the Cultural Revolution, it was the military that stepped in to fill the void and rebuild the system, both at the local level where they re-built control through revolutionary committees, and at the central level where the green uniforms of the PLA dominated the scene at the 9th Party Congress in 1969.

. . .

## MAOISM AND LENINISM: THE BASIS OF POLITICAL CONFLICT IN BEIJING

Important as local leaders and military figures were for Mao, the main challenges to his authority came from within the central party-state leadership itself. Mao had very clear ideas about how the new state should be organised, and how the party should continue the revolution once in power. Unfortunately for Mao, and ultimately for the rest of the Chinese population, these ideas were not widely shared by Mao's colleagues within the central leadership. Their rejection of Mao's ideas, and Mao's refusal to accept this rejection, was in many ways the key determinant of the tumultuous events that China experienced between 1959 and 1976.

Mao's visions of the new political order were in many ways shaped by his experiences before 1949. Particularly important here are Mao's struggle with the Bolsheviks, both the Comintern in Moscow and those following a Leninist approach to revolution within China. Time and time again, Mao had fought to impose his view of the revolution over those who wanted to adhere to the Leninist orthodoxy, and he had been proved right. Yet when the new political order was being established after 1949, Mao faced the possibility of the resurgence of Leninism. For Steven Levine, this is a function of the revolutionary struggle.[13] Whilst Mao's colleagues had supported his revolutionary strategies which had brought them to power, once the revolution was over and they were ensconced in power, they reverted back to type.

The legacies of the revolution before 1949 were profound for the new state. On one level, we see a Mao who had supreme self-confidence that his ideas were correct – a sort of superiority complex. He also had supreme confidence in the Chinese masses. In 1933 the party had been virtually wiped out, but it survived. At the end of the Long March, the party was again all but wiped out, and found itself in one of the most inhospitable areas of China facing potential attack from both the Japanese invaders and the Guomindang. Not only did it survive, but in the space of 14 years it was in power. If the people could be inspired to achieve these victories, what was to stop a correctly inspired population reaching even greater targets?

But on the other hand, Mao retained deep suspicion of those who tried to block him, both at home and in Moscow. On one level here, we see Mao's desire to impose the primacy of the Chinese experience over dogmatic Marxism. On another level, we see Mao's growing concerns over what the experience of the Soviet revolution might mean for China. In both the Soviet Union and further west in the satellite states, Mao saw a revolution that had become routinised and bureaucratised. Organisation and control had replaced revolutionary zeal. Whilst this was not only a waste of revolution, it also, for Mao, represented a dangerous abandonment of the people. The party was no longer acting as a vanguard of the proletariat, but instead had become an inward-looking elite, isolated from the masses, which was acting to protect its own narrow interests as the new ruling class.

. . .

## THE THEORETICAL PRINCIPLES OF MAO ZEDONG

In understanding Mao's political ideas and the strategy that resulted from them, it is important to recognise that these ideas evolved in response to changing internal and external factors. For example, his revolutionary strategy in Jiangxi, with an emphasis on building up the military as an agent of revolution, was very much shaped by the party's position of weakness in the early 1930s. Once in power, Mao's ideas were very much focused by the examples of other communist states. In the Soviet Union, he saw an example of how revolutionary states could become routinised and bureaucratised and take on a road to revisionism – from the dictatorship of the proletariat to the dictatorship of the party-state bureaucrats. In the Polish and Hungarian uprisings of 1956, he saw the potential pitfalls awaiting a state which allowed itself to become too isolated from its own people's demands and aspirations, and the pitfalls of allowing Moscow's priorities to take precedence over your own national conditions. In the Hungarian case, he also saw the danger that anti-revolutionary forces might be hiding in the party waiting for the chance to subvert the revolution, and take a path towards capitalist restoration.

But Mao's ideas were also shaped by the constant challenges of his colleagues, who, as noted above, appeared determined to ignore his ideas and return to their more orthodox Leninist approach to revolution. As time went by, Mao became increasingly convinced that his colleagues were the main obstruction to the implementation of his correct ideas, and that to get China back on the correct revolutionary track he must first get rid of these opponents.

Mao's ideas also evolved in response to the challenges of his own policies. For example, his emphasis on the importance of educating the masses before revolutionary change could be effective was partly a consequence of the failure of his own Great Leap policies. Unable to accept the notion that his ideas might be wrong, he instead blamed both obstructionist cadres and the ignorance of the masses. If only he could educate them correctly, then his ideas would reap dividends.

### Economics or Politics in Command?

For many of Mao's colleagues, the example of the Soviet Union provided a blueprint of a sort for the establishment of a new political order in China. This is not to say that they followed the Soviet model in toto, but that they shared many of the principles that underpinned the Soviet system. Perhaps the first place to start is with an understanding of the revolutionary process itself, and the relationship between economic change and political or 'spiritual' change – put more simply, the relationship between the way the economy works and the way that people think.

For the Leninists within the party, the primacy was on economic recovery and development. Changing the way people think was not unimportant, but as China was a backward and underdeveloped country, they argued that the main task was to (re)build the economy. Once this was completed, then the party could move on to other tasks. For Mao, this approach was anathema, and was based on an over-strong acceptance of what he called 'dogma' and the rejection of the lessons of the Chinese experience. He too believed that China should develop, and develop as quickly as possible. It was not the goals that Mao objected to, but both the methods and the underlying principles that guided these goals.

Mao warned that whilst the Leninist proposals might lead to economic development in China, it would be to the detriment of building communism. The methods they planned to use would generate new forms of oppression, control and authority that would leave the Chinese masses as powerless as they had been before the revolution. If managers and experts controlled the revolution, then they would come to see themselves as superior to the workers (and the workers would perceive themselves as inferior). If bureaucrats and planners took control of the revolution, they would come to see themselves as superior to the proletariat, and the proletariat would either through coercion or habit develop a passive acceptance of the party's right to dictate. Worse still, they might become alienated from the revolutionary state controlled by bureaucrats who would simply tell them what to do and not listen to their views. Mao was also concerned that if economic incentives were utilised to sponsor growth, then the people would become selfish and self-interested and materialist – the antithesis of the mutual aid, comradeship and political conviction that was needed to build communism. In short, if you concentrate on economic change before worrying about the social cultural dimension, by the time that you have reached economic development, the people will need another political revolution to overthrow the dictatorship of the party planners, the managers and the experts.

To prevent this, Mao argued that the party should only implement economic changes that simultaneously increased socialist awareness. For example, introducing mutual aid teams in the countryside could not only increase agricultural production by utilising economies of scale, but also display the benefits of co-operation and working together as opposed to selfish individualism. Mao argued that his approach would lead to a China that was both developed and socialist. Indeed, his policies would generate faster economic growth than those of the

Leninists. The people had already proved that if they were correctly motivated, then they could achieve anything – just witness the revolutionary victory itself. China did not possess many financial resources, but it did have another source of capital in its people. If the party could now convince the people of the superiority of socialism, then they would be mobilised and motivated to work for the revolution. The state would not need to pay them more or offer financial incentives to work, or even force them to work – they would do it willingly because they believed.

Furthermore, Mao and the Leninists disagreed on the specifics of policy, as well as the general principles. While the Leninists were committed to collectivisation of agriculture, they thought that urban industrial development should come first. In the Soviet Union, forcing the peasants to provide more and more finance and raw materials for the cities had facilitated industrialisation. Whilst the Chinese Leninists did not want to 'squeeze' the peasantry quite as much as their Soviet predecessors, development of the urban sector would have to rely on the transfer of some resources from the countryside. Once the urban-industrial base had been developed and could provide tractors, chemical fertilisers, and skilled managers and experts, then rural collectivisation could proceed and be successful.

For Mao, this approach ignored the realities of the Chinese revolution, and placed too much emphasis on emulating the Soviet experience. Mao argued that if, and it was a big if, the Leninists' approach had been relevant in the Soviet case, Chinese conditions dictated an entirely different approach. Could the party really justify 'squeezing' China's peasants – around 90 per cent of the population – for the benefit of urban industrialisation? And if it could justify it theoretically, was it wise for the party to risk alienating such a large section of the population in its drive for industrialisation, particularly the sector of the population which had been the party's main constituency of support in the revolution?

Furthermore, Mao opposed the approach on practical grounds. If industrial development was so dependent on surplus from the rural sector, then surely it made sense to develop the countryside first to provide even greater surplus for industry. Rather than expend scarce capital on the development of the industrial sector, the party should mobilise the peasantry to attain shared political goals. By promoting the political revolution in the countryside, then the rural population would engender rural development that would in turn facilitate urban-industrial revolution.

Crucially, Mao was not swayed from his beliefs even when the evidence suggested that he had been mistaken. As we shall see in the following chapter, Mao's attempts to mobilise the peasantry – to arouse their political enthusiasm to generate economic advances – resulted in mass starvation and economic chaos at the end of the Great Leap Forward. Indeed, if any-thing, the spectacular failure of the Great Leap strengthened Mao's convictions that political mobilisation and ideological training should be the party's primary task. The Great Leap had failed because the masses did not yet accept the correct-ness of the policies – even many party cadres had not properly understood what they were meant to be doing. What was needed now was a new national campaign to educate the masses and even party members themselves of the wisdom of Mao's ideas and of how communism would work to benefit the people.

So where Mao had previously argued that economic change and socialist education had to go hand in hand, by the early 1960s he argued that the people should be first correctly edu-cated as good socialists, and economic change would then fol-low. By this stage, Mao had virtually turned orthodox Marxism on its head. Rather than economics determining politics, Mao's emphasis had turned even more to the importance of political will – an approach which distanced him even further from the ideological approach of much of the rest of the CCP leadership.

## The Relationship Between the Party and the Masses

Another key area of cleavage between Mao and his colleagues was over the role of the party, and the party's relationships with the masses. For the Leninists, the position was clear. The party was an elite vanguard ruling over the people, but on their behalf. The people were largely naive and ignorant of the principles of socialism and if you listened directly to what they said, then you might actually act against their own best inter-ests. They would only look at the local situation and assess their short-term views, often overly influenced by old feudal ideologies. Party members, however, had sufficient knowledge of the principles of socialism and an understanding of the 'wider' long-term picture – they viewed the world through the correct socialist paradigm and were thus best placed to implement correct policies.

In practice, this meant that only party members should be involved in the decision-making process. There would be channels for the normal people to have a say. These were the 'transmission belts' between the party and the people: trade union organisations, agricultural co-operatives, national federations and so on. However, the party should not act on the views expressed in these forums if it thought that they were misguided. Ultimately, the party remained the sole arbiter of what the people's interests were, not the people themselves.

Again, Mao argued that these ideas followed the Soviet Leninist orthodoxy too closely, and disregarded the lessons of history. Mao feared that the party risked becoming isolated from the normal people and ignoring their true wishes. At best, this could result in the party ignoring what the people wanted, and instead making policies that only served party members' interests. At worst, the party risked alienating the masses, as Mao later believed was the cause of the popular uprisings against ruling communist parties in Poland and Hungary in 1956. Notably, both the Polish and Hungarian parties had remained very close to Moscow, suggesting that their policies were based more on what the Soviet Union wanted than what the Polish and Hungarian people themselves wanted and needed.

The party, then, risked becoming a smug and complacent new ruling class that paid more attention to what had happened in the Soviet Union than it did to its own revolutionary situation. For Mao, the way to prevent this danger was to immerse the party in the masses. The people would act as the correct check and balance on arbitrary party rule. Rather than confining discussion to party members (often referred to as 'small democracy'), the masses themselves should take part in the process ('big democracy'). The people were the font of true wisdom. The party should go down to the masses to discover their ideas and their desires. It should then transform these disparate ideas into concrete and coherent policy, and return them to the people who would embrace and accept them as their own. Furthermore, in order to prevent the isolation of the party from the people, cadres should immerse themselves in proletarian culture by working in the factories and the cities, to 'proletarianise' themselves through work and study with the masses themselves.

Mao was also concerned that the party was discriminating against workers and peasants in its drive to increase party membership. On one level, the desire to win the support of intellectuals and experts to aid economic development had resulted in them being given a stake in the new political order through party membership. On another level, the system of recruiting new party members placed an emphasis on those who already had the 'correct' political background – typically the sons and daughters of existing party members. As party membership increasingly became an important criterion in gaining access to higher education, this meant that the party, by the 1950s, was becoming a self-replicating, isolated and inaccessible ruling elite.

This evolution of party membership after 1949 clearly irked Mao. Why should the people's party become a haven for intellectuals and managers, and why should access to the party be denied to the normal people? It was not that Mao hated intellectuals *per se*. On the contrary, he realised that if China was to modernise and reclaim its rightful place in the world, then it needed skilled and able individuals in all walks of life. However, he was very much opposed to 'intellectualism' which had underpinned the Confucian social order – the idea that intellectuals were of a higher moral worth than the normal people. Mao feared that the intellectuals' view of their own moral worth had not been changed by the revolution, and that they continued to perceive themselves as being more worthy, whilst too many ordinary people considered themselves to be inferior. If China was to move towards a classless society, then these old social norms had to be eradicated – the proletariat had to bring forth its own intellectuals.

Finally, he resented the increasingly closed nature of party membership and the inter-generational transmission of party membership. Why should accident of birth become the main criterion for party membership? Mao was concerned that class attitudes could be passed on through generations. He was very wary of attitudinal hangovers from the past, and, as we shall see below, this had significant implications for Mao's notions of class and class conflict in the post-revolutionary state. But while he was wary of 'bad class' elements permeating the party, he was equally suspicious of attitudinal hangovers in managers, experts and intellectuals. And why should the proletariat be denied entry simply because they were not the offspring of party members?

For Mao, class background was important, but not necessarily enough on its own. Equally important was political activity. If those with the correct class backgrounds were not politically active, then they were denying their revolutionary role. So where the Leninists tended to judge political correctness in terms of an individual's family background (those who were 'red by birth'), Mao preferred to judge people on what they actually did (those who were 'red by action').

## Revolution and Stability

Whilst forcing the party to engage with the masses was one method of ensuring that the party remained part of the people that it was supposed to represent, this was not enough in itself. Even this form of party–people relationship could lead to complacency and stability, and perhaps above all else Mao feared the implications of this stability for the revolution. Once things became stabilised, routinised and bureaucratised, then revolutionary zeal would disappear. The revolution would thus, as it had in the Soviet Union, become stagnated in bureaucratic control by the party, and even popular participation in decision-making could become bureaucratised and sanitised. As such, new forms of dominance and oppression (this time by the party) might emerge to replace the old feudal and colonial forms of oppression.

Mao thought that once stable forms of relationships emerged, new forms of unequal relationships formed around them. For example, the cadre's position of power over the peasant would lead to an unequal relationship, with each considering themselves to be unequal to the other which would result in a new form of 'class' oppression. Mao's notion of 'class' was thus very different from the way that most Marxists understood the term. In the Marxist tradition, one's class is determined by one's socio-economic relationship to the means of production. Put more simply, if you own the means of production, then you belong to a different class from those who do not own the means of production, and simply rely on their own labour.

As we have seen, in defining his revolutionary strategy before 1949, Mao played around with these strictly socio-economic definitions of class to distinguish between different classes within, for example, the peasantry. Nevertheless, these definitions were largely still related to one's relationship to the means of production. After the revolution, Mao's notions of class were further transformed to take on new determinants and new non-economic definitions, with crucial consequences for his notions of class conflict, and for the evolution of conflict within the Chinese political elites.

In accordance with the orthodox approach, class conflict should not occur in the post-revolutionary state once the state has undertaken the full nationalisation of the means of production. Thus, once land reform accomplished the goal of giving land to the tiller, and the industrial and commercial sectors were under state control (in the Chinese phraseology, under the ownership of the entire people), then everybody had the same class since everybody equally owned the means of production. In this sense, then, class conflict should have finished in China at the 8th Party Congress of 1956 when Liu Shaoqi announced that the economic transformation was essentially complete. Class conflict would still exist, but this would be conflict between the Chinese people and external enemies of the Chinese people.

It is difficult to ascertain whether Mao agreed with this view or not at this stage. There is some evidence from Mao's earlier writings in the 1940s that he was already thinking of class more in terms of a state of mind, rather than in strictly economic terms. However, Mao did not oppose this view at the 8th Party Congress (in public at least). But 1956 was in many ways a defining year in Chinese politics, as will be discussed in greater detail in later chapters. Internally, Mao's plans for agricultural development were defeated by his colleagues, who instead chose a more moderate adaptation of Soviet central planning for the Second Five Year Plan. In addition, the events of the Hundred Flowers Movement in 1956 and 1957 (see Chapter 3) brought the question of internal opposition to both Mao in particular, and the CCP in general, into sharper focus.

Externally, the lessons of the Polish and Hungarian uprisings suggested that in these socialist states at least, class struggle was far from over. On one level, the two ruling parties had apparently isolated themselves so much from their people that they took on the characteristics of an exploiting class. The workers in Poland and Hungary had no way of getting their voices heard other than through rebellion. On another level, Nagy's rise to power in Hungary was, for Mao, an example of how a bourgeois class enemy had joined the party and waited for his chance to usurp power and turn the revolution over to capitalist restoration. If this was not evidence enough of the need to maintain the class struggle, Khrushchev's denunciation signalled, for Mao, the end of radicalism in the Soviet Union. The Soviet revolution was now run by 'revisionist' managers and bureaucrats – a new party class which ran the country for their own benefit and ignored their own people.

By the end of the 1950s, and probably from the end of the Hundred Flowers, Mao's notions of class and class struggle were clearly departing from those of his Leninist colleagues. The revolution must continue to ensure its survival, and the continued class struggle was the key to maintaining the revolution. If the people and the party relaxed for a second, then the revolution could be lost.

At the risk of over-simplification, we can identify five major class enemies that Mao thought would destroy the Chinese revolution if the Chinese people let them. The first was external enemies. Initially this meant the United States and its allies, who appeared committed to crushing communism in Asia. However, as time passed, Mao's increasing suspicion of Moscow led him to designate both the United States and the Soviet Union as imperialist superpowers intent on destroying China. The second was new classes which Mao feared were appearing in the Chinese countryside. For example, he was concerned that the process of land reform in the countryside might generate new classes of rich peasants. The third was what we might call the continuation of 'attitudinal' classes – people who despite the revolution considered themselves to be superior to the masses. The fourth was agents of foreign powers who were waiting in society or (worst of all) in the party to distort and ultimately overthrow the revolution. Given the links (either personal or ideological) that many Chinese communists had with the Soviet Union, many party members ran the risk of being identified with aggressive foreign powers once the Sino-Soviet alliance gave way to Sino-Soviet conflict in the 1960s.

This brings us to the fifth and final potential class enemy. Mao believed that permanent revolution and class struggle were essential to guard against the party becoming a ruling class in itself. This idea has much in common with the Yugoslav communist leader Djilas's notion of 'The New Class' – a new exploiting dictatorship of the party-state bureaucracy over the people.[14] It was not that party members deliberately set out to become a new class, but their positions of power in the state gradually altered their perceptions and actions.

Thus, Mao believed that the revolution faced numerous challenges from both within and without, and these class enemies were a much bigger danger for the revolution than economic underdevelopment. Thus, where the Leninists emphasised development as the main goal for the revolution, and required political stability to pursue developmental goals, for Mao class conflict and continual revolution were the *sine qua non* for all policy.

. . .

## MAO'S POLITICAL IDEAS: REVOLUTIONARY PURITY OR POLITICAL PRAGMATISM?

It is notable that Mao's emphasis on ideology and politics reflected those areas where he was most able to set the political agenda. His ideas were not particularly strongly held within the party-state bureaucracy. As Lieberthal notes:

> Mao's own position in the system would be affected by the type of economic development strategy pursued. The Chairman's personal political strengths lay in the areas of foreign policy (especially towards the great powers), rural policy, and issues of revolutionary change.[15]

It was thus to his advantage to maintain the primacy of the ideological debate and focus on those areas where his voice was most likely to be heard.

Furthermore, Mao's prestige was high amongst the rural masses and the young, partly as a consequence of the mass mobilisation campaigns and the development of the personality cult that will be discussed in detail in the next chapter. Again, it played to his strengths to emphasise the primacy of rural development. With the Leninists dominating policy-making, subjecting them to supervision and control from the masses who were more sympathetic to Mao's views was also to his political benefit. Similarly, promoting party entrance for those who were politically active created a new pro-Mao constituency in the party to challenge the existing status quo and the technocratic party membership.

Another consideration here is the relationship between Mao's goals for the Chinese revolution and the influence of Soviet Marxism. The extent to which Mao ever had a firm and good grasp of the canon of Marx and Engels is open to question. It certainly appears that he came to the original works *after* he had already developed his main ideas about the class basis of the Chinese revolution. Whatever the case here, Mao was very much concerned with ensuring the correct balance between theoretical principles and concrete experiences. For Mao, the works of Marx, Engels and Lenin provided the theoretical base for the revolution. This theoretical work provided the abstract principles for Marxists to follow, but did not provide universally correct policies. After all, had Lenin himself not reinterpreted the Marxist guidance to suit the specifics of the case in revolutionary Russia?

For Mao, then, there were no abstract theoretical truths. The only real truths came from applying these guiding principles to the specific case in hand. Thus, the Marxist class analysis that forecast revolutionary potential in Europe could not simply be applied to the Chinese case to identify a Chinese revolutionary struggle between the oppressed proletariat and the bourgeoisie. But if you used the basic class analysis – the guiding principle – and applied this to the specific Chinese case, then you came up with a different class-based revolutionary strategy. Practice, then, was the only criterion of truth – you had to seek truth from facts, not in the abstract works of Marx and Engels, or in the experience of the Soviet Union. As the Soviet Marxists had correctly adapted Marxism to fit their own conditions, then wasn't it being anti-Marxist to accept the Soviet experience (a result of specific conditions) as a blueprint or model for Chinese communism?

The key distinction here is between Theory and Thought. Marxism-Leninism, not just Marxism, provided the abstract theory. Mao Zedong Thought represented the specific application of the theory to the Chinese case. Thus, Mao believed that slavish or dogmatic adherence to not only the original writings of Marx and Engels, but also to the Soviet experience, was not only inappropriate to the Chinese situation but also anti-Marxist. In practical terms, Mao much resented the over-reliance on Moscow as a model for China. Such an approach denied the validity of the Chinese experience in the revolution before 1949, and threatened to subvert China's national interests to those of Moscow. Surely the lesson of the victorious revolutionary struggle was that the CCP only succeeded when it sought truth from facts rather than from Moscow.

Mao's resistance to interference from Moscow played an important role in the evolution of conflict between Mao and his colleagues after 1949. Mao thought that Moscow had never given him sufficient credit for all that he achieved before 1949, and now felt that his colleagues' Leninism was profoundly unsound and ungrateful. Mao had not fought to liberate China from Japanese influence simply to swap this now for Russian influence. Indeed, one gets the feeling that he would have opposed any policy that appeared too Soviet in inspiration even if it had been wildly successful. Note that the first major leadership purges after 1949, those of Gao Gang and Rao Shushi, were in no small part due to those leaders' close relations with Moscow. Peng Dehuai, dismissed as Minister of Defence at the Lushan Plenum of 1959, was also very close to Moscow, and an adherent both of following the Soviet model and of closer military reliance on the Soviet Union. Similarly, when Liu Shaoqi was purged during the Cultural Revolution, he was typically referred to as 'China's Khrushchev', and many other purged leaders were branded as 'black hands painted by Moscow'. Even Mao's closest comrade during the radical years of the Cultural Revolution, Lin Biao, was branded as a pro-Soviet traitor when he too fell foul of his patron in 1971.

Maintaining the independence of the Chinese revolution was important for Mao because the concrete circumstances in China were the main determinant of correct policy. But maintaining independence was also important in its own right. The Chinese revolution was, of course, intended to produce a communist society in China. But it was also designed, in Mao's mind at least, to produce a strong China which could take its rightful place on the world stage.

. . .

## MAO THOUGHT OR MAOISM?

Mao's vision of what the revolution should achieve, and how it should be achieved, departs considerably from Marx's original view. It also departs considerably from the Leninist interpretation of revolution. Indeed, some would argue that Mao's ideas move so far away from Marx, and at times deny its basic essentials, that you cannot consider the two to be part of the same ideology. Mao did not so much add new interpretations and applications to Marxism (Mao Thought) as develop a totally new and distinct ideology (Maoism).[16]

The debate over whether Mao was a Marxist or not is a complex and tortuous one to follow.[17] At the risk of over-simplification, those who argue that Mao did create a new distinct ideology argue on three main points. The first, perhaps least significant, revolves around the class-based nature of Mao's revolutionary strategy. With no real proletariat to speak of, and no bourgeois revolution in place, then how do you get to a proletarian revolution? Second, and very much related to this, can a peasant-based revolution be a Marxist revolution?

The third point is the most substantial and pertinent. By defining class more as a state of mind than as an economically determined state, surely Mao moves too far away from Marx's original works? Marxism is, perhaps above all, an economically deterministic ideology. If you deny the importance of economics as the determinant of social and political change, then you must be denying the basic building blocks of Marxism itself. How can class struggle be possible after the revolution when the establishment of the proletarian dictatorship has removed class divisions? Mao compounds the crime by ultimately arguing that transforming human thought can be the precursor to economic change (rather than economic change transforming human thought). Mao, then, is a 'voluntarist', who turns Marx on his head by emphasising the primacy of willed social change as a precondition for economic change.

Those who see Mao as being part of the Marxist tradition do not dispute these major differences between Mao and Marx, and even between Mao and Lenin. However, they argue that the 'Maoists' miss the point about Marx and Marxism, even if they are correct about Mao. Marx, they argue, was less of an economic determinist than they suggest, and that he did discuss the importance of willed 'cultural' change. Reducing Marx to a simple economic determinist is over-simplifying the thousands of words that Marx wrote. Furthermore, Marx never intended his ideas to be a blueprint for all countries to follow. He was writing about the specific situation in one or two European countries at a specific moment in time. Even Marx toyed with the notion that other forms of oppression (and therefore class conflict) might exist in oriental nations, of which he knew very little. The important thing here is not following Marx's exact prescriptions for revolutionary change, but using his class analysis approach.

Thus, if you take the Marxist approach of identifying class conflicts in society, and apply it to the Chinese situation, then you end up with a different notion of the oppressing and revolutionary classes in China than you would if you used the same approach to investigate Britain and France in the nineteenth century. The main oppressing classes in China were the agents of feudalism (landlords, the Guomindang and the Confucian bureaucratic/imperial structure) and the agents of colonialism. Thus, in the Chinese case, the oppressed classes were the peasantry and those classes facing the brunt of colonialism. It was therefore entirely Marxist to develop a revolution based on the support of the peasantry and those urban groups which had been alienated by both the foreign colonisers and the Guomindang's response to those foreign colonisers. Marx may not have developed a notion of a semi-feudal semi-colonial state, but that was because he hadn't been interested in China. Although the term is not found in Marx's works, the idea of semi-feudal semi-colonialism emerges from deploying Marxist perspectives. Whether you see Mao as a Marxist or not essentially depends on your view of Marx and his works – was it a blueprint, or merely an approach?

Furthermore, if Mao is not a Marxist, then what about Lenin and the Soviet revolution? Where did Marx talk about imperialism as the highest stage of capitalism? Marx argued that revolution would occur in the most advanced capitalist nations, so how does Lenin come to the conclusion that it can occur in the weakest links of the international capitalist chain? And where did Lenin find his justification for an elite group of revolutionaries leading a revolution of an undeveloped proletariat in the works of Marx? The answer is that he applied basic Marxist approaches to the specifics of the Russian situation to develop an understanding of the revolutionary situation in a specific and unique case study. And if Mao denies economic determinism, then what about the policies adapted in the New Economic Policy in the Soviet Union to build the economic base that Marx said was a prerequisite for developing revolutionary consciousness in the proletariat? Surely, once Lenin had done this, and still remained a Marxist, then anything that Mao was doing was in exactly the same vein?

So while there may be a clear and real distinction between Marx and Mao, the key link lies in Lenin's reinvention of Marxism to fit the Russian situation. If Lenin can reinterpret

Marxism, then surely Mao can reinterpret Leninism? Only very few authors would not consider Lenin a Marxist. Gregor, for example, argues that once Lenin 'compromised' Marxism and tried to 'fabricate the entire missing industrial base', then the path to Mao's deviations and a new Maoist ideology were clearly set in place. What Mao adapted to the Chinese situation wasn't Marxism, but Stalinism, so Mao could not have been a Marxist.[18]

The debate will continue. But does it matter? Does the peasant dying from starvation at the end of the Great Leap Forward accept his fate more readily because it was a Marxist policy which led to his fate? The answer to the second question is no, but the answer to the first question is a resounding yes for three main reasons.

First, Mao was convinced that he was right and convinced that his was the correct Marxist approach. While it is true that Mao wanted power, he did not just want power for its own sake. He was also motivated by ensuring that his correct Marxist ideas were followed, and if people got in the way and relied on inappropriate Russian models, then these obstacles had to be removed.

Second, and following on from the above, we return to the importance of Sino-Soviet relations, and Mao's attitude towards Soviet Marxism. In the international communist debate, it was important for Mao to ascertain that his ideas were not only part of the Marxist canon, but also the best model for others to follow in promoting revolution in the third world.

Third, and more important for this study, Mao had to argue that his ideas were the correct Marxist ideas in competition with those Chinese leaders who instinctively and ideologically looked to Moscow for their inspiration. Unable to dominate the specifics of policy-making on a day-to-day level within the party-state bureaucracy, Mao's major way of reasserting himself in the political arena was to maintain the importance of ideology on the political agenda. By continually keeping the ideological debate alive, and by continually emphasising the correct Marxist approach of seeking truth from facts and asserting the primacy of the Chinese experience, Mao could reassert his views over and above those of his colleagues, and use the Marxism debate as a tool to attack his opponents. Defending his ideas as the only correct interpretation of Marxism in the Chinese case was a crucial component of Mao's political strategy.

## PARTY CLEAVAGES IN MAO'S CHINA AND SOURCES OF POWER

One of the apparent paradoxes of Mao's China is that a man who was so influential, so important for the Chinese revolution, was in many ways relatively weak. Yes, he was the figurehead of the revolution, and yes he was the main architect of the CCP's victory in 1949. But once the party after 1949 established a party-state system based on the Soviet Leninist model, then Mao found his position much weaker in this formal power structure than he had in the more informal personality-based days of the revolutionary struggle.

But it is exactly because Mao was relatively weak in the formal party-state structure that he exercised his influence in the way that he did. Unable to influence policy through the day-to-day decision-making framework, Mao was forced to act outside the formal structure. At the highest level, he kept major ideological decisions on the political agenda. In this respect, Mao's control of the terms of the Sino-Soviet dispute was also an extra-system attempt to attack the Leninists within the Chinese party. At lower levels, Mao utilised his popular support within the peasantry and students to spark political campaigns from the bottom up as a means of bypassing the formal decision-making structure. And on a parallel level, Mao utilised his supporters within the military, particularly after 1959, to create an alternative power structure to the party-state organisations. In terms of pursuing his policy preference, this entailed embarking on mass campaigns that created such a momentum that the rest of the party were all but forced to go along with them. In the case of the Cultural Revolution, this 'organised' spontaneity was directed against the party-state structure itself – the very arena where Mao's opponents were most heavily concentrated.

. . .

## NOTES

1. Mao Zedong (1977) 'lun shi da guan xi (On the Ten Great Relationships)' (April 1956) in *Mao Ze Dong Xuan Ji: Di Wu Juan (The Collected Works of Mao Zedong: Volume 5)* (Beijing: Renmin Chubanshe) pp. 275–77.

2. Reflecting their predominantly military character, these regions were initially called military administrative commissions. Despite the later change in title to administrative commissions, many of the new 'civilian' leaders simply transferred out of the military into the new party-state. They were, in effect, soldiers in civvies.

3. There were 29 provincial level units in China at the start of the 1980s. These included three cities, Beijing, Tianjin and Shanghai, which were given provincial status due to their importance to the national economy. They also included the supposedly 'autonomous' regions of northern and western China with large ethnically non-Chinese populations (for example, Tibet and Inner Mongolia). The number has now increased to 31, with the separation of Hainan Island from Guangdong province, and the 1997 decision to grant the city of Chongqing (formerly in Sichuan province) provincial status.

4. These were Anhui, Henan, Gansu, Guangdong, Shandong, Qinghai, Zhejiang, Hebei, Guangxi, Liaoning, Xinjiang and Yunnan. Teiwes, F. (1972) 'Provincial Politics in China: Themes and Variations' in Lindbeck, J. (ed.) *China: Management of a Revolutionary Society* (London: Allen and Unwin) pp. 126–27.

5. Ibid.

6. Goodman, D. (1986) *Centre and Province in the People's Republic of China: Sichuan and Guizhou 1955–1965* (Cambridge: Cambridge University Press).

7. Vogel, E. (1969) *Canton Under Communism* (Cambridge, Mass.: Harvard University Press).

8. Donnithorne, A. (1972) 'China's Cellular Economy: Some Economic Trends Since the Cultural Revolution', *China Quarterly* 52, pp. 605–19.

9. Whitney, J. (1969) *China: Area, Administration and Nation Building* (Chicago: University of Chicago Press).

10. Whitson, W. and Huang, C. (1973) *The Chinese High Command: A History of Communist Military Politics, 1927–71* (New York: Praeger); Whitson, W. (1969) 'The Field Army in Chinese Communist Military Politics', *China Quarterly* 37, pp. 1–30; Whitson, W. (1972) 'Organizational Perspectives and Decision Making in the Chinese Communist High Command' in Scalapino, R. (ed.) *Elites in the People's Republic of China* (Seattle: University of Washington Press) pp. 381–415.

11. Having earlier been evacuated to the Soviet Union for medical treatment.

12. For example, there are now seven Military Regions, each controlling military affairs in between two and six provinces. The Military Regions are named by the cities that house the military

regional commands – Beijing, Chengdu, Guangzhou, Jinan, Lanzhou, Nanjing and Shenyang.

13. Levine, S. (1987) *Anvil of Victory: The Communist Revolution in Manchuria* (New York: Columbia University Press).

14. Djilas, M. (1957) *The New Class: An Analysis of the Communist System* (New York: Praeger).

15. Lieberthal, K. (1993) 'The Great Leap Forward and the Split in the Yan'an Leadership 1958–65' in MacFarquhar, R. (ed.) *The Politics of China 1949–1989* (Cambridge: Cambridge University Press) pp. 87–147.

16. See Schwartz, B. (1960) 'The Legend of the "Legend of Maoism"', *China Quarterly* 2, pp. 35–42.

17. John Starr provides an excellent overview of these debates in Starr, J. (1986) ' "Good Mao". "Bad Mao": Mao Studies and the Re-Evaluation of Mao's Political Thought', *Australian Journal of Chinese Affairs* 16, pp. 1–22. See also Knight, N. (1983) 'The Form of Mao Zedong's "Sinification of Marxism"', *Australian Journal of Chinese Affairs* 9, pp. 17–33.

18. Gregor also argues that Mao did not use a Marxist class analysis at all. Mao believed that the peasantry would rebel because they were poor – and poverty is not the same thing as class. Gregor, A.J. (1995) *Marxism, China and Development* (New Brunswick: Transaction Books).

# Chapter 3

# THE FIRST MAJOR CLEAVAGE: 1949–1957

. . .

## RECONSTRUCTING THE COUNTRYSIDE

It did not take long before the different interpretations of the best road for Chinese development began to manifest themselves in political conflict. As we saw in Chapter 2, Mao's notions of the relationship between the party and the people, and the importance of maintaining revolutionary zeal and class conflict, generated instability and conflict during 1956 and 1957. The result of the Hundred Flowers Campaign was also to have a significant impact on the evolution of the second major area of conflict: that over the best development strategy for the Chinese revolution.

Teiwes argues that in the early stage of the post-revolutionary period, Mao was rather orthodox in his approach.[1] He accepted the establishment of a rather Leninist party-state structure, and the need to rebuild the economy on the basis of the First Five Year Plan. Nevertheless, it was in the countryside that Mao was probably most active and most concerned. Mao saw rural reform as his area of expertise, and one where he had a key advantage over his colleagues; it was also the area where his personal prestige and profile was the highest. Developing the countryside, and developing it along his own lines, was therefore a major consideration for Mao in the immediate post-1949 period.

The process of land reform began even before the liberation in those areas under Communist Party control. But in the years following the establishment of the new republic, the process of land reform was extended to the entire country. After thousands of years, the social and economic structure of the countryside was torn apart, and a new system put in place – perhaps the greatest episode in social and economic engineering that the world has seen.

On a very simple level, the aim of land reform was to give land to the tiller. The landlords were to be destroyed as a class, but not as individuals.[2] But there was another element to the land reform process. Rather than having policy imposed from above, peasants were encouraged to participate, and make the key decisions themselves. Thus, rather than the party simply reallocating land, it was for the people of the countryside to decide who had been the exploiters, who had been the exploited, and to make their decisions accordingly. This isn't to say that the party simply stepped back from the decision entirely. Work teams of dedicated communists were sent to the villages to educate and to explain, but they weren't meant to intervene actively.

All rural dwellers had to submit themselves to classification by their peers, a process that is sometimes referred to as 'passing the gate'. If they were classified as a landlord or a rich peasant, then they would lose most of their land and property, but would retain enough to live on from their own endeavours. If they were classified as a poor peasant or a landless labourer, then they would gain land and property from the dispossessed. Middle peasants, however, were allowed to keep their land and property. In this way, the party hoped to build the active support of the ordinary people, but without alienating too many middle elements. Similarly, early policy in the cities was built around attacking only the biggest bourgeois families, whilst initially allowing the smaller industrialists and businessmen to thrive. Indeed, more people were employed in private industry in 1951 than in 1949, as property seized by either the Guomindang or the Japanese was restored to previous owners. In this early stage at least, the party's policy was one of radical change tempered by a desire not to alienate middle classes. Once the party felt more secure in power by 1953, then it hardened its approach and implemented a policy of forced nationalisation.

Land reform did not always go smoothly. In his description of land reform in Shanxi province, Hinton shows the difficulty that the party work teams faced in persuading the peasants to attack the landlords.[3] The peasants had lived under the old system for so long that they could not conceive how they could live without the landlords – who would employ them? The challenge, then, was to explain to the peasants that it was not the ordinary people who were dependent for their existence on the landlords, but the landlords who were dependent on them. It also took a very brave individual to come forward from the crowd to accuse landlords of past evils.

In some areas, fear of a possible re-invasion from the Guomindang, and the resultant restoration of the landlords, meant that peasants were reluctant in the extreme to be too aggressive. Rather than identify people as landlords, they took the safer path of classifying them as middle peasants. But this meant that there was not enough land being reclaimed from the old landlords to go around. In such cases, the party often insisted on second rounds of classifications, with stricter guidelines for classifying landlords and middle peasants. Frustrated by the lack of action by the peasantry, the work teams frequently imposed the judgements themselves.

In other areas, the reverse problem emerged (particularly in those areas with a firmer communist base, and notably in the north-east). When they were given the chance to identify past evils, peasants threw themselves into the campaign and attacked the landlords with gusto. Reliable figures are difficult to come by, but a figure of two million landlord deaths during the land reform process appears to be pretty close to the mark. Again, the party had to intervene directly, but this time to temper peasant enthusiasm because of fear that it would alienate the middle classes.

Two million deaths are not inconsiderable. Defenders of the process would argue that under the old system, mass deaths from starvation were commonplace, and that the land reform merely shifted the threat from peasant to landlord. Given the longevity of the old feudal system, the transformation of the countryside was indeed dramatic. But the transformation wasn't complete. If the peasants thought that gaining land was the end of the revolution in the countryside, they were greatly mistaken – if anything, land reform was only the start of the process.

One of the problems with land reform was that there was simply not enough high-quality land and equipment to go around. In addition, the move towards everyone having their own little plot of land wasn't necessarily leading towards the development of socialist ideas. Rather than emphasising the importance of communal action and proletarian solidarity, it rather suggested personal motivations and selfishness. Thus, even before the land reform process had been completed in some areas, the party moved on towards re-assessing rural production within its heartland.

The next step was to create mutual aid teams (MAT). Again, the emphasis was placed on peasants making the decision to co-operate themselves, rather than being forced into co-operation from above. Work teams were again sent down to the countryside to explain to the peasants the benefits of working co-operatively – if you've got an ox, and your neighbour has got a plough, then surely it makes sense to share your resources. The MATs were very small-scale, with a few households joining together to work co-operatively during busy times (sowing, harvest, etc.). Importantly, the peasants still very much controlled their own bit of land – you worked together and shared your resources, but what was yours was yours.

The move towards MATs was relatively successful. And again it is worth emphasising that the move came from the peasants themselves, and that they retained a notion that their land was their own – a significant comparison with what was to come later. But again, the process was not without its problems. The scale of farming was still often very small, and the benefits of economies of scale were still unfulfilled. Furthermore, there had been a tendency for peasants with good land or decent resources to work together to maximise their benefit, while those with the poorer quality land or fewer resources were often left out of the process. As such, even at this early stage, divisions began to re-emerge within the countryside between the 'haves' and 'have-nots', and the main beneficiaries were the old middle peasants who usually had started off from a higher base.

Almost as soon as the MATs were established, the moves began to replace them with a new form of rural organisation. By transferring from MATs to co-operatives, the number of households involved in co-operation was increased, thus bringing more people into the benefits of co-operation. Members of the co-operatives now pooled all their land and agricultural property, and worked the land together. Importantly, there was still a notion of what was yours was yours – earnings were still related to what you put in in the first place. Thus, if one person put in one unit of land, and another put in two units, the second person would receive twice as much from the harvest as the first.

Thus, in the space of five or six years, the countryside went through three stages of transformation. Whilst the initial land reform was by far the most radical of these, the subsequent transitions to MATs and co-operatives were not inconsiderable themselves. By around 1954, the debate moved on yet again, and this time with far-reaching consequences.

## THE DEBATE OVER COLLECTIVISATION

Despite the successes of the land reform process in the countryside and the First Five Year Plan in industry, it became clear by about 1954 that a new path had to be found for future developments. Even at this early stage, Mao came up against considerable opposition to his ideas from colleagues within the party-state elites. For Mao, the issues were clear. Unless the co-operativisation of the countryside was speeded up, then China would suffer both economic and social problems. On the economy, Mao argued that only through increasing the pace of collectivisation in the countryside would the rural sector both produce sufficient food for itself and for the rapidly growing urban sector. In the longer term, it would also facilitate the growth of light industry in both urban and rural centres. The collectives would soon produce more than enough grain to meet demand, and they could then produce cash crops like cotton which would spur the development of China's textile industry.

Socially, Mao pointed to the still growing disparities between the well-off peasants and those who were losing out. Many were so poor that they were being forced to sell off their land or rent it out to others, thus putting them back in a position of dependence on their labour in a manner similar to that before the revolution. Finally, Mao pointed to the great successes of the rural population in not only prosecuting the revolution before 1949, but also in undertaking land reform after 1949. He argued that the peasantry had great enthusiasm for the collectivisation programme, and that the party should not waste this great opportunity.

For Mao, then, the move should be accelerated. Not only should the party strive to complete basic co-operativisation, but it should ride on the high tide of peasant enthusiasm and move on to a new form of organisation. These were to be collectives (sometimes referred to as higher stage co-operatives), which differed from what went before in two main ways. First, they were bigger still than the co-operatives, typically encompassing between 150 and 200 households. Second, and perhaps more fundamental, they struck at the heart of existing notions of private property. The collectives moved to a socialist system of distribution. Rather than your rewards being dependent on your original input – your capital shares in the co-operative – they were now entirely dependent on the work that you put in. To each according to his deeds.

Mao's views were opposed by key figures within the party elites, notably by Liu Shaoqi, Chen Yun and Vice-Premier Li Fuchun. They argued that without modern inputs from the industrial sector, co-operatives could not flourish. The priority must be production, even if there were some small class and social problems in the countryside, and this meant that the pace of collectivisation should be gradual. Furthermore, the point of rural collectivisation was to serve the cities, by providing food for the workforce, raw materials, and capital. To sum up, there was, as Blecher puts it, a deep division between those leaders who wanted to collect from the peasants (the Leninists) and those who wanted to collect the peasants together (the Maoists).[4]

These debates over the best path for development were aired within the party during 1953 and 1954. During this time, there were three main attempts to speed up the process, but each met with opposition not only from party leaders, but also from local-level party administrators, and from the peasantry themselves. On this last point, we have to question whether Mao's understanding of the peasants' enthusiasm for collectivisation was more in his own mind than in theirs. This opposition to rapid collectivisation was enforced in an official State Council (government) directive in March 1955, which called for a cautious approach. Rather than pushing ahead towards collectivisation, local cadres should instead ensure that the new co-operatives were consolidated and made to work properly. This approach was supported in July when the Vice-Premier Li Fuchun set a rather cautious target of only one-third of all households to be in basic co-operatives by the end of 1957. To make matters worse, Deng Zihui initiated the dissolution of over 200,000 co-operatives during the spring of 1955.

When he responded to these moves in the summer of 1955, Mao began to refer to a new political entity called 'the party centre'. It seems that the 'party centre' simply referred to Mao himself – Mao was trying to convey the idea that he was the party, and the party was Mao. Any action in violation of Mao's views was therefore an action against the party, even if it was other party leaders or the party's Central Committee itself that was taking that action. Mao was clearly irked that the decision to dissolve the co-operatives had been taken without his consent, and indeed in violation of an April 1955 resolution.

However, it is difficult to get a real idea of who Mao actually blamed for his defeats at this stage. Parris Chang notes that in one speech, Mao referred 20 times to 'some' or 'certain' comrades who had obstructed reform, without ever mentioning specific names.[5] During the Cultural Revolution, Mao claimed that Liu Shaoqi was the main opponent of collectivisation at this stage. Liu clearly had reservations (at the very least) about collectivisation, reservations that he openly outlined as early as 1951. Yet at the time, Liu did not actively oppose Mao's policies, although neither did he act to prevent the dissolution of collectives in 1955.

Our problem here is that Chinese history was rewritten on a number of occasions after 1949 as the past was used to justify the present. During the Cultural Revolution, Mao was keen to justify the lengths he had gone to in overthrowing Liu by emphasising Liu's long-term and consistent opposition to Mao's correct policies. The suggestion that Mao really thought that Liu was the major obstacle to reform and a 'capitalist roader' at this stage is a little far-fetched. As Li Fuchun and Deng Zihui were the most active opponents of collectivisation in 1955, it is much more likely that they were the real focus of his displeasure.

Despite his protests, it appeared that Mao's view had lost, and that his opponents had won the day. The scene appeared set for a new development plan which, despite modifications, still resembled the original Soviet blueprint more than it resembled Mao's own proposal. China was to embark on a moderate and relatively slow path to development with an emphasis on industrial development first, limited international economic contacts, and even a minor role for market forces and private plots in the countryside.

But Mao was not the sort of man to sit back and see his ideas rejected, even if they had been rejected by a combination of formal decision-making processes and popular opposition to his strategies. As he would do time and time again, if he couldn't get his ideas passed through the formal processes, then he was more than ready to use informal processes instead. Thus, Mao embarked on a tour of the country, visiting various provincial leaders in an attempt to build a wide base of support for his ideas. Mao was using his own prestige and authority to appeal to a section of the party (the provinces) to attack another part of the party (the central party-state organisation).[6]

*guerilla warfare – bypasses*

Having established his support base, Mao then convened a special *ad hoc*, and in some respects illegal, meeting in Beijing in July 1955. Mao criticised the abolition of the co-operatives, and called for a new movement to sweep the country. His own targets were radical compared to the views of many of his colleagues, but rather moderate in comparison to what happened. Mao envisaged a relatively modest pace of collectivisation, and set a target of all households being in co-operatives by 1960, with some of the more established making the transition to collectives.

*like the emperors of China – immerse in local politics*

In the event, provincial and lower-level cadres implemented the collectivisation drive with such verve that the process of co-operativisation was completed well in advance of Mao's targets. As actual policy on the ground became increasingly isolated from the party's (as opposed to Mao's) official policy, the central leadership had little option other than to fall in line and implement Mao's proposals. Mao also significantly took the opportunity to place some of his own men in leading positions. Perhaps the most notable here was Chen Boda, who took a senior position in the party's rural decision-making body.[7]

The party leadership had essentially been outflanked. But Mao's victory was far from total. The new collectivisation drive in many ways countered the initial programmes of agricultural reform. Rather than the peasants being persuaded to take the initiative themselves, this new reform was much more of a top-down movement. This is not to say that China witnessed the same level of violence that accompanied forced collectivisation in the Soviet Union. But there was resentment from many in the countryside, manifest more in a policy of non-compliance than violence.

*What*

Within a year, the initiative moved back towards the Leninists. With the emphasis in the countryside on grain production and land reclamation, cash crops had been neglected. As these were a major source of both raw materials for industry and capital for investment, the state began to face a financial crisis.

*No one has absolute power.*

For the opponents of collectivisation, this is what they said would happen all along. They also pointed to the lack of management and planning expertise in local cadres, another factor they had previously stressed. The Leninists were not slow in exploiting these problems to force a re-think of strategy. First through the media, and then in internal political meetings, criticisms of the push to collectivisation began to appear ever more strident. When Khrushchev denounced Stalin and the personality cult in February 1956, Mao's opponents were given further ammunition to attack his work style. Throughout the spring and summer of 1956, the ideas of economists such as Chen Yun gained the ascendancy. The drift away from collectivisation and towards a new emphasis on light industry gathered pace, and Mao's opponents became ever more confident.

So by the 8th Party Congress of 1956 – the first party congress since the establishment of the new People's Republic – Mao's views appeared once again to be losing ground. Mao's proposals for agricultural development were shelved, and a new moderate Five Year Plan was instead put forward. To make matters worse for Mao, the party's constitution dropped 'Mao Zedong Thought' from its list of ideological sources, leaving 'Marxism-Leninism' as the party's guiding principles. As managers and experts were increasingly brought back into the state and administrative structure, Mao's position became increasingly weak. Time for him yet again to bypass the party structure and to appeal to his other constituencies to reassert his views.

## THE HUNDRED FLOWERS CAMPAIGN

Despite these problems within the Communist Party leadership in Beijing, the story of the Chinese revolution up to 1955 was one of repeated successes. In 1936 the Communist Party had been holed up in one of the most desolate areas of China, facing the distinct possibility of elimination from hostile Guomindang forces. And if the Guomindang didn't get them, then the Japanese might finish them off instead. By 1955, the Japanese and the Guomindang had been seen off, and a new People's Republic had been established. A new party-state structure was more or less intact, with party control extended over a wide range of political, economic and social activities. The threat of American invasion through Korea had been averted, and

China's borders had been more or less stabilised. In the countryside, a massive programme of land reform had resulted in perhaps the most fundamental economic and social restructuring that the world has seen in the space of around three years. And in the cities, the First Five Year Plan had been a great success, with economic recovery going well, and a new heavy industry base well on the way to completion.

On the face of it, then, communist rule had been a great success, and the party had every right to expect that the population would endorse its performance to date. But Mao was growing increasingly concerned about the way that the party was running the country, and in 1956 he embarked on a new radical experiment to alter its relationship with the masses in what became known as the Hundred Flowers Campaign.

In the west, the Hundred Flowers was originally taken as a sign of liberalisation and a political thaw in China. With the Stalin personality cult under attack in the Soviet Union, some in China and abroad perceived Khrushchev's de-Stalinisation as partly an attack on Mao's own growing personality cult (probably correctly). Thus, when on 26 May 1956 Mao issued the call to 'Let a Hundred Flowers Bloom, A Hundred Schools of Thought Contend',[8] and given the specific context of what was happening in the Soviet Union, it was perhaps not that surprising that many mistook its relevance.

The confusion over what was going on was exacerbated by the way in which the policy came about. Rather than using the formal structures of power, Mao's 26 May speech was an *ad hoc*, almost extra-system way of bringing the issue onto the political agenda. This was a tactic he was subsequently to deploy on two further occasions. Having seen his agricultural proposals defeated in the Central Committee, Mao took his proposals to a special meeting of provincial leaders to reassert his ideas. At the onset of the Cultural Revolution, Mao similarly used the East China Conference on Art and Literature to air his first attacks on the party, although this time through the proxy of his wife, Jiang Qing. On all three occasions, these non-formal mechanisms proved highly successful in placing his ideas back on the agenda with significant consequences. Of all China's leaders, only Mao had the political presence to use a speech to change fundamentally the direction of Chinese politics.

In the case of the Hundred Flowers Campaign, Mao's speech was only circulated in draft form through universities and

*competing his interpretation*

colleges by the Director of the Party's Propaganda Department, Lu Dingyi. There was considerable confusion over what the speech actually meant for policy in practice, and, perhaps unsurprisingly, many intellectuals were wary to speak up and air their thoughts on the revolution when they were unsure how far they were allowed to go in their comments. When the famous writer Guo Moro, who was also head of the influential Academy of Sciences, found his interpretation of what the movement meant criticised in a *People's Daily* editorial, then the sense of confusion was only deepened.

So what, then, were Mao's motives for launching the Hundred Flowers Campaign? For some, the Hundred Flowers was a machiavellian attempt to flush out opponents of the new regime so that they could be chopped down. It was all a sham of liberalisation with the explicit aim of hoodwinking opponents into exposing themselves. The conspiracy theorists place specific attention on Mao's February 1957 speech on 'The Correct Handling of Contradictions Amongst the People'. This speech was seen by many as a green light for airing all grievances and criticisms in an open manner. But when it was finally published in June, the paper had been revised to include sections that essentially laid strict limits to what was permissible criticism. Furthermore, Mao and his acolytes later argued that Mao had been in control of the process all along, and that it was indeed a subtle plot to flush out class traitors – but then again, they would wouldn't they? The suggestion, then, is that the intelligentsia were deliberately deceived, and then found that *ex post facto* criteria had been imposed which made their criticisms unacceptable and counter-revolutionary.

For Han Suyin, who was very close to the official Maoist explanation, the Hundred Flowers was indeed part of a deliberate strategy by Mao.[9] The primary target of the movement, for Han, was the party leadership itself. Mao was frustrated that his notions of the importance of class struggle after the revolution were not being accepted. He feared that the party was becoming a smug and isolated elite that refused to allow non-party members to participate in policy. Mao's objectives for the Hundred Flowers were thus two-fold: first, to force the party to accept the importance of immersing itself in the masses to prevent the dangers of revisionism and bureaucratisation; and second, to display that class conflict was alive and well, and that class enemies were waiting for the chance to overthrow the

*bring peasants in again - keep empowering them*

revolution, not only from within society as a whole, but even within the party itself.

An alternative hypothesis sees Mao as much more of a reactive rather than proactive actor. Having achieved so many great victories, he expected the Hundred Flowers to bring a ringing endorsement of the revolution. When intellectuals and even party members began to raise fairly severe criticisms, then he was shocked by the response. Rewriting the Contradictions speech was not a reflection of a machiavellian manipulator at work, but more a reflection of Mao changing his mind and reassessing his ideas accordingly. Whereas the more manipulative interpretations are built on the notion that Mao had already developed his ideas about class struggle after the revolution, the reactive approach rather suggests that the Hundred Flowers Campaign actually shaped Mao's notions of class conflict.

Finding a way through this minefield of conflicting interpretations is not easy, but I would argue that the answer to the issue lies somewhere in between the two extremes. I suggest that scoring points against his colleagues in the party leadership did indeed initially motivate Mao. Khrushchev's ascendancy to power in Moscow raised the real spectre of the complete death of revolution in the Soviet Union, and the danger that a bureaucratised, smug party elite might follow the same path in China. He was also concerned that the party was too concerned with wooing experts, managers, intellectuals and technocrats into the party, and ignoring its proletarian base. Finally, he was irked that his own proposals for agricultural reform were facing severe obstacles in the party decision-making machinery.

Thus, Mao went back to his main constituency, the people themselves, to attack the direction of the Leninist party leadership. By asking for a verdict on the party's record so far, he expected a ringing endorsement of his own policy, thus strengthening his hand *vis-à-vis* his colleagues. Immersing the party in the masses was thus a means both of proving the correctness of Mao's ideas regarding the party–masses relationship, and of utilising his main power base. Indeed, the evidence suggested that the Leninists' strategies were becoming unpopular in the country. The summer of 1956 saw a wave of strikes and student unrest as popular expectations were not met by the party. In particular, the party's bureaucratic work style and the growing power of managers and cadres over the people were a focus for much criticism. There were also problems in the countryside as a poor harvest combined with stable consumption created the first food shortages since the revolution.

During the movement itself, Mao's ideas were in a state of evolution. This was partly a response to events outside China, notably the workers' uprisings in Poland and Hungary. But it was also partly a response to events within China itself. After Mao's initial calls for a blooming and contending had met with strictly limited response, the call was renewed in January 1957. Again, the calls met with a limited response, and the debate was renewed at a special conference on propaganda work in March 1957. The aim of the conference was to strike against resentment from party members that they were being asked to subject themselves to criticism from the people. The call was to 'listen to opinions, especially unpleasant ones . . . let people speak up'. If the party didn't listen and take heed, then how could it respond to what the people wanted? The party was not infallible and had to accept this. Nevertheless, key party leaders, notably Liu Shaoqi and Peng Zhen, remained sceptical in the extreme, and argued that only party members should be allowed to participate in the blooming and contending.

Han Suyin argues that at this point, the right decided to go along with the campaign and allow full freedom of expression. They thought that the comments that would emerge would prove that allowing non-party members to participate in decision-making was both folly and dangerous. So in the spring of 1957 the entire country became engaged in the process of criticism. Editorial freedom soon emerged, supported by the growth of *dazibao*. These 'big character posters' were put up across China, expressing open and uncensored criticisms of the party. The movement was particularly strong in the universities, where the proletariat was still poorly represented, and many students came from traditional 'bourgeois' backgrounds. During April and May of 1957, the criticisms became more and more radical, calling for Mao and Zhou Enlai to stand down, and to let the intellectuals share power.

To be sure, it was Mao himself who had set this process in motion, and probably to serve his own political ends. Nevertheless, it appears that even he was surprised by the plethora of criticisms that the movement brought forth. The party, or at least the Maoist wing of the party, was not as popular as Mao had thought, and the extent of the rightist criticism was a worrying danger for the future of the revolution.

The blooming and contending was brought to an official halt on 6 June with a strident *People's Daily* editorial. If the Leninists really thought that they had won the day, the publication of Mao's speech on the correct handling of contradictions, including the subsequent revisions, placed Mao's objectives firmly back in the ascendancy. In this new version, Mao made an explicit reference to the existence of antagonistic contradictions remaining within the people – in simpler terms, the idea that class conflict had to remain the main priority of the Communist Party even after the revolution. In an antagonistic contradiction, the two sides that are in conflict are in a fight to the death – if we don't defeat them, then they will defeat us. By identifying the existence of antagonistic contradictions within the party itself, Mao was already starting on the road that would lead to the Cultural Revolution.

Mao's attentions had not yet turned towards the top members of the party elites. The role of Deng Xiaoping is particularly notable here. During the Cultural Revolution, Deng was named as 'the number two person in authority taking the capitalist road' (after Liu Shaoqi). However, at this stage, Deng was if anything a member of the Maoist camp. The anti-rightist campaign was largely conducted under Deng's tutelage, and, as we shall see, Deng was also influential in promoting Mao's Great Leap strategies. It was only once the Great Leap began to fail that Deng rather jumped ships – something that says much about Deng's own 'profile in power'.

There was, however, an extensive campaign launched against rightists within the party, particularly at the provincial level, with a number of major local leaders removed from power. It is important to note here that party members who overstepped the boundaries of criticism received much harsher treatment than non-party members – they were more dangerous, and more was expected of them. The anti-rightist campaign was also prosecuted at lower levels. A programme of re-education through labour was introduced to break down the barriers between mental and manual work. Furthermore, managers were forced to participate in manual labour, and workers were conversely given the right to participate in all decision-making. The party administration was also plunged into the masses, with 800,000 cadres employed in manual labour in the countryside by the autumn. Finally, over a million students were exposed to proletarian values by participation in manual work.

The consequences of the Hundred Flowers were ultimately far-reaching. As noted above, it was the start of a process of party rectification and submission to scrutiny from the masses (albeit a controlled and one-sided Maoist scrutiny) which was ultimately to lead to the Cultural Revolution. Along with Mao's agricultural development programme, it also further widened the existing gulf between Soviet Marxism and Mao's own approach. Ultimately this party-party conflict was to emerge as full-blown inter-state conflict. More immediately, managers, intellectuals and experts (and many of the next generation of experts in the universities) were either alienated from the new regime or physically removed from their positions as they were sent to labour camps or to do manual labour. The anti-rightist campaign created an atmosphere of fear that pervaded the party from top to bottom. So when Mao subsequently called on the party to implement his Great Leap Forward strategies, many complied for fear of being branded a rightist if they demurred, or if they pointed out the obvious failings of the policy once they began to emerge.

What the Hundred Flowers also achieved was to place Mao's ideas back at the top of the Chinese political agenda. Having seen his ideas for development rejected in 1956, the Maoist approach was very much back in vogue by the end of 1957. People felt unable to oppose Mao and Maoist strategies, and this enabled Mao to implement his developmental strategies, and ultimately provides many of the explanations for why they failed so spectacularly.

.  .  .

## THE GREAT LEAP FORWARD

Mao was back. The Hundred Flowers had reasserted his agenda and his presence on the political scene. Whether intentional (or predetermined) or not, Mao's notions of the importance of maintaining class struggle as the party's number one object-ive were firmly in place. His idea that the Chinese experience should take predominance over Soviet-inspired Marxism was also back in place.

By returning the political debate to his 'own' sphere of ideology, Mao had outflanked his colleagues. In the newly re-radicalised political atmosphere, and with opponents scared of being branded rightists, Mao moved to reinvigorate his proposals for agriculture and to restore his own vision of the best – indeed, the only correct – path for Chinese development. With rightist cadres sent down to the countryside for their opposition to Mao's policies, the process of collectivisation was renewed with vigour. Throughout the country, the co-operatives were re-installed, and the amalgamation of co-operatives into collectives was accelerated.

Despite the victories of 1957, Mao was still not in total control of affairs. Chen Yun, in particular, remained unconvinced of the wisdom of Mao's views. Nevertheless, the tide was moving inexorably in Mao's direction for four main reasons. First, the decentralisation of power to the provinces undercut the ability of central leaders to block Mao's proposals. If the provincial leaders were implementing policy, then the central party leadership had little choice other than to go along with it. If they didn't, then central policy would become increasingly out of touch with reality. Mao's use of the provincial leaders in 1956 to try and reinvigorate his policies was replicated by his strategy in 1957 and 1958. Again, he went on an extensive tour of the provinces to build up support for his ideas. Again, their implementation of his policies forced the central leadership to subsequently fall in line. Again, the provincial leaders' participation at national meetings and conferences helped Mao win the vote and the day.

In addition, provincial leaders proved useful in providing external criticisms of the central party elites. Chang notes that a number of provincial leaders criticised conservative central leaders in letters published in the national press.[10] And this brings us to the second main factor. The *People's Daily* in particular, but the media and cultural organs in general, were particularly pro-Mao at this stage. With the Hundred Flowers Campaign weeding out 'rightist' cultural intellectuals, the left had a relatively free hand. Whilst the support of the provincial leaders was important, their criticisms would not have been published had it not been for the pro-Mao elements within the *People's Daily*. With the media on his side, Mao could launch a new propaganda campaign, blaming any previous failures of collectivisation on obstructionist officials, and lauding the benefits of his new programme.

The third factor is very much related to the above. With the purges of the anti-rightists and the new media campaign attacking conservatism and critics, the atmosphere of fear meant that some leaders simply kept quiet, while others took a tactical step to the left. So by the summer of 1958, Mao was able to get his policies approved by the central party apparatus even though considerable *latent* opposition to his ideas remained in place.

Fourth, and finally, Mao's ideas gained more credence because they were seen to be working. The renewed pace of collectivisation appeared (at least) to be relatively problem free. Furthermore, Mao used positive experiences provided by experiments in loyal provinces to show the wisdom of his approach. It is always helpful if a theoretical approach is backed up with practical experience, and competing policy packages in China are often only brought to the central arena after they have already been tried and proved in test areas. Thus, Mao returned to his native Hunan province to tour the newly established Sputnik Commune. Not surprisingly, Mao was shown an example of a highly successful commune in action, and he went back to Beijing convinced that even the collectives could now be replaced by an even more advanced form of organisation.

Thus, the idea of the Great Leap Forward was born. Collectives were all well and good, but why stop there? With the peasants' enthusiasm for communism apparently knowing no bounds, and with opposition to his ideas silenced (for the time being at least), Mao was keen to make his policies irreversible and so struck forward on the combined tides of optimism and fear that he had created.

The idea of the Great Leap was in many ways the high point of Mao's period in power. During the heady revolutionary days of 1958, it seemed as if China, having only just escaped from the ravages of colonialism and feudalism, could make a rapid transition to a truly communist society. The aim of the Great Leap was to create sprouts of communism in the countryside. The short-lived collectives would be transformed into communes. These communes were to be much larger in size – covering as many as two million people in the extreme case – and were to move from socialist distribution of resources (to each according to his deeds) to communist distribution (to each according to his needs). The communes were an attempt to combine party, state and military activity in one organisation. The Great Leap's plans were to be facilitated both by releasing the revolutionary enthusiasm of the masses and by eliminating inefficient modes of production. Thus, the old family system was broken down, and with it the old rural structure built around villages as the centre of activity.

In its place, new systems were built. All private property was to be pooled, and the commune would take control of everything. Rather than living in families, people were assigned to specialist work teams and allocated to dormitories. Rather than women being forced to stay at home to look after children and prepare food, new crèches were established to take over childcare, and communal kitchens established for all to eat at. As the emphasis was now on communist distribution, you could eat as much as you wanted without any correlation to payment or work points.

With only a few people now needed to provide food and child-care, women were brought more into the productive forces. In addition, as traditional boundaries between land were broken down to create huge fields, economies of scale were introduced and fewer people were needed to farm each unit of land. This created an excess labour source that was detailed to push forward the frontiers of development. On one level, teams were dispatched to reclaim waterlogged land, to build irrigation canals, to establish a local infrastructure to move produce around, and so on. On another, equally important level, teams were dispatched to establish an industrial base in the countryside. Under the slogan 'take steel as the key link', each commune was set a target for steel production (irrespective of each commune's raw material resources). Work teams were established to find sources of iron ore and coal, and then to build the transportation system required to bring the raw materials back to the heart of the commune. Small scale 'back-yard' steel furnaces sprang up across the countryside in an attempt to establish the wherewithal for establishing a rural industrial base.

By establishing a new industrial base in the countryside, the industrial sector would be free to look after itself. With more food and raw materials anticipated to arise from communisation, industry could make even greater advances. For Mao, then, the Great Leap was not so much a choice between rural development or industrial development but the simultaneous development of both – 'walking on two legs'. Furthermore, with rural industrialisation looking after itself, the industrial sector could diversify into light industry. Thus, the Great Leap combined the best of all worlds, and would lead very quickly to the creation of a new, strong, prosperous and communist China. And the beauty of it was that it could all be achieved by unleashing the revolutionary enthusiasm of the people, rather than by paying them more.

Mao's motivations for launching the Great Leap were primarily from his ideological convictions. The Great Leap would not only transform the way people viewed their work, the revolution, and the superiority of communism, but it would also generate rapid growth – much more rapid than the now shelved moderate Second Five Year Plan. It would also break down the divisions between town and county, with the establishment of the new rural industrial base. And the role of managers and experts would be diminished as the masses themselves took charge of their own destiny – power was to be given back to the proletariat from the managers, intellectuals and bureaucrats. In the cities, a similar attempt to break down the divisions between town and countryside was also attempted, but with minimal success. Workers were encouraged to participate in agricultural production where possible, but it was not always possible to find suitable land on which to grow food. There was, however, a far-reaching attempt to reduce the power of factory managers by both encouraging worker participation in factory management and increasing the power of party officials in the workplace. Despite the new power of the party in the factory, it is fair to say that the radicalism of the Great Leap was felt more in the countryside than in the cities.

Despite Mao's clear ideological objectives, communisation and the Great Leap also served other ends. First, it had an international relations dimension. On one level, Mao was keen to show to the outside world (and particularly to Moscow) that his brand of Chinese socialism was working. On another level, national security issues were also very important. Despite the relative easing of tension with the US after the stalemate in Korea, Sino-US relations remained on rocky ground. These tensions were exacerbated by the Chinese bombardment of offshore Taiwanese islands, a factor which will be dealt with in more detail in Chapter 6. The fear of invasion from the United States remained high, and as relations with the Soviet Union began to deteriorate in the 1950s, it seemed pretty clear to Mao that Moscow could not be relied upon to defend China if it came under attack. The creation of relatively self-contained communes with their own industrial capacity did not reduce the risk of invasion, but it did have military implications. If the United States did launch an attack on China, for example, then the country would not be paralysed if the key industrial centres were taken out. The communes would be able to continue functioning because their reliance on the cities had been much reduced. Also, the communes were charged with the task of military training. Everybody was to become a soldier, and with so many soldiers to rely on, the Chinese could fight and fight and fight. The Great Leap not only saw the mobilisation of the masses to attain socialist goals, but also mobilisation around Chinese goals of self-determination and independence. Intense nationalist fervour and a propaganda campaign that appealed to inherent nationalist tendencies accompanied the communisation process. Thus, we can argue that the initial enthusiasm and euphoria that the Great Leap did engender was perhaps more based on nationalist, than socialist, aspirations.

Second, the commune system struck at the heart of the traditional Leninist approach to development. Having already somewhat emasculated the central authorities by devolving power to the provinces, the Great Leap went a step further and placed a greater emphasis on decision-making within the communes themselves. In this respect, while the Great Leap was clearly an end in itself, it was also a means to the greater end of undercutting the power of the central party-state leadership – power was to be placed in the hands of those who were more receptive to Mao's ideas.

· · ·

## FROM GREAT LEAP TO GREAT FAMINE

The Great Leap was a startling success, or at least that's how it appeared at first. Grain production soared. By the end of 1958, the countryside appeared to be awash with grain. More of it was brought into the cities, and China began to pay off some of its debts to the Soviet Union by exporting it. With so much available, the party leadership decided to decrease the amount of land sown for grain and to grow cash crops instead and concentrate on industrial production in the communes. Furthermore, buoyed up by the successes of 1958, targets for industrial and agricultural production were revised further upwards – if the masses could achieve this much, then how much more could they achieve?

Table 1

| Author | Year of Study | Amount of Deaths | Time Phase |
|--------|---------------|------------------|------------|
| Coale | 1981 | 16.5 million | 1958–61 |
| Coale | 1984 | 27 million | 1958–63 |
| Aird | 1982 | 23 million | 1960–61 |
| Mosher | 1983 | 30 million | 1960 |

But between 1959 and 1963, China was plunged into a desperate famine. Many years after, it is still difficult to gauge the full extent of the famine, but Penny Kane's analysis of four different approaches to the body count (see Table 1) gives us some indication of the size of the problem.[11]

Apart from the mortality rates, the Great Leap had serious economic consequences. Grain production was 170 million tons in 1955, but fell to 143 million tons in 1960, and throughout the 1960s China was forced to spend scarce foreign currency importing grain on international markets. Over 50 per cent of imports during this period were grain imports. Between 1958 and 1961, GNP fell by around 15 per cent.

What happened to make the great successes turn into such a great disaster? First, we should perhaps note two mitigating factors. The years 1959 and 1960 saw the worst weather conditions in Chinese recorded history, with over half of all cultivated land hit by droughts or floods, or in some cases both. While it is very easy to blame the deaths entirely on the failings of the Great Leap, we cannot know what impact the weather would have had whatever system existed. The second mitigating factor was the withdrawal of all Soviet advisers to China in the summer of 1960. This move hit hard in the industrial sector, as the Soviets also took home their blueprints and cut China off from many key components for industry. Nevertheless, we should recognise that the withdrawal was in part caused by Khrushchev's belief that the Chinese were adopting an at best foolhardy development programme by following the Great Leap. And as MacFarquhar notes, the Chinese did much to make a continued Soviet presence in China untenable:

the Chinese did not follow Soviet technical advice and often demonstrated their scorn for it; the Chinese had created intolerable conditions for Soviet advisers, spying on them, searching their belongings, opening their mail; in some cases, Soviet specialists had been molested and even attacked.[12]

Nevertheless, the Great Leap was in many ways a catalogue of errors. First, the decentralisation of power to the communes followed the earlier decentralisation of decision-making power to the provinces in 1956 and 1957. With both provinces and communes encouraged to become self-sufficient in all agricultural and industrial commodities, the centralised planning and distribution system that the party had built up in the preceding years stopped functioning effectively. Thus, when the famine began to hit, it proved difficult for grain to be transported around the country from surplus to deficit areas. In some areas, grain supplies were hidden and stockpiled for local consumption rather than being turned over to starving comrades in other parts of the country.

Perhaps more fundamentally, we have to consider Mao's own over-estimation of the revolutionary enthusiasm of the masses. When the needs of subsistence existence were removed from the rural population, they didn't respond in a measured 'socialist' manner. Instead, many of them took the opportunity of increasing food consumption in the new communal and free kitchens. Furthermore, many peasants proved reluctant in the extreme to pool their resources when they were being forced into communal living. Rather than see the communisation process as beneficial for all their comrades, many peasants did not want to give up their hard-earned resources. Rather than pool their produce, many slaughtered and ate their livestock, and ate (or secretly hoarded) their grain supplies. For example, Kane notes that the pig population of China was decimated during the communisation programme, as a result of both the reluctance to pool private property and the over-consumption in communal kitchens. When the famine began to hit, the usual supply of carefully and previously reserved stockpiles – amassed for just such an occasion – had long since been consumed.[13]

One of the key points here is the way in which over-zealous local party officials often pressured the peasants into joining the new communes. Whereas the original land reform and mutual aid teams had been established through the active participation of the peasants themselves, the collectives and the communes were developed more by political pressure and compulsion. Much of the blame for the subsequent failings of the

Great Leap was placed on the local cadres for pushing people to accept what they were not ready for. But in many respects, the blame was misplaced. Yes, the cadres took an overly aggressive stance towards communisation, but can you really blame them? The Great Leap occurred in the wake of the anti-rightist campaign and the provincial political purges of 1958. Indeed, without this anti-rightist atmosphere, then the Great Leap might not have happened at all. It was Mao who thought that the peasants were ready to abandon their private property and traditional family basis of life, and to work for the revolution for the love of their comrades and the motherland.

Once these criteria had been set, it would have taken a brave individual to suggest that things might not all be as rosy as they appeared. Once the momentum for communisation got underway, any reluctance to communise might be taken as a sign of resistance – the very sin which had caused a number of local cadres to be attacked after the earlier slowdown in the collectivisation campaign. The more areas reported successful communisation, the more the pressure increased for others to follow suit.

This competition to prove one's Maoist credentials by attaining and surpassing production targets was to have far-reaching consequences. For example, steel production targets were in many cases simply unattainable. At best, many communes expended considerable time and effort trying to find sources of iron ore and coal to produce steel of such low quality that it often couldn't be used. In some communes, cadres ordered the melting down of pots and pans to ensure that they met their targets. There are also stories that factories produced unusable goods simply to meet their targets.[14] The drive to increase steel production took on such an important role that grain was often left to rot in the fields as work teams were too busy trying to find raw material sources and to build steel furnaces. With national grain production apparently so high, then why waste time on harvesting when steel output targets were still to be met? When Peng Dehuai, who opposed the communisation programme all along, visited a village during the high-point of the steel production drive, he remonstrated with the peasantry: 'hasn't anyone of you given a thought to what you will eat next year if you don't bring in the crops? You're never going to be able to eat steel.' The response in many ways sums up the mood at the time: 'True enough; who would argue with that? But apart from when the centre send down a high-ranking cadre, who would stand up against this wind?'[15]

Here we see one of the paradoxes of Mao's approach to the Great Leap. Communisation was supposed to give more autonomy to the communes themselves. But with the central authorities setting targets and quotas, the theoretical power of local leaders was vastly constrained by the political necessity of meeting these quotas. The above examples might seem amusing or even laughable, but they had grave consequences. At the very least, they wasted manpower and scarce raw materials in the search for the unattainable. Mao's notions that the Great Leap could also aid the development of a light industrial base were pretty much scotched at source given that so many of the rural industries were producing unusable steel.

But there were also farther-reaching consequences that China is still dealing with to this day. Where coal was in short supply or even non-existent, communes embarked on programmes of deforestation to provide fuel. Deforestation also occurred in a search for more arable land. Furthermore, in the desire to increase grain-sown land, many communes simply ploughed straight up and down hills. Once the rains came, then the seeds and the soil were simply washed away, creating severe problems of soil erosion.

And indeed, it was in the search for greater grain production that we see perhaps the most severe consequences of the Great Leap. The desire to prove oneself to be redder than red took on an intensely competitive nature. With the spectre of the anti-rightist campaign and attacks on cadres who were cautious over collectivisation hanging over them, many – perhaps not surprisingly – placed their own political survival above what was best for the commune. Thus, once other communes began to report that they had reached their grain targets, it became almost politically necessary for others to say that they too had met their quotas, even if it wasn't strictly true. Once other communes began to proclaim that they had vastly exceeded their quotas, it became necessary for others also to claim that they had exceeded their quotas.

So one of the reasons that the great successes of 1958 turned into the great famine is that the successes weren't really there at all. There was a vast over-reporting of grain production across the country. For example, Endicott's interviews with local leaders in Sichuan province reveal that local cadres were often told to go back and revise their grain output figures if higher-level officials felt that they were not telling the story that Mao wanted to hear. In one commune, grain was transported from several fields and replanted in one field, so that the local cadres could show a visiting inspection team that they had an output of 2,000 kilos per unit of land, rather than the real figure of only 500 kilos.[16] The notion that the country was awash with grain was therefore built on falsified output figures. Again, the local cadres were blamed, but the real blame should lie on Mao's shoulders, for both over-emphasising the revolutionary enthusiasm of the masses and creating the culture of fear that made cadres act in the way that they did.

In many ways, then, the failure of the Great Leap was a direct consequence of Mao's strategy for implementing it in the first place. His over-exuberance, over-confidence and over-certainty that he was right proved an unstable starting point for the Great Leap. The manner in which he managed to launch the Great Leap through the anti-rightist campaign and the decentralisation of power to the provinces only compounded the problems. Perhaps Mao had simply been too successful in his earlier political career, and in too much of a hurry to get his ideas in place.

.  .  .

## ABANDONING THE GREAT LEAP

The euphoria of the Great Leap was only a very temporary and short-lived affair. By as early as the autumn of 1958, central leaders began to become aware of problems in the country-side, and many toured the provinces to find out what was going on. In November and December, the party met in the city of Wuhan to reconsider the experiences of the Great Leap. The winter of 1959 was a confusing time, with contradictory signals emerging from the party leadership – a sign of the contradictory approaches of different leaders.

On one level, the party took a step back from communisation. Local cadres were criticised for forcing the pace of commun-isation, and for believing that communism could be achieved in the near future. The pooling of all property was also criticised, and peasants were allowed to restore their private property and to engage in 'private' (or at least individual) activities.[17] But at the same time, the party issued other statements that supported the overall direction of the Great Leap, and set even higher output targets for 1959.

This confusion was further heightened by Mao's decision not to stand for re-election as Chairman of the State and his subsequent replacement in the spring of 1959 by Liu Shaoqi. Was Mao accepting the blame for the problems and standing down? While it is possible that Mao was making a partial retreat, he significantly retained the more important post of Chairman of the Party.

There was clearly dissatisfaction if not outright opposition to the Great Leap policies, but it was still difficult for Mao's colleagues to implement their explicit reversal. But in the spring of 1959 they utilised the same tactics that Mao himself had deployed to initiate the Great Leap. They went to the provinces, or sent down investigation teams on their behalf, to gain the evidence that they needed to overturn the Great Leap. At the central level, Chen Yun attempted to re-centralise the economy, and to re-establish the state planning organisation control. Even Mao appeared to become more aware of the problems in the countryside, and personally criticised local cadres for being over-zealous.

In the summer of 1959 the party leadership met at Lushan to discuss the Great Leap. Here, Mao met the fiercest attack yet on his policies. Although the communes remained in name, they were in practice broken up, and to all intents and purposes the collectives were restored. Private plots and private activity were encouraged in order to stabilise production in the countryside, and managers and experts were slowly brought back into position.

Mao's plans had been knocked back, but not fatally. Although much of his programme for development was overturned after 1959, he did achieve one significant gain. Minister of Defence, Peng Dehuai, had long been a severe critic of Mao's policies, and he used the Lushan meeting to launch a bitter attack on Mao. Peng's conflict with Mao was primarily a function of conflicting views over the relationship with the Soviet Union. Peng had been in charge of Chinese military operations during the Korean War, and was convinced that China could not defend itself without Soviet military support. Mao's growing disenchantment with the Soviet Union both angered and worried Peng. The Great Leap Forward not only further exacerbated tensions between Moscow and Beijing, but also took China further down the dangerous line of relying on the new people's militia to defend China, rather than on a professional and expert military elite.

But Peng's attacks on Mao were not just based on military strategy and foreign policy. Peng was a firm advocate of following the Soviet model of development. As Minister of National Defence, he was a leading party figure as well as being China's major military leader, and the Lushan meeting gave him the opportunity to air his grievances. Unfortunately for Peng, while many other leaders shared his views of what had been wrong with the Great Leap (even if they hadn't thought so in the first place), Peng found himself in a distinct minority when he openly criticised Mao at Lushan.

Perhaps the memory of the anti-rightist campaign was too fresh. Perhaps they too shared Mao's scepticism over the wisdom of leaning too close to Moscow (even those who by and large wanted to accept the Soviet model). Perhaps they were prepared to let Peng do their work for them without having to expose themselves, or they were simply happy to overturn Mao's policies without attacking the man himself. Perhaps they realised that while they might not need Mao's policies, it would have damaged the party's own legitimacy if they openly attacked the architect of the revolution himself. Or perhaps they were aware that Mao had the ability and the support to unleash the peasants and the army against the party if the need arose: 'I will go to the countryside to lead the peasants to overthrow the government. If . . . the army won't follow me, then I will go and find a Red Army. But I think the . . . Army will follow me'.[18]

If anybody doubted Mao at this stage, he was to prove both prepared and able to lead a fight against the party before too long.

Whatever the case, Peng was dismissed. This move proved important for two major reasons. First, for Lieberthal, Mao broke apart the accepted norms of inner party behaviour:

Mao seems at Lushan to have broken the unwritten rules that had governed debate among the top leadership to that point. Before Lushan, it was accepted that any leader could freely voice his opinions at a Party gathering, and debate could be heated. Nobody would be taken to task subsequently for what he said, as long as he formally accepted and acted in accord with the final decision reached.[19]

The new message was clear: criticising Mao could be damaging to your health.

Second, Peng's purge was followed by the elimination of many of his followers within the military. Crucially, Mao's loyal supporter, Lin Biao, replaced Peng as Minister of Defence. This was not merely a consolation prize for Mao in recompense for losing his development plan. Lin had an exemplary military record during the revolution, and with the elimination of Peng and his followers, he was a leading candidate for the job. But as we shall see in the next chapter, the establishment of Lin as head of the military was to play a significant role in Mao's recovery from the disasters of 1959 in the second half of the 1960s.

.    .    .

## NOTES

1. Teiwes, F. (1993) 'The Establishment of the New Regime, 1949–1957' in MacFarquhar, R. (ed.) *The Politics of China 1949–1989* (Cambridge: Cambridge University Press), pp. 5–86.
2. In theory, they were allowed to keep a small plot of land to farm just like everybody else. In practice, millions of landlords suffered and died at the hands of vengeful peasants, particularly in the north-east.
3. For an excellent example of this process in Shanxi province, see Hinton, W. (1966) *Fanshen: A Documentary of Revolution in a Chinese Village* (New York: Vintage Books).
4. Blecher, M. (1986) *China* (London: Pinter) p. 61.
5. Chang, P. (1975) *Power and Policy in China* (University Park: Pennsylvania State University Press) p. 13.
6. It is also significant that the party decentralised considerable control to the provinces during 1956 and 1957. This move undercut the power of the 'obstructionist' central leaders to dictate policy across the country.
7. Chen Boda was a Marxist theoretician, and a close ideological adviser to Mao. Indeed, he is thought by some to have been the original author of some of the works carrying Mao's name, and was, at the very least, a close political ally at this time.
8. These terms were taken from traditional Chinese political culture and activity. Mao and the communists frequently deployed the language of the past to describe their policies, as it gave the population some sort (at least) of reference point to understand what they were talking about. For example, when referring to the communist utopia of the future, the CCP frequently used

the phrase '*datong*', which in Confucianism referred to the perfect state of harmony.

9. Han Suyin (1976) *Wind in the Tower: Mao Tsetung and the Chinese Revolution, 1949–1975* (London: Cape).

10. Chang, *Power and Policy in China*, p. 78.

11. Kane, P. (1988) *Famine in China, 1959–61: Demographic and Social Implications* (London: Macmillan).

12. MacFarquhar, R. (1983) *The Origins of the Cultural Revolution Vol II: The Great Leap Forward, 1958–1960* (Oxford: Oxford University Press) p. 279.

13. Kane, *Famine in China*.

14. Targets were usually set for tons of output, and not for units of output. Thus, if you were producing screws, it made some sense to produce huge screws with very little waste rather than usable but more wasteful screws.

15. MacFarquhar, R. (1983) *Origins of the Cultural Revolution Vol II: The Great Leap Forward, 1958–1960* (Oxford: Oxford University Press) p. 195.

16. Endicott, S. (1988) *Red Earth: Revolution in a Sichuan Village* (London: I.B. Tauris) especially pp. 44–67.

17. As long as they fulfilled their quota of supplies to the state, then they were allowed to grow other crops or raise livestock which they could then treat as their own property.

18. Schram, S. (ed.) *Mao Tse-tung Unrehearsed: Talks and Letters, 1956–71* (Harmondsworth: Penguin).

19. Lieberthal, K. (1993) 'The Great Leap Forward and the Split in the Yan'an Leadership 1958–65' in MacFarquhar, R. (ed.) *The Politics of China 1949–1989* (Cambridge: Cambridge University Press) pp. 87–147.

# Chapter 4

# TOWARDS THE CULTURAL REVOLUTION

The failure of the Great Leap might have ruined other men. Mao had at last managed to implement his ideas, only for them to fail with disastrous consequences. However, he was so supremely self-confident that he didn't let the small matter of the collapse of the Great Leap deflect him from his purpose. He did not deny that things had gone wrong, but this didn't mean that the policies were flawed. The basic idea was correct, but others had incorrectly implemented the ideas. It wasn't Mao's fault, but the fault of the local-level cadres who had been implementing communisation in the wrong way; it was the fault of the peasants for not being sufficiently aware of the supremacy of his ideas; and it was the fault of opponents within the party who had tried to obstruct him. The ideas were not flawed, it was just that the conditions were not ripe for implementing them effectively.

During the Cultural Revolution, Mao was specifically to blame Liu Shaoqi and Deng Xiaoping for obstructing his policies. But both of these men had actually gone along with the Leap at the time. Indeed, Deng Xiaoping had been one of Mao's more active proselytisers until he saw the damage of 1958 and 1959. If anybody had obstructed and opposed the Great Leap, it had been Peng Dehuai (now out of the picture), Chen Yun, and Premier Zhou Enlai.[1] Mao's hostility to Liu and Deng had much more to do with what happened after the Leap, than during the Leap itself.

So by the end of the Great Leap the divisions between Mao and his colleagues in the central leadership had grown in both number and depth. Mao's prestige amongst the leadership (if not the people) was also much diminished, and he had lost the support that Deng Xiaoping and Liu Shaoqi had once been prepared to give him. Yet it is still difficult to conceive why Mao decided to throw the party and the country into chaos by launching the Cultural Revolution. Nor is it easy to see how Mao, from his new position of relative isolation in the political elite, was *able* to launch the movement.

In order to gain a better understanding of why Mao did what he did, this chapter will trace the continuation of conflict between Mao and other communist leaders in the first half of the 1960s. It will then turn to the *how* side of the issue by identifying Mao's sources of power within the political system in the 1960s. As we shall see, a key element here was Mao's prestige and standing within the general population – a prestige that many of those who suffered during the Cultural Revolution had helped create themselves.

. . .

## SOCIALIST EDUCATION AND CULTURAL REVOLUTION

Writing on the Cultural Revolution, the former Belgian ambassador to China, Simon Leys, argued that 'The Cultural Revolution had nothing revolutionary about it but its name, and nothing cultural about it except the initial tactical pretext'.[2] Whilst Leys might be correct that the Cultural Revolution was nothing more than a political tactic by a desperate man to get back to power, this statement in some ways obscures what Mao meant by a cultural revolution.

'Cultural Revolution' does not simply refer to culture in the sense of art and literature. Instead, the word 'culture' (*wenhua* in Chinese) here is used in a much broader sense to refer to 'civilisation' or perhaps 'political culture'. The notion that the phrase *wenhua* encapsulates is the dominant mode of thought that pervades society. Put another way, what perspectives and ideas influence the way that people perceive events, society, economics, their future? The point of a cultural revolution, then, is to bring about a fundamental change in the way that people view the world – to change their mode of thought. In this particular instance the aim was to cast off old feudal or other attitudes and replace them with new socialist modes of thought and attitudes, to win the hearts and minds of the people and persuade them of the superiority of socialism.

Mao was far from original in talking about a cultural revolution in these terms. Indeed, Marx's original explanation of communist revolution was built around a notion of cultural revolution. But Mao was original in his notions of how the cultural revolution would be brought about. For Marx, it would be a result of economic changes: oppression and exploitation would lead to the proletariat changing their attitudes about society and politics, and they would then rise up to overthrow the exploiters and build a new communist society. However in China, the exploiters had been overthrown and the Communist Party had come to power before the vast majority of the population had undergone this transformation in their attitudes and ideas. Furthermore, the revolution had been achieved in a backward, underdeveloped and predominantly agrarian society. In China, then, Mao argued that the cultural revolution could be achieved by persuasion, education and indoctrination by the party. And if this job was accomplished successfully, economic development and modernisation would follow the cultural revolution.

When the Great Leap didn't work out as Mao expected, Mao increased his emphasis on the importance of carrying out a cultural revolution. The lesson of the Great Leap was that local-level cadres and the masses themselves had not fully altered their way of thinking and embraced the correctness of the ideas. If only he could first re-educate the people and achieve the cultural revolution, then the ideas could be put into practice again, and this time they would bear fruit. So far from being de-radicalised by the experiences of the Great Leap, Mao was sparked into embarking on an even more radical attempt to politicise the entire country.

The urgency of implementing this cultural revolution was intensified by what Mao saw as the worrying growth of new class cleavages in the countryside. Rich peasants seemed to be reasserting themselves and their power. For Mao, the return to radicalism was not just to create the basis for the long-term implementation of correct policies, but to overcome the immediate problems that he saw in the countryside.

Despite the failings of the Great Leap, Mao by and large escaped the opprobrium of the people. They instead turned their hostility on local cadres who had forced them into communisation against their will. But while Mao's popular image remained relatively untarnished, the position in the party elites themselves was somewhat different. By the end of the 1950s, Mao was facing even greater opposition to his ideas and policies than he had done at the start of the decade. Where opponents may have been suspicious before, they now had concrete evidence of the failings of Mao's policies. Perhaps crucially, Mao lost the support of two key leaders. Whereas Liu Shaoqi had always leaned more towards the Soviet model than Mao's own approach, he had nevertheless been a faithful follower once Mao had initiated the Great Leap. Deng Xiaoping had been even more faithful to Mao, and had personally taken the lead in prosecuting both the anti-rightist campaign and the Great Leap. By 1960, both men had distanced themselves from Mao, and were committed to following non-Maoist strategies.

Throughout the first half of the 1960s, Mao's ideas came under attack from all directions, and it seemed as if they might have had their day. Despite his formal position of power as Chairman of the Party, Mao did not, as a matter of choice, involve himself in day-to-day affairs. He also later complained that Deng simply ignored him during the 1960s and didn't consult him about any policy changes. When the two men met in party meetings, Mao complained that Deng, who was deaf in one ear, would sit far away from him at meetings so that he couldn't hear the great man's advice!

In the economy, Chen Yun was charged with implementing a recovery programme to stop the famine and to stabilise production. Chen was devoted to allowing some private activity in the countryside to motivate the peasants to produce more. Whereas Mao put his faith in mobilising the peasants through revolutionary zeal, Chen thought that material incentives were more important. At the same time, Chen was keen to re-centralise control in the hands of planners and the central authorities. Where Mao put his faith in the initiative of local cadres and planners, Chen thought that only through central control – viewing the country as a single chessboard – could the party ensure measured and logical development.

Chen's ideas are often referred to as the 'bird-cage' theory of development. The bird is the free market, and the cage is the central plan. Without the cage, the bird would fly away. But if the bars of the cage were too restrictive, then the bird would be unable to move and would die. The challenge, then, was to ensure that the cage was strong enough to keep the bird in, but to allow it some freedom and room to exist.[3]

This dual emphasis on central control and market forces was the antithesis of Mao's developmental strategy. Where Mao had placed politics (and class struggle in particular) at the forefront of all decisions, the new leadership emphasised the importance of economic recovery. If it helped boost the economy, then a policy should be adopted even if it meant taking a temporary step backwards socially and ideologically. This notion that economic recovery was paramount has become most clearly associated with Deng Xiaoping. In a speech which was to come back to haunt him in both the Cultural Revolution and again in 1976, Deng argued that the political consequences of a policy are irrelevant as long as it bears economic fruits in the short run. Or in his own words, it doesn't matter whether a cat is black and white; if it catches the mice, then it is a good cat.

In addition to these changes, other areas of policy increasingly reflected the Leninist view at the expense of Mao's ideas. For example, managers and experts were increasingly brought back into positions of influence. In education policy, academic ability and the correct political background became increasingly important for gaining university entrance (as opposed to political activity). And in cultural policy, political and ideological criteria were increasingly ignored with a resurgence of the notion of 'art for art's sake'. In short, all Mao held closest to his heart was under attack.

If Mao was annoyed by these attacks, he became particularly frustrated by the moves to block any resurgence of his ideas. On one level, the Leninists in the party moved to reverse the anti-rightist campaign of 1957. Liu and the party leadership rehabilitated many of those criticised during the aftermath of the Hundred Flowers Campaign. Indeed, the left and 'leftism' were now the major focus of official criticism. While this dealt a psychological blow to Mao, it also provided more practical problems for the restoration of his policies. With local levels of the party increasingly controlled by the restored right, it would be difficult to use the localities to attack the centre again as he had done in 1956.

Perhaps 1962 was the key watershed in the evolution of conflict within the party. Not only did the party leadership begin its policy of restoring previous rightists, but Mao's attempts to restore his ideas and his policies met with only very limited success. On the face of it, Mao was relatively successful in the two major party meetings of 1962. After all, he managed to reaffirm the importance of class struggle as the guiding principle for party policy. In addition, his idea that the party should embark on a Socialist Education Movement (SEM) to re-educate the backward masses and facilitate a cultural revolution was also successful. But these successes were more apparent than real. The party leadership might have affirmed the primacy of class struggle in theory, but practical policy remained guided by the primacy of economic concerns. Perhaps more important, Mao's vision of what the SEM should achieve was very different from his colleagues'. Indeed, in many ways, Mao's political successes of 1962 appear to be little more than tokens to keep him quiet while others got on with the real job of running the country.

The debate over the SEM was a defining moment in Chinese politics. Before the Great Leap, Mao had been able to reassert his principles by bringing the issue of ideology back onto the agenda. This time, however, Mao found his moves stymied by an increasingly sceptical and powerful party elite headed by Liu Shaoqi and Deng Xiaoping. Mao saw the SEM as a means to two ends: to reassert his ideas and his own political primacy, and to undertake a radical revolution by educating both the masses and local party cadres and persuading them of the superiority of socialism (by which he meant Mao's version of socialism). It was to be a mass campaign entailing the participation of the whole country. If it succeeded, then he could go back to his successful policies of communisation, and this time they would work.

For Liu, Deng and many other central leaders, it was simply inconceivable that the party should embark on another mass mobilisation campaign while the situation in the countryside was still critical. Furthermore, many within the party-state system itself – including many who had themselves suffered from the anti-rightist campaign – opposed the move from more pragmatic grounds: did they really want to start a ball rolling which might eventually roll on them? For the first time, Liu did not simply go along with his master's voice, but instead decided to assert his own line.

By the spring of 1963, Mao was clearly frustrated by the slow, not to say obstructionist, implementation of the SEM by the central party-state leadership. As he had done before, Mao decided that if he couldn't get his way through the system, then he would go outside the system and use his own popular support to reinvigorate the SEM. Thus, Mao called on his capital of mass support by issuing a ten-point plan for prosecuting the SEM. If anything, this document made the implementation of the SEM less, rather than more, likely. Mao's vision of the SEM involved subjecting party cadres to self-criticism and to criticism from the masses themselves. It seems, then, that Mao was asking the turkeys not only to vote for Christmas, but to organise the Christmas meal themselves.

The conflict over the SEM returned the leadership to the unresolved issue of the relationship between the party and the masses, the same issue which had resulted in the Hundred Flowers Campaign. Mao wanted the party to immerse itself in the masses, while the rest of the party leadership were convinced that only party members should get involved in the decision-making process. But 1963 was not 1956. Mao's position within the leadership was less powerful than before, and his opponents were not only still grappling with the aftermath of the Great Leap, but had also witnessed (and in some cases suffered from) the anti-rightist campaign in 1957. So this time, the Leninists were more forceful than before, and responded in kind to Mao's document with their own programme for the SEM. Both Deng Xiaoping and Liu Shaoqi issued their own ten-point plans, which contained little of Mao's original impetus. While the campaign was not explicitly shelved, it was to be conducted under tight party supervision. The masses could be educated, but the process would be under the control of party work teams. And whatever education was to take place, it should never be allowed to impinge on economic recovery in the countryside. In short, it was not to become a mass campaign, and it was to remain under strict party control.

The significance of the SEM should not be underestimated. Here we see Mao using his 'usual' tactics to get the party to accept his view. He had tried to pull the debate back from day-to-day policy-making to matters of grand ideological design. But this time it hadn't worked, and largely because Liu and Deng had done their best to ensure that it hadn't worked. With Mao getting older, his ideas ever more out of favour, and key leaders openly obstructing his policy initiatives, it was clear to Mao that he had to do something quickly. Furthermore, he had to eliminate those people at the top of the party who were getting in the way.

. . .

## CREATING AN ALTERNATIVE POWER BASE

Given that the party structure was increasingly unreceptive to his ideas, Mao was forced to use other means of re-establishing his primacy. The development of the personality cult, particularly amongst young people, ensured that his prestige remained high within the general population. But Mao also retained significant and ultimately crucial bases of support in other areas, notably within the military, in important provinces in eastern China, and in sections of the media and propaganda organisations. These were to prove powerful tools in mobilising the population to achieve his ends in the Cultural Revolution.

### The Military

When Peng Dehuai was dismissed as Minister of National Defence in 1959, Mao was not just removing a powerful opponent. By securing Lin Biao's elevation to replace Peng, Mao ensured that the military was led by one of his most loyal followers. The transition from Peng to Lin is sometimes portrayed as the transition from a professional to a political military. While this slightly exaggerates the transition (the military in fact maintained its military role and upgrading), it is certainly true that Lin vastly increased the army's political role. Importantly, in politicising the army, Lin ensured that a greater emphasis was placed on Mao than on any other leader, or even the party as a whole.

Even under Peng Dehuai, the party had always played an active role within the military. For example, at each level of military leadership, political commissars of equivalent rank were charged with ensuring that party policy was considered in all decision-making. What Lin essentially did was to take these existing trends a step further. For example, the role and status of these political officers was strengthened, and soldiers were required to attend more political education classes. Typically, the soldiers would study Mao's dictums and ideas, not those of Liu or Deng, and not Marx, Lenin or Engels. Lin collected Mao's major works together and published them. This volume was distributed widely, first through the army, and then through society as a whole, and became better known in the west by the title 'The Little Red Book'.

The politicisation was accompanied by an attempt to raise the profile of the army in the minds of the general public. In 1964 a new campaign was launched calling on the people to 'Learn from the PLA'. Soldiers were put forward as paragons of socialist virtue. They were imbued with the correct Maoist ideology and were utterly selfless in their devotion to the revolutionary cause and to their fellow proletarians. The implication was that the party, by comparison, was smug, complacent and self-serving.

This campaign provided three main advantages for Mao. First, it showed that he, or at least his followers in the relevant organisations, still had the ability to initiate new political campaigns. Second, it generated an emulation of the military, particularly in terms of studying Mao and reading the Little Red Book. Third, it brought Mao's suspicions of the party leadership out into the open, raising the spectre of the need to purge even the highest levels of the party if they were following the wrong path. Although it still came as something of a shock when Mao later called on the people to bombard the party headquarters and seek out the capitalist roaders, the 'learn from the PLA' campaign at least sowed the seeds of doubts about the party's (but not Mao's) ability to rule.

Whilst Lin Biao was super-loyal to Mao, we must take care not to imbue the military with a single cohesive view. Indeed, the military was in many ways fraught with the same tensions as the party itself. At the central level, Lin and Mao faced considerable opposition from the Chief of Staff of the PLA, Luo Ruiqing. The main line of conflict here was over China's position between the two superpowers, an issue brought into sharper focus in the 1960s by the escalation of American involvement in Vietnam.[4] For Luo, China should support the communists in Vietnam in their struggle with the Americans. The implication, and perhaps no more than an implication, was that China should shelve its differences with the Soviet Union and form an alliance to oust the Americans. Luo further insisted that Vietnam showed that the United States was still committed to defeating communism in Asia, and the only way forward for China was to establish a strong professional and technocratic military along the lines of the Soviet Red Army.

For both Mao and Lin Biao, this approach was totally wrong. First, relations with the Soviet Union had now deteriorated to such an extent that any alliance, even in a third country like Vietnam against a common enemy, was unthinkable. Second, the Chinese experience showed that guerrilla warfare supported by mass mobilisation was the way forward – Luo Ruiqing, like Peng Dehuai before him, was placing the Soviet experience above Chinese experience. Thus, Lin and Mao argued that China should keep out of the Vietnamese conflict, and only allow limited aid in the form of allowing Soviet supplies to pass through China on the way to the Vietnamese communists.

Despite some support for Luo's views from Deng Xiaoping and Liu Shaoqi, they were not prepared to push the issue. We might suggest that they feared sparking political upheaval by opposing Mao at this stage. It is also true that embarking on a costly war in Vietnam would not exactly have aided domestic economic recovery. Luo found himself increasingly isolated and was removed from power in December 1965. With the benefit of hindsight, perhaps this was the first purge of the Cultural Revolution. Mao had fought an argument on what he believed to be one of his main areas – relations with the superpowers – and he had won.

Despite the removal of a powerful opponent from the central military leadership, there was still considerable opposition to Mao's views within the military at the regional level. Regional military commanders possessed considerable autonomy as they were in direct control over the troops – if they didn't order their men to fire, then they wouldn't fire. So when the Cultural Revolution began to unfold, military reactions were somewhat divided. While some local leaders followed Mao's call to support the left, others actively supported the right and tried to fight off the Cultural Revolution, while a third group of leaders initially chose to do nothing. Crucially, though, Mao had enough support from the military to start the movement rolling. He was also able to rely on support from the 8341 unit, the special forces guarding the central committee headquarters in Beijing. These forces were under the command of Mao's old bodyguard from the Yanan days, Wang Dongxing. Wang's loyalty to Mao transcended his loyalty to the party as a whole, and was a key factor in launching the Cultural Revolution.

.   .   .

## THE PERSONALITY CULT AND POLITICAL SOCIALISATION

Whilst support from the military was an important component in launching the Cultural Revolution, Mao also benefited from enormous support from the population in general, and students and young people in particular. The almost godlike status that Mao held in China was the consequence of many years of ideological and propaganda work. As such, to understand fully how and why so many Chinese participated in the Cultural Revolution, it is important to take a step back to establish the origins and implications of mass mobilisation, political socialisation and the personality cult.

*Encouraging Political Participation*

In creating a new political order after 1949, the CCP faced a considerable task in creating a new political culture within China. In pre-revolution China, there was no strong tradition of active political participation. Politics was considered the preserve of the intellectual elite, an occupation reserved for those who had passed the Confucian examination system. For the average Chinese, the tradition was one of relative passivity and acceptance of control from above. The only time that politics became a popular and mass activity was when conditions became so bad that ordinary people were forced to rebel.[5] Once the rebellion had been successful in overthrowing the illegitimate ruler, then normal politics and popular passivity were resumed.

This tradition created a number of problems for the new leadership. First, they feared that if they could not create a new political order entailing widespread popular participation in politics, then the peasantry would not necessarily feel a shared common interest in keeping the party in power. If they simply accepted communist rule passively, then might they not accept Guomindang rule passively?

Thus, the party thought that if the people were encouraged to participate in political action, it would create a closer relationship between the party and the people. The masses would gain a better understanding of the party's goals and ideas through participating in attaining them. The people would also feel that they had a stake in the new political system, and would be more prepared to defend it against external and internal threats. Like their Soviet counterparts, the Chinese authorities did (and still do) lay great store in attaining or even surpassing their self-imposed targets. If the people were encouraged to participate in a campaign and fulfil or exceed its targets, then they would feel an immense sense of pride in themselves, as well as in the party.

But for Mao, participation was not just a means to an end, but an end in itself. Simply being involved in the political process was seen as being a legitimating force, and one that tied the people much more closely to party policies and goals. Indeed, in some cases, the result of the participation was perhaps less important than the process of participation itself. Perhaps the best example here is the campaign to kill the sparrows. Having dissected a dead sparrow and counted the amount of grain in the bird's stomach, a well-intentioned individual calculated that if all the birds were killed, then this would have an enormous impact in terms of the extra amount of grain available for human consumption. Thus, it was decreed that the entire population be mobilised on a specific day to kill all the birds. And this is exactly what happened. The whole country took pots and pans and anything that would make a noise, and each time a bird tried to rest, it was scared from its perch by a cacophony of noise until it fell to the ground dead through exhaustion. The fact that the birds also ate bugs and hence there was a resultant explosion in insect life that caused its own toll on agriculture was almost beside the point. Everybody had participated, and the goal had been achieved.[6]

### Promoting Gratitude

Legitimacy through popular participation was important, but not the only way in which the party tried to build up its popular legitimacy. The party deliberately built a cult of personality around Mao. Mao was very useful for the party. He was a figurehead, a hero, and a great leader who had led China out of the wilderness. In doing so, they promoted the idea that Mao was the embodiment of the revolution – an idea that Mao and his followers were not slow to utilise when they needed to. So while the image of Mao the Great Helmsman was initially designed to provide legitimacy for the party, it created a stronger loyalty to Mao as an individual than it did to the party as a whole.

In order to establish legitimacy, the party placed great emphasis on reminding the population of what life had been like before the communist liberation.[7] This was particularly important for inculcating a deep gratitude to the party in the younger population who had no personal knowledge of the old bad days with which to compare the new system. Thus, the party charged its propaganda departments with the task of extolling the great virtues of the Long March generation, the people's army, and the Great Helmsman himself. The message was clear, if not to say a little blunt: look what great deeds these people performed for you, and remember how awful life was before Mao came along. It is perhaps worth noting here that the party's propaganda departments were one of the few areas of the party-state organisation where Maoists held significant influence.

### Mobilising Control of the Media and Art and Literature

Mao placed great faith in the power of art and literature to change the way people thought. He, like many others of the May Fourth generation, had himself been inspired and politicised by reading the works of Ibsen and the ersatz works of young Chinese liberals. As early as 1942, Mao had made his pitch for leadership of Chinese culture. At the Yanan forum on art and literature, Mao laid down prescriptions for all art and literature that were to continue to influence policy throughout his life.

Mao argued that writers and artists had a duty to 'serve the people' – a byword in many ways for 'serve the party'. Rather than showing things as they were, cultural intellectuals should deploy 'socialist realist' perspectives. The type of literature that Mao wanted extolled new socialist virtues and clearly contrasted them with the evils of the old feudal past. The result was a very stark delineation of characters between wholly bad representatives of the old guard and wholly good representatives of the new. Life and the revolution were to be displayed in black and white, and the only grey characters were temporarily unsure of the best way forward. Inevitably, grey turned to white as these characters ultimately saw the light in a cathartic recognition of the superiority of socialism. Psychological development of characters was also taboo, with the only personal progression permissible being the acceptance of class consciousness. Finally, familial and other bases of friendship were replaced by comradeship and shared class consciousness – you must do something for the love of socialism, love of the party, and love of the proletariat, and for no other reason.

This approach was not confined to literature. The visual arts, music, plays and opera all had to conform to these principles. Though Mao initially faced resistance from the literati, there can be little doubt that his prescriptions for art and literature were an important component in installing a new cultural policy – a policy which perhaps aided Mao more than it did the party as a whole. And it is no mere coincidence that when the Cultural Revolution was in its early emerging days, the arena through which the Maoist left chose first to criticise the Leninists was cultural policy.

## Revolutionary Heroes and Emulation Campaigns

Like the Soviets before them, the Chinese communists unveiled a number of socialist heroes for emulation by the people. Initially, these were heroes of the revolutionary struggle who had done so much to liberate the people from past evils. To be good citizens, the people were encourged to follow their examples. However, as time went by, the CCP realised that it was creating expectations that could no longer be fully realised. Once the Korean War had achieved its stalemate by 1953, it was increasingly difficult to find avenues through which people could actually emulate these great heroic deeds. Furthermore, with the number of university places strictly limited, and the number of 'exciting' revolutionary jobs few and far between, there was a danger that the young people might find themselves frustrated in their goals.

Thus, a new revolutionary hero appeared in the shape of Lei Feng.[8] Unlike the previous heroes, Lei Feng was not particularly glorious or heroic. He was, in many ways, an anti-hero. The whole point of the Lei Feng campaign was to emphasise that doing boring mundane things was as revolutionary as fighting the Japanese. If you do the small things correctly – or 'socialistly' – then the combined impact of these small acts will be to develop a glorious socialist China. Or in the words of Lei Feng himself:

A man's usefulness to the revolutionary cause is like a screw in a machine. It is only by the many interconnecting and fixed screws that the machine can move freely, increasing its enormous work power. Though a screw is small, its use is beyond estimation. I am willing to be a screw.

Lei Feng emerged on the scene in 1962 in a double-page spread of *China Youth Daily* with a hand-written exhortation in Mao's own calligraphy to 'Learn From Lei Feng'. Lei Feng had been orphaned by the combined excesses of brutal landlords and Japanese aggression, and he had only been saved by the appearance of communist forces which took him under their wing and nurtured him. Lei Feng developed a deep love for his fellow proletarians, and he became profoundly grateful for everything that the party, and particularly Mao, had done to save him and the Chinese people from past evils. Lei Feng unfortunately suffered an early death, but fortunately for us and China, his diaries were posthumously found and published in a number of serialisations.

What these diaries show is a young man who subverted all his own selfish interests to aid the socialist revolution out of love for the party and his fellow proletariat. If he was on a train, Lei Feng would grab a brush and help the staff clean the carriage, always denying any thanks. In his dormitory, he would secretly mend his comrades' clothes or creep into the kitchen to prepare the evening meal – always in secret and never in the hope of gaining personal glory or thanks.

More important for this study, Lei Feng was a voracious reader of Mao's works. Whenever he faced a problem, he would find the solution in reading Mao. Every problem found a solution in Mao. Only by studying Mao, and by studying Mao continuously, could an individual really hope to understand the truth and become a good socialist. And as everybody had to learn from Lei Feng, then the message for all young people was that they too must study Mao's works.

The fact that Lei Feng emerged in the 1960s is of no small significance. At a time when Mao was perhaps at his weakest in the formal power structure after the failings of the Great Leap Forward, Mao and his followers were trying to bolster his prestige and image in other arenas. In the Lei Feng case, it is important to note that students were told that it was Mao's works and Mao's ideas which could resolve all problems and lead towards a correct understanding of socialism, and not the ideas of the party as a whole, or of other key leaders. As we shall see, this attempt to separate Mao and the party was to be of crucial importance to Mao in the launching of the Cultural Revolution.

## Ideological Training and the Personality Cult

Students and soldiers were not the only targets for such political education. Through the party's organisation, propaganda, and ideological departments, the new communist creed was spread throughout the country. Mass meetings were held at all workplaces, and in rural areas, where the message was repeatedly rammed home. Although these meetings were meant to be a two-way process allowing the people to have their input into politics, in practice they were essentially forums for outlining the party's message.

In schools and colleges, and in workplaces, people were required (not always formally, but in practice) to attend political education classes, where they would discuss the wisdom of Mao's works, and why Mao was correct. But it was not just in these formal meetings and classes that the political message was promoted. It was all but impossible to escape the political process. The press and the spoken media carried the Maoist message continually. With censorship ensuring that there were no unofficial sources of news and other information, the message became an unchallenged and unilateral one. The front page of the *People's Daily* became a tribute to Mao and repeated his words *ad nauseam*.

Even if you didn't read the papers, or listen to the news, you still could not escape the message. Posters, statues and monuments of Mao appeared across the country, portraying Mao as an almost superhuman figure, and as a great statesman. Thanks to Mao's prescriptions for art and literature, the political message was also ubiquitous in novels, in films, in music, in plays. And increasingly, Mao's role in the revolution and his great deeds became the focus for these cultural works. And just in case you managed to avoid looking at these, loudspeakers piped the music and the latest news across factories, in schools and colleges, and on public transport. There was essentially no escape.

For a party that theoretically believed that great men did not make history, the cult of personality was a rather odd concept. But it was not without precedent. By the time the CCP came to power, the cult of personality had already been strongly established – perhaps taken to extremes – in the Soviet Union. Indeed, it is not too fanciful to suggest that Mao's own personality cult was designed to place him on an equal footing with Stalin. It also had a quasi-historical precedent in China. Under the old imperial system, power was visibly (at least) vested in the hands of one man – the Emperor. In many ways, the Mao cult filled the void of the loss of the imperial system by creating a new Emperor – the people's Emperor.

The point of the personality cult was to establish a clear link between the revolution and Mao. The two became inseparable. Mao was the revolution, and the revolution was Mao. If you even dared to question Mao, you were being utterly ungrateful for all that he had done to free you from the tyranny of the past. Even if what Mao says appears strange – for example, rise up and bombard the headquarters, attack those party members who are taking the capitalist road – then don't question that Mao might be wrong. Hasn't he been right every time so far?

The strength of the personality cult poses huge problems for political succession. How can you replace the great leader? This task was to befall Hua Guofeng, who found himself hamstrung by his adherence to Mao and Maoism, the very things which had caused most of the problems that China faced in 1976. More immediately, it posed huge problems for the rest of the party. By allowing (even supporting) the Mao cult to grow, the party faced a situation where the people had more loyalty to Mao than to the party itself. Furthermore, how could they themselves criticise Mao in public, when the man had an image of invincibility and infallibility? Having built up this image, Mao's critics risked placing themselves in danger if they openly opposed him, and even risked undermining the position of the party itself. When it came to the Cultural Revolution, these were to be crucial considerations in explaining Mao's ability to mobilise key sections of the population in an assault on the party itself.

## The Education System

A final consideration here is the way in which the education system was used to promote socialist virtues in a manner that aided Mao during his major struggles with the party leadership. Mao viewed mankind as essentially malleable – people's thoughts could be moulded. Whilst this approach was applied to the entire Chinese population, the younger generation provided a particularly good avenue for spreading socialist thought. Here were people untainted by any feudal instincts, and if you could get them persuaded at an early age, then they would be persuaded for life. By winning the hearts and minds of the younger generation, the future of the revolution would be secure.

The approach to indoctrination in the classroom entailed a combination of controlling ideas and controlling activity. In terms of ideas, the entire school curriculum was designed to promote socialism. The first elementary reading primers were laden with socialist virtues. Children first learnt the vocabulary of socialism in their initial learning experiences. All subsequent texts were similarly designed to promote revolutionary ideals. For example, the psychoanalytical approach of people like Freud was banned as it placed an emphasis on individual psychological development and did not deal with the primacy of class struggle and comradeship. Unsurprisingly, market economics were not taught, except to give a negative example of the evils that capitalism inevitably brought.

China's feudal past was dealt with in a slightly different manner. While the old feudal system was clearly wrong and evil and acted against the interests of the Chinese people, Chinese history was considered to be an important area for discussion. On one level, this entailed emphasising the harsh treatment that China suffered at the hands of the western imperialists from 1840 onwards. This was not intended to excuse the imperial system for its own failings. Indeed, the imperial bureaucracy was portrayed as being incapable of defending the interests of the Chinese people, and as having capitulated to the foreign powers. Nevertheless, the colonialists had no right to compound the oppression of the Chinese people further with their imperialist interventions. On another level, the party extolled traditional notions of national pride, and the concept that China was the centre of world civilisation. The Chinese people should strive to return China to its rightful position of global preeminence, and be proud of its long history of innovation and invention. Building communism was clearly important, but so was restoring China to its rightful place in the world order.

In terms of organisation, the classroom gave the party an excellent opportunity to inculcate an atmosphere of obedience and respect. Participation in the revolution was important, but it had to be disciplined participation – an almost tautological obedient spontaneous participation. Students were taught to accept what they were told about the revolution, and to have unbounded love for comrades and unbounded hatred for class enemies. They should not question the correctness of the party and/or Mao.

Within the class, the horizontal ranks of desks were organised into sub-groups of the classroom committee. The vertical ranks were similarly sub-divisions of organisation, but this time for the Young Pioneers (in many ways replicating the overlapping of party-state relations in China). The Young Pioneers were the first rung on the long ladder to party membership. In order to gain entry, students from the age of five had to display political action. Obviously for young children, this did not mean fighting in Korea to ward off the American threat, but more mundane socialist activities such as helping to tidy up, or helping old people – the boy scouts meet Marxism.

Enrolment into the Young Pioneers was accompanied by much pomp and congratulation, and the award of the coveted red neckerchief. It was also staggered, with only the best allowed in during the first wave of enrolment. The idea here was that this would force those who had been left out to re-double their efforts and to become more politically active. Eventually, all students would be admitted (with the exception of those from the worst class backgrounds – sons and daughters of particularly evil landlords or Guomindang officials).

Within the schools and the Young Pioneers, the students would engage in self-struggle sessions, admitting their socialist failings in public in an attempt to become a better socialist. One of the key objectives here was to increase their chances of gaining membership to the Communist Youth League. Unlike the Young Pioneers, membership here was strictly limited, and only the best communists were allowed in. But membership was worth striving for, as it brought with it an excellent chance of ultimately joining the party. As party membership also increased the chances of getting a university place and a good job, personal rather than ideological motivations may well have inspired some young Chinese to become politically active.[9]

The impact of student socialisation on Mao's political strategies has become an area of contention. On one side, Chan,[10] Unger[11] and White[12] portray student activism during the Cultural Revolution as an internal class struggle. Those who felt that they were being denied access to rewards used the Cultural Revolution to attack the sons and daughters of party members who were monopolising the Communist Youth League, and through this, access to the party, university entrance and good jobs. Those who were not 'red by birth' used Mao's attacks on the party establishment to promote 'red by action' as the main criteria for personal advancement. It was a class conflict, but not the type of class conflict that Mao desired.

On the other side, Forster's analysis of Red Guard activism in Zhejiang province led him to different conclusions.[13] Whilst admitting that his case study may not be universally applicable (Zhejiang was one of the most radical Maoist provinces), he argues that what the Cultural Revolution did was remove certainty. After years of being told what to do, the breakdown in order in the Cultural Revolution meant that vague and at times contradictory orders were being issued from conflicting power centres in Beijing. The divisions that emerged within the Red Guard movement were not a result of competing student 'classes' but between competing interpretations of what Mao had said, or more clearly, what he meant.

The two approaches are not necessarily mutually contradictory. Guangdong, the focus of Chan's and Unger's investigations, and Zhejiang, the focus of Forster's, had developed in different ways after 1949. Whereas Guangdong under Tao Zhu and his young deputy, Zhao Ziyang, veered towards the liberal economic spectrum of the Leninists, Zhejiang was always more firmly in the Maoist camp. But whichever is true, the fact that the intense politicisation of China's youth was an important component in enabling Mao to launch the Cultural Revolution is not contested.

.  .  .

## NOTES

1. Lieberthal, K. (1993) 'The Great Leap Forward and the Split in the Yan'an Leadership 1958–65' in MacFarquhar, R. (ed.) *The Politics of China 1949–1989* (Cambridge: Cambridge University Press) pp. 87–147.

2. Leys is the pen-name of Pierre Ryckmans. Leys, S. (1977) *The Chairman's New Clothes: Mao and the Cultural Revolution* (London: Allison and Busby).

3. For more details on Chen Yun's approach, see Lieberthal, K. and Lardy, N. (1983) *Chen Yun's Strategy for China's Development: A Non-Maoist Alternative* (Armonk, N.Y.: M.E. Sharpe).

4. We have to be aware that the victors write history, and Mao's vision of what Luo wanted may of course have been distorted to justify the action taken.

5.  This right to rebel had become part of the Confucian doctrine of the mandate of heaven. If an Emperor was failing to fulfil the requirements of the people, then the people not so much had a right as a duty to rise up and overthrow him. Indeed, the only real indication that an Emperor had lost the mandate of heaven was his overthrow by a successful rebellion.

6.  Of course the problem with this type of participation is that we can't be sure why people participated. Did they really share the party's goals and want to participate, or were they simply scared of what would happen to them if they didn't? The public face might show compliance, but the private face might have an entirely different demeanour.

7.  Just one example here is the Recall Bitterness sessions organised in Chinese schools. Peasants would be brought into the schools to explain how dreadful their lives were before the communists. See Chan, A. (1985) *Children of Mao: Personality Development and Political Activism in the Red Guard Generation* (Seattle: University of Washington Press).

8.  This section draws from Anita Chan's excellent account of the Lei Feng phenomena in *Children of Mao.*

9.  Ibid.

10. Ibid.

11. Unger, J. (1982) *Education Under Mao: Class and Competition in Canton Schools, 1960–1980* (New York: Columbia University Press).

12. White, G. (1976) *The Politics of Class and Class Origin: The Case of the Cultural Revolution* (Canberra: Contemporary China Centre Papers No 9).

13. Forster, K. (1990) *Rebellion and Factionalism in a Chinese Province: Zhejiang, 1966–1976* (Armonk, N.Y.: M.E. Sharpe).

# Chapter 5

# LAUNCHING THE CULTURAL REVOLUTION

During the first half of the 1960s, the Chinese economy gradually recovered from the devastation of the Great Leap. Rural production was stabilised, and domestic food supplies were complemented by imported grain as China's leaders sanctioned a pragmatic limited engagement with the international capitalist economy. But just as things were improving, Mao embarked on a new radical campaign which was to prove even more devastating than the Great Leap.

From a historical perspective, the Cultural Revolution can be seen as the culmination of the debates and conflicts that had surrounded Mao's position within the Chinese communist leadership after 1949. Indeed, in some respects, the origins of the Cultural Revolution go right back to Mao's refusal to accept the Comintern's plans for revolution in China in the 1930s. But even while the Cultural Revolution was being launched, Mao's opponents in the party could not have guessed that he was preparing to risk destroying the party itself to rid them from the scene.

Mao's failure to push through his ideas for the Socialist Education Movement taught him that an open political-ideological campaign would face huge obstacles from the central party organisation. The right were not going to countenance a mass campaign which would disrupt the economic recovery. Nor were they, or party cadres throughout the system, prepared to sanction a political purge against themselves. So when the Cultural Revolution was launched, it was not, immediately at least, identifiable as a political campaign against the top of the party, but appeared to be a rather limited debate over cultural policy. The extension of the initial limited campaign into the wider political field caught many of its victims unawares. And as the movement developed a momentum of its own through the radicalism of China's youth, even those who initiated the Cultural Revolution in the first place were surprised by the way that events unfolded.

. . .

## STARTING THE CULTURAL REVOLUTION: THE DEBATE ON ART AND LITERATURE

The Cultural Revolution began as a relatively minor debate over cultural policy (hence the confusion sometimes over what the cultural part of the Cultural Revolution actually meant). Cultural policy provided a fruitful arena for Mao to reassert himself for two reasons. First, it was an area where he had much more influence than Liu Shaoqi, Deng Xiaoping or other party leaders. It was Mao who had established the criteria for art and literature under communist control in Yanan in 1942, and his voice still carried authority and weight. Second, while a debate over cultural policy might cause some unease amongst intellectuals, it would have only a minimal impact on the economy. It was not (or at least, did not appear to be) a mass movement, and Liu and Deng were thus less likely to block the debate, or try and control it as they had done with the Socialist Education Movement.

During the first half of the 1960s, writers and artists had increasingly ignored Mao's 1942 assertion that all art and literature should promote the revolution. Rather than writing about the party and the class struggle, authors slowly began to return to traditional themes. They returned to art for art's sake rather than art for the revolution. Whilst this was bad enough for Mao, the fact that party leaders at both national and local levels were turning a blind eye to these changes was even worse.

Under the old imperial system, intellectuals had a duty to act as the representatives of the people. No matter how dangerous it might be, they were morally mandated to speak out if they felt that the emperor was ignoring or harming the people. So, for many intellectuals, the call to support the party and the revolution unreservedly denied them their traditional role as the conduit between the rulers and the led. If they were not to speak up for the people, then who would?

In the relatively liberal atmosphere of the early 1960s, some writers returned to what they perceived to be their natural and rightful role in society, producing work that questioned party policy. It was not that these writers opposed the party *per se* and wanted to overthrow it, but that somebody needed to speak out when the party made mistakes. Significantly, the majority of this type of critical literature – what the authors themselves saw as loyal criticism – focused on the way that the radical policies of the 1950s had harmed the people. Not surprisingly, it was this critical work which caused Mao most displeasure.

The most important of these critical works was 'Hai Rui Dismissed From Office' by Wu Han. The story was a rather straightforward historical account of an imperial officer who had been dismissed by a belligerent Emperor for daring to suggest that imperial policies were harming the peasantry. This apparently innocuous story became the focus of intense opposition from the left (and essentially marks the starting point of the Cultural Revolution) for two reasons. First, it was taken by Mao and his followers to be an attack on Mao's dismissal of Peng Dehuai in 1959.[1] Second, in addition to being a noted writer, Wu Han was also Vice-Mayor of Beijing. Attacking Wu Han thus had an overtly political, as well as cultural connotation, and also brought into light the role of Peng Zhen. As Mayor of Beijing, Peng Zhen could be criticised for allowing his subordinate to act in this way, and it was probably no coincidence that Peng Zhen had been one of the more vocal critics of Mao's policies and strategies from the early 1950s.

Mao and his followers had established a basis for launching the movement, but they still faced considerable problems in finding an audience for their views. With the central leadership and the Beijing city leadership largely hostile to Mao's ideas, Mao turned his back on the capital and sought support from loyal leaders in the provinces. The left were particularly strong in Zhejiang province, and also in neighbouring Shanghai, a city that had gradually fallen under the influence of a group of radical Maoists headed by Mao's wife, Jiang Qing.

Jiang Qing was Mao's third wife,[2] and her revolutionary credentials stood in stark contrast to her predecessor's. Mao's first wife, Yang Gaihui, was the daughter of the philosopher who had inspired Mao into political action, and had helped secure Mao a job in the library at Beijing University. Even though Mao had abandoned her for his second wife, He Zhizhen, Yang Gaihui remained loyal to the revolution and to Mao. When Yang was arrested by the Guomindang after Mao's failed attempt to lead an uprising in the city of Changsha in 1930, she refused to renege on her husband and was executed.[3] He Zhizhen also developed a reputation for revolutionary activism. She took part in the Long March despite being seriously ill, and her courage won her support and admiration from the party leadership.

By contrast, Jiang Qing's political credentials were somewhat questionable. She had first come to prominence in Shanghai in the 1920s. Known variously as Lu Ping and Lan Ping, she had developed an acting career and become a firm fixture on the Shanghai social circuit. Jiang courted media attention, and through a string of relationships with leading men, became an almost permanent topic in the gossip columns of the city's magazines and newspapers.[4]

There were many in the Chinese leadership – notably Zhou Enlai and Deng Xiaoping – who viewed Jiang Qing's subsequent conversion to communism with intense suspicion. This suspicion turned to outright hostility when Jiang Qing arrived in Yanan during the revolution and became romantically involved with Mao. After giving birth to her and Mao's fifth child, He Zhizhen had been finally persuaded to move to Moscow for medical treatment. Given all that she had been through, Mao's betrayal of his wife dismayed many of his colleagues, both for personal reasons and for the fear of alienating the largely socially conservative peasantry. The fact that he had betrayed her for a politically suspect former socialite was even worse.

Mao's marriage to Jiang Qing was reluctantly accepted by the rest of the party leadership on the condition that Jiang did not play a prominent public role or gain any political position.[5] So despite her marriage to the most important man in China, Jiang Qing was unable to wield any power. Given her very clear pleasure in playing the role of China's 'first lady' during and after the Cultural Revolution, it seems that Jiang's political ambitions had been thwarted by her relationship with the man who could have given her what she wanted. While it would be going too far to portray the Cultural Revolution as Jiang's strategy for finally gaining political power, it seems that she did use the movement to re-impose herself on the political scene, and to settle some old scores along the way.

In addition to Jiang Qing, the group of radical Maoists in Shanghai consisted of Wang Hongwen, Yao Wenyuan and Zhang Chunqiao – a group that later became known as the Gang of

Four. Wang Hongwen was a true proletarian, a factory worker whose labour activism in the Cultural Revolution earned him a position in the national political elite.[6] Crucially, Yao Wenyuan and Zhang Chunqiao were both leading figures in cultural affairs: Yao was a literary critic and editor, and Zhang was the head of cultural affairs in Shanghai. As such, while Mao might not be able to launch his attack on Wu Han and the Beijing leadership in Beijing, Shanghai provided a more than suitable alternative.

Indeed, it was the Shanghai radicals, rather than Mao himself, who took the lead in launching the Cultural Revolution in 1965. Jiang Qing had reappeared from her political exile at the East China drama festival in the summer of 1965, where she railed against the abandonment of her husband's cultural principles. This was followed by a more ferocious and specific attack on Wu Han by Yao Wenyuan in November 1965. Whilst the national press simply ignored Yao's paper, he had no trouble in publishing it in Shanghai. It was subsequently reprinted in the army's own national newspaper, the *Liberation Army Daily*, thus giving Yao's attacks a national platform.

Despite the best intentions of the right in Beijing, Mao's support base within Shanghai and within the military had brought the debate out into the open. Not surprisingly, the right countered using the same tactics that they had deployed to sideline Mao's Socialist Education Movement in 1962: they took up the movement in an attempt to turn it into something that they could control. Thus, when the *People's Daily* responded to Yao Wenyuan's article, the right published it with an editorial stressing the importance (and problems) of studying history. It was thus portrayed as an abstract intellectual question, and nothing to do with the contemporary political system. Furthermore, when a Cultural Revolution Small Group was set up to investigate the issues being raised, the right packed it with its own supporters. Indeed, Peng Zhen was appointed as the head of the new small group – one of the very men that Mao and the left were trying to attack.

These attempts to side-track the Cultural Revolution proved to be, at best, a temporary setback. At worst, they actually increased the evidence for Mao and his followers that the central party leadership was protecting the unprotectable from the verdict of the people. Perhaps the key point in moving the momentum away from the right came with Liu Shaoqi's departure for a tour to south-east Asia in the spring of 1966. By the time he returned, the tide had moved considerably. Mao and his followers had called a special Communist Party meeting in Hangzhou where Peng Zhen had effectively been removed. Crucially, Premier Zhou Enlai did nothing to block the campaign to criticise Peng Zhen. Whilst Zhou may not have taken a leading role in prosecuting the Cultural Revolution, his acceptance of the new radicalism was an important aid for Mao in establishing the new political wind.

With Peng Zhen in disgrace, the movement took on a new sense of urgency. Many in the cultural sphere began their retreat (either enforced or often self-imposed) and the left went on the offensive. The rightist-dominated Cultural Revolution Small Group was disbanded and replaced by a new group staffed by Mao's most loyal followers. Furthermore, this new group was not simply confined to studying culture in the narrow definition of the term, but extended its remit to assess political crimes and the pervading political climate.

Another important aid to the left was the reluctant acquiescence of Liu and Deng to the *fait accompli* of the dismissal of Peng Zhen. Faced by a growing momentum for a change in polity, they decided to run with it rather than fight it. Indeed, they participated in the great mass rallies of the Cultural Revolution, even once a wider political movement had replaced the early limited purge. So when the movement first extended into the universities, Liu and Deng sent in their own work teams to try and limit the new revolution to a minor attack on university officials.[7] In essence, they tried to turn the focus of student radicalism onto specific individuals, rather than the political system itself.

The work teams also imposed order and organisation: they decided who should be criticised and what should be done rather than allowing the student activists to run amok. Just like with the SEM, it was to remain a movement of the party by the party, not a mass movement as Mao and his followers both wanted and needed. So while a number of high-ranking university officials were purged by these rightist work teams, those at the top of the educational system escaped criticism.

This time, however, Mao was not prepared to see his movement hijacked by the party, and he was prepared to go to whatever lengths were needed to obtain his objectives. Thus, Mao called for the students and the masses to bombard the headquarters – to seek out and destroy those at whatever level who were taking the capitalist road. Initially, this did not explicitly include those at the very apex of the political system, namely Deng Xiaoping and Liu Shaoqi, but as the revolutionary momentum increased, then both men fell foul of the revolution and into disgrace. Both Liu and Deng produced 'self-criticisms' in October 1966, admitting that they had made some mistakes. But rather than save them, these self-criticisms only provided further ammunition to their enemies.

Liu Shaoqi was not formally dismissed from the party and purged until the autumn of 1968. Indeed, for much of the Cultural Revolution, he was not directly criticised by name, but referred to as 'the number one person in authority taking the capitalist road' or 'China's Khrushchev'. But while they might not have been criticised by name, both Deng and Liu suffered in person: both men were paraded in front of mass meetings and vilified for their crimes against the revolution. Liu was to die a miserable death in jail, untreated by his captors, and broken by the criticism. Deng removed his hearing aid so that he couldn't listen to his tormentors, wrote a rather non-committal self-criticism, and even told his children to condemn him to save themselves. This did not stop one of his sons, Deng Pufang, from victimisation from the Red Guards resulting in his paralysis.

The wave of revolutionary enthusiasm was supposedly a spontaneous outburst by the people against the party which was taking the wrong road towards capitalism. In reality, it was more a case of organised spontaneity. As we saw in Chapter 4, it was partly the result of the development of the cult of personality over a number of years, and the emphasis on loyalty to Mao above loyalty to the party. It was a reaping of the seeds of loyalty which had been sown (and even sown by Mao's opponents) over the preceding two decades.

Crucially, the military played a leading role in allowing the Maoist left to unleash this loyalty into political activism. On one level, the military provided a political constituency for Mao in launching the Cultural Revolution through formal party channels. When Mao was not sure that he would win a vote in the Politburo or Central Committee, then military units helped by preventing opponents from attending the meeting. On other occasions, Mao called 'enlarged' Politburo meetings and invited loyal military leaders to act as representatives of the masses. Whichever method was used, Mao's majority was assured, giving the impression at least that the Cultural Revolution had the support of the entire party leadership.

On another level, the military provided vital support for the Maoists by organising a mass holiday for the young people of China. The railway system was essentially requisitioned by military units acting on behalf of the Maoist left, and young people were taken, free of charge, to Beijing to attend mass rallies in favour of the Cultural Revolution. These mass rallies were also well orchestrated and organised. In the best (or worst) traditions, the minor celebrities would appear first extolling the virtues of Mao – or in the words of his main acolyte, Lin Biao, the 'genius' of Mao. The correctness of everything Mao had done and said so far was emphasised so that his policies would not – could not – be questioned, irrespective of what he said. And eventually the great man would make his own contribution. Mao was in many ways remarkably uncharismatic. His strong, rather high-pitched Hunanese voice did not in itself raise the audience to action. His method of delivery was also rather mundane and deliberate. But charismatic authority and appeal is much more to do with the aura and the wider campaign than it is with the abilities of a single individual. These people had come already inspired and already sure of Mao's brilliance. Armed with their red books, the mass rallies verged on mass hysteria.

When the rallies were over, the students and young people were shipped back to their homes and told to prosecute the Cultural Revolution by seeking out power-holders taking the capitalist road. And seek out these people they did. The call to bombard the headquarters fell on relatively fertile soil. During the 1960s, there was considerable discontent in much of China at the growth of party control and of the limited opportunities available for those who were not part of the new party class. Furthermore, the youth of China had been socialised into accepting the wisdom of Mao, and that political action was the best way of making a mark on society. Thus, when they were given the green light to rebel by Mao, they rebelled because Mao could not be wrong, and because rebelling gave them an opportunity to prove their political credentials.

These young people also found supporters within the urban working class as well. For those with secure jobs and benefits within the state-owned sector, the Cultural Revolution was dangerous as it threatened their position and their wealth. For the

30–40 per cent of urban workers who were not part of this privileged state-owned working class,[8] the Cultural Revolution was also very welcome. And with the official trade unions acting much more as a catalyst for party policy and the status quo, it gave them a channel to attack the privilege and security that they had been denied.

But while the Cultural Revolution might have originated with organised activism, once unleashed it proved a difficult beast to control. The people had been told that the party was a smug and complacent isolated elite that told the people what to do rather than listening to what they wanted. If anybody tried to control the way that the movement was moving, or criticise its excesses, then they would be committing exactly those crimes that the Cultural Revolution was intended to detect and correct. The movement was, in its very inception, uncontrollable.

An attack on those in the party who were taking the capitalist road would have been enough on its own to cause widespread chaos. But the Cultural Revolution was more than just a purge of party officials. It was an attack on all modes of thought and behaviour that were not conducive to promoting the correct (i.e. Mao's) vision of socialism. Thus, traditional ideas and practices were attacked as being feudal in origin. In practice, this meant destroying traditional Confucian and Buddhist relics and temples, and the verbal and physical abuse of the religious. It also meant attacking anything and anybody who had a link with China's pre-revolutionary order. If you had served in the Confucian bureaucracy, or worked with or for the Guomindang, or if you had been a landlord, then you were fair game for the revolutionaries. Furthermore, even if you were the grandchild of somebody with a dubious past, then your class origin also made you a suspect and usually also a victim.

Western influences also came under severe attack, not simply those overt capitalist influences, but anything western at all. So even those who had returned to China from the west to aid the revolution came under attack, as they must have suffered spiritual pollution while they were away from China. Homes were ransacked, and foreign books and music were taken as a sign of impure thoughts, and their owners dealt with accordingly. If you wore western dress, or even wore your hair in a western manner, then you too were subject to attack. Even owning a pet suggested bourgeois thoughts, and there were severe penalties for the pets, if not the owners as well. Intellectuals in particular suffered extreme measures. Designated as the 'stinking ninth class' – the very bottom of the rung in the ladder of class worthiness – intellectuals came under vicious attack.

As the revolutionary momentum increased, the scope of the revolution also increased. Indeed, the momentum created its own drive to increase radicalism – if you weren't seen to be redder than red, then you too might find that you came under attack. Thus, the Cultural Revolution almost created a competition to be more radical. In some cases, this was manifest in bizarre tokenism: for example, the renaming of the street housing the Soviet Embassy to 'Revisionism Street', or the rather short-lived attempt to alter traffic lights so that red now meant go.

But there were many more, less trivial consequences. Once identified as class traitors, the victims were subjected to psychological and physical abuse. It became almost *de rigeur* to subject the victims to ritual humiliation – to dress them up in dunces' caps and parade them around towns and cities encouraging people to vent their anger at these traitors. The most important figures were also subject to mass criticism in football stadia and other public places. Many others were beaten to death by the crowds, executed by kangaroo courts, or committed suicide to end the torment. As with the Great Leap Forward, Mao was not directly to blame for the many deaths and other hardships inflicted in the Cultural Revolution. But as with the Great Leap, Mao must ultimately take the blame for creating the conditions in which the terror occurred. Mao did not pull the trigger, but he loaded the gun.

Faced with this hostility, those under attack not surprisingly fought back, and by 1968 the country was on the verge of civil war (if not in one). Power-holders established their own Red Guard units to defend themselves from the radical Red Guards. Rival radical Red Guard units fought each other as they disagreed on targets, methods and solutions. In Wuhan in the summer of 1967, units of the Chinese military supporting the left were deployed against other units in Wuhan who were resisting the Cultural Revolution and defending the status quo.[9] The city of Wuzhou, for example, on the banks of the Li River in southern China was all but destroyed by fighting between rival units in April 1968 that killed thousands of young Chinese men and women. And these are just two examples (although extreme ones) of the terror and conflict that swept the entire country.[10]

. . .

## MAO'S RESPONSE

The way in which Mao initiated the Cultural Revolution almost made the resulting chaos inevitable. It could not be controlled because attempting to control it would undermine the movement's *raison d'être*. But in Mao's reaction to what occurred, we see perhaps the key characteristic of his notions of power, politics and revolution. Mao wanted the people to participate spontaneously and take the reins of the revolution back into their own hands. But he wanted and expected their participation to be along his own clearly defined lines for the revolution. When events moved in undesired directions, then Mao was quick to try and impose his own visions where possible.

Perhaps the best example here is the establishment of a new form of government in Shanghai during the height of the Cultural Revolution in early 1967. The radicals took the initiative to establish their own new form of control based on the model of the Paris Commune of 1871. The new Shanghai Commune was intended to combine all functions of government, economics and society into a self-contained and self-governing organisation. Whilst Mao was generally in favour of combining functions in lower-level units of government, he was not prepared to see the party lose its dominant role by the creation of these quasi-autonomous organisations. Thus, Mao ordered the commune to be closed down, and instead promoted a new form of organisation called the revolutionary committee. These new committees were also intended to merge party, state and army functions, but the role of the party as the dominant organisation (albeit in partnership with the military and the radical mass organisations) was reaffirmed.

The new revolutionary committees were to be established at all levels. While they were to include representatives of the mass organisations and the radicals, it soon became clear that the new power structure resembled the old power structure more than it resembled a radical redistribution of political power. Indeed, in many cases, the personnel of the old power structure were re-appointed to the new power structure. As Domes points out, while the revolutionary committees did contain radical mass elements, the real power in the new committees lay in the standing committees. These standing committees typically saw only a minority (token?) role for the masses, with real power in the joint hands of the military and the party. Indeed, as early as 1967, some of those party officials who had been purged and attacked by the Red Guards only months earlier were now being rehabilitated and restored to power.

From 1967 onwards, then, Mao actually began to rein in the Cultural Revolution, but not always with great success. In addition to the establishment of the revolutionary committees, Mao criticised the radicals in Beijing, telling them that they had gone too far in prosecuting the Cultural Revolution and that the move to Paris Commune type organisations was striking at the heart of the party. The radicals, for Mao, had let him and the Chinese people down. Throughout the rest of 1967 and 1968, Mao, in conjunction with Zhou Enlai, tried to restore order and de-radicalise the Cultural Revolution. At the central level, key leftists left the scene. Perhaps the most notable was Chen Boda, Mao's personal secretary. Mao's wife, Jiang Qing, who had played an important role in launching the Cultural Revolution, also lowered her profile as Mao began to react to the ultra-leftism of some of his acolytes.

The process of de-radicalisation was in many ways much more difficult than the initial radicalisation of the Cultural Revolution. What had been unleashed could not easily be re-leashed, and with the Cultural Revolution raising many new conflicts and establishing many scores to be settled, restoring control was an immensely difficult task. Mao was not aided in this process by the continued radicalism of his second in command and chosen heir apparent, Lin Biao. Having done so much to lay the foundations for the Cultural Revolution himself, Lin's own political standing was very much tied in with the maintenance of the radicalism he had helped unleash. Furthermore, while Mao might have been happy with a relatively minor purge of top leaders to put his policies back on the rail, Lin required something more than this. If he was really going to succeed Mao, then the more top people (perhaps including Premier Zhou Enlai) that were removed from the scene, then the greater were Lin's own chances of gaining power on Mao's death. Lin's promotion of radicalism proved to be a thorn in the side of the de-radicalisation process, and, as we shall see, was ultimately to lead to Lin's own political downfall.

For some, the most confusing thing about the Cultural Revolution is why Mao decided to de-radicalise the Cultural Revolution so quickly after unleashing it. But this confusion stems from a misunderstanding of what Mao actually wanted, and a misunderstanding of Mao's position within the remaining power structure. Mao did not want to destroy the party in the Cultural Revolution, but to remove those who were getting in his way and preventing the implementation of his correct policies. The party had to remain the dominant force in society – but *his* party, not Liu's or Deng's. Mao did not originally conceive that the Cultural Revolution would go as far as it did. The purge of capitalist roaders was only meant to be a limited purge. Most cadres and even high officials who had been seduced into taking wrong paths could be re-educated as part of the new Socialist Education Movement.

What the Cultural Revolution became, then, was not what it was meant to be. The evolution of the Cultural Revolution was more a consequence of left-wing elements seizing the opportunity and taking events further than they should, and of the unintended conflicts and chaos that were unleashed at local levels. But if Mao really thought that the Cultural Revolution would proceed along clearly defined lines, then his faith in both the masses' and his colleagues' political ambitions had been misplaced. Perhaps Mao was deluded by the successes of the revolution before 1949. But it is probably more correct to say that the priority of removing the people that were getting in his way – and removing them sooner rather than later – obstructed a rational understanding of the full implications of what he was doing.

With the country on the verge of collapse, some form of de-radicalisation was also essential. The country was being plundered by the radicalism of the Cultural Revolution, and Mao recognised that unless order was restored, China's development would be (already had been) severely jeopardised. Order had to be restored, or China would not become the strong country that Mao so desperately wanted it to be. Furthermore, growing tensions with the Soviet Union increased the urgency for a restoration of order. The chances of the Soviets using chaos in China as either an excuse for military involvement or as an opportunity to launch a pre-emptive attack could not be ignored. With China totally isolated at this stage, she had no allies to fall back on, and this real fear of a Soviet attack was the main motivation for overtures towards the United States, which initially took place through the respective diplomatic agencies in Warsaw in 1969.

But the de-radicalisation was not just Mao's decision alone. Despite all his presence and influence, Mao simply could not govern on his own, and relied on alliances with key figures and groups. Key amongst these was Mao's alliance with Premier Zhou Enlai. While Zhou was, at the very least, initially prepared to go along with the Cultural Revolution, he became concerned about the direction the movement was taking. Indeed, Zhou is credited with sending his own personal bodyguards to protect Deng Xiaoping from the ravages of the radical Red Guards after Deng's official fall from grace. Whether myth or not, it is certainly the case that Zhou did much to bring Deng back to power from his disgrace in 1973, and provided a bulwark against the Gang of Four and the left until his death in 1976.

More to the point, Zhou had devoted most of his career after 1949 to developing China's international profile and encouraging the non-communist world to establish diplomatic relations with Beijing. Domestic chaos in China did nothing to convince the west that China was a reliable member of the international community. But worse was to come when radical Red Guards burnt down the British representative office in Beijing in August 1967. Ten days later, Zhou called for all Red Guards to return home and stop attacks on the foreign community – a call that at this stage went unheeded. It is notable that the move to de-radicalise the Cultural Revolution also came hard on the extension of Red Guard criticism of Zhou's position, and questions about his own revolutionary credentials. All in all, whatever sympathy Zhou may have had with the Cultural Revolution was severely dented, and his pressure on Mao to call in the students, to distance himself from the Gang of Four, and to rebuild the party, was a significant determinant of the course of Chinese politics from 1967 to 1976.

Finally, Mao was also influenced by pressure from key military figures. While Lin Biao may have been keen to further prosecute the Cultural Revolution, the same was not true for many military commanders on the ground. They had seen the chaos and conflict at first hand. Furthermore, once the radicals had cleansed the party of capitalist roaders, they began to turn their attention to the military. Before the Cultural Revolution, soldiers had been portrayed as paragons of socialist virtue – they were everything that many party members weren't. But during the Cultural Revolution, many military units had failed to support the radical left in their struggles with the right, and some had even defended the right. Furthermore, the army in many areas was at the forefront of the attempt to rebuild party structures and end Red Guard radicalism.

Not surprisingly, then, the army came to be seen as the main obstacle to the continuation of radicalism. When the military began to be criticised in the same language that Mao and his followers had used to describe the party immediately prior to the Cultural Revolution (as 'arrogant' and 'complacent'), then the prospect of a new phase of radicalism against the military increased. Notwithstanding Lin Biao's own personal reasons for wanting to maintain the Cultural Revolution, many of his men had different opinions. And as relations with the Soviet Union declined, making the prospect of war with China a real possibility, the last thing that either Mao or Zhou Enlai wanted was discord and chaos in the army.

. . .

## THE RETREAT FROM THE CULTURAL REVOLUTION AND THE FALL OF LIN BIAO

In combination, then, the conditions were ripe for a retreat from radicalism and the return to normal politics, or as normal as was possible under the circumstances. With considerable effort, the Red Guards were cleared from the streets. Unable and unwilling to blame himself, Mao instead put the blame for the excesses of the Cultural Revolution on the students and radicals themselves. As early as July 1968, Mao had reprimanded Red Guard leaders for their excesses, and as the radicalism of the Cultural Revolution was brought to an end, millions of young people were subsequently 'sent down' to the countryside. The process was meant to be a temporary measure to rusticate the young people: to provide them with a real education of what life was like for the peasant masses. However, there was no early return to the cities for many, and the temporary rustication soon became permanent.

For many of the sent-down youth, the response in the countryside was less than warm. The Cultural Revolution had largely been played out in the cities, with only relatively minor impacts in the countryside. With the influx of the sent-down youth into the villages and countryside, the Cultural Revolution took a new turn. The rural peasants didn't want to – indeed, in many cases, couldn't – waste precious food on these unproductive young people. They were an unwanted burden on the rural population, and were treated as such. By the end of the 1960s, those who had been the main agents of the Cultural Revolution only a few months earlier were now in many ways also the victims of the movement that they had fomented.

The party met to pass its verdict on the Cultural Revolution in the 9th Party Congress in 1969, the first such major party meeting for 13 years. In his report to the congress, Lin Biao hailed the successes of the Cultural Revolution which he portrayed as the spontaneous and undirected rising of the masses against those in authority who were trying to overthrow the revolution.[11] Despite the up-beat nature of Lin's key-note speech, the congress was not the victory rally of the radical left that it appeared to be at first sight. In many ways, the congress marked a watershed in the Cultural Revolution, and indicated the changing political environment. For example, the Gang of Four, who had done so much to start the movement from their heartland of Shanghai in the first place, were conspicuously silent.

It was also notable that almost half of the delegates at the congress wore military uniforms. Although Lin was nominally in charge of the military as Minister of Defence, this large military presence within the new party Central Committee did not consolidate his power. Throughout 1969 and 1970, Mao increasingly distanced himself from the radicalism associated with Lin Biao, and Mao's former secretary, Chen Boda. Indeed, even before the August Party Congress, Mao had signalled a change in policy by calling for a more controlled movement against a narrow group of leading party officials. Furthermore, in his New Year's Day 1969 speech, Mao argued that these officials might be 'saved' rather than dismissed: they could be re-educated to see the error of their ways rather than being purged. While Lin Biao was still using the language of the Cultural Revolution and talking about the importance of political virtues for party cadres, Mao was now emphasising professional skills necessary for cadres to undertake their work effectively. Lin was calling for a continuation of radicalism, but Mao was now talking about the need to rebuild the party-state system.

If Mao thought that Lin would now fall in line, he found instead that he was increasingly out of step with his chosen successor. The position of chosen heir apparent was something of a poisoned chalice. If you sat around and simply followed exactly what your patron did, then you ran the risk of being ousted from power once your patron left the scene. But if, like Lin, you tried to build your own power base, then you ran the risk of irking your patron and losing his patronage. Having risen to power on the back of his ultra-loyalty to Mao and radical Maoist policies, Lin was reluctant in the extreme to moderate his view and follow Mao's line of de-radicalisation. Furthermore, the rebuilding of the party would bring back people who opposed Lin Biao both for ideological and personal reasons. Lin could not countenance de-radicalisation because it would damage his own position. But by trying to push ahead with the revolution when Mao was beginning to abandon it, Lin Biao alienated the man who had brought him to power in the first place, and the one man who could keep him in power.

In the late winter of 1969, Mao effectively signalled the end of the Cultural Revolution by abolishing the Cultural Revolution Small Group, which had organised the Cultural Revolution and had become the main power base of Chen Boda and Lin Biao. Significantly, there is no subsequent record of Chen Boda, a man who is thought to have helped Mao formulate many of his ideological principles, making any major policy statement. An additional indication of a further move away from the Cultural Revolution came with an investigation into the activities of the extreme and ultra-radical May 16th Red Guard Unit. Perhaps most important of all was the decision in March 1970 to remove the position of Chairman of State from the new draft constitution. With no position of Chairman of State, this meant that the leading position within the state sector was the Premier. So when Mao died, Lin Biao would only be able to succeed to the position of Chairman of the Party, and face the equal claims to power of Zhou Enlai, or whoever was the Premier at the time.

Events ran away from Lin throughout the rest of 1970. On 1 July, the national holiday in commemoration of the foundation of the CCP, a *People's Daily* editorial established new criteria for selecting new party members that overturned the previous criteria laid down by Lin Biao. In August, a mere year after Lin had apparently held sway at the party congress, the Central Committee instructed the army to adhere to Mao's call to rebuild the party. It also took the first steps to restore party control and leadership over the military.

Political conflict amongst China's elites was rarely carried out in a direct and overt fashion. For example, even when Liu Shaoqi was under fierce attack in the Cultural Revolution, he was not referred to directly by name. Conflict was often carried out by allegory, in obscure and labyrinthine debates over traditional Chinese stories, where only those in the know understood which character from *The Water Margin* corresponded to which contemporary political leader. In this context, the political changes in 1970 amounted to a relatively open attack on Lin Biao. Certainly, Lin felt that he was under attack, and countered at the Central Committee by attempting to restore the position of Chairman of the State, and intimating that Zhou Enlai had revealed his opposition to Mao. This strategy was entirely misconceived, and Mao, now closer to Zhou than Lin, rejected the proposal and the intimations behind it.[12]

What happened next is the subject of some conjecture. The official story says that Lin tried to assassinate Mao and fled to the Soviet Union when the plot was uncovered. However, the escape plan was devised in a hurry, and the plane, lacking sufficient fuel, crashed in Outer Mongolia killing all on board. The claim that Lin fled to Russia is plausible. Having been seriously injured in battle in 1937, Lin was sent for treatment to the Soviet Union where he became an official CCP representative. Some reports also suggest that Lin fought with the Soviets in the Second World War at the battle of Leningrad. If he did feel pushed into a corner, there was probably nowhere else for him to run. However, Soviet investigators who did find a wrecked plane insisted that none of the bodies on board could conceivably have been Lin's.

The problem that we have in determining the truth is that both China and the Soviet Union had good political reasons for lying. Mao faced the problem of explaining why this man who had once been his chosen heir apparent, his closest comrade in arms, had now fallen foul of the Great Helmsman. So whether true or not, the supposed direction of Lin's flight was important for Mao. He could portray Lin as being an agent of Moscow all along, a man who had only been pretending to be a leftist to cause disorder in China. Thus, although Lin was originally called an ultra-leftist, Mao and the party leadership later did an about-turn and branded him a rightist who had hidden behind the Cultural Revolution for unscrupulous political reasons. Conversely, the last thing that Moscow wanted was any suggestion that it had been interfering in domestic Chinese politics, and that the chaos of the Cultural Revolution in China was a result of a devious Soviet plot.

The Lin affair shows something of the conundrum that Mao was in by the end of the Cultural Revolution. The movement had gone way beyond his original intentions and had produced many problems for the country. Yet it was difficult for Mao to criticise it in essence, as he had done more than most to initiate the movement in the first place. Mao had benefited considerably from the removal of opponents in the central authorities like Luo Ruiqing, Peng Zhen, Bo Yibo, Liu Shaoqi, Deng Xiaoping and others. If he allowed criticism of the Cultural Revolution, then he might undermine all that he had achieved and his own position.

Twenty-eight years later, when Zhao Ziyang was dismissed from power during the Tiananmen Incident, the party did not turn round and dismiss all of his achievements as being wrong or counter-revolutionary. Here was a man who had done good things in the past, but he had made a mistake that meant he couldn't stay in power. Such a moderate and measured appraisal of an individual was unthinkable under Mao. Everything was either black or white, and shades of grey were to be avoided if at all possible. So when Lin fell, he became totally black, totally wrong. This reappraisal of Lin then had an inevitable knock-on effect. If Lin was totally wrong, then were his followers totally wrong as well? And if they were totally wrong, then had the people that they criticised been wrongly attacked?

Lin's purge, then, resulted in a wider reappraisal of past activities, which had a crucial impact on the evolution of politics. It was a minor anti-leftist campaign which in many ways laid the foundations for the later reversal of Mao's ideas and strategies under Deng Xiaoping, although there was still a long way to go and a number of sharp deviations to follow before Maoism would be laid to rest. In the year after Lin's disappearance, half a dozen top military leaders and over 30 provincial leaders who had been associated with Lin also disappeared from the scene. Not all were purged once and for all, but in keeping with the newly 'moderate' culture of the post-Cultural Revolution, a number of leaders were said to have been 'duped' by Lin and his followers. As should have happened in the Cultural Revolution, these leaders should not be killed or jailed, but given the chance to re-educate themselves and then return to the fold.

Alongside this purge of the ultra-left (now, of course, called the right), many of the victims of the Cultural Revolution were rehabilitated. The highest-profile rehabilitation came in April 1973, when Deng Xiaoping reappeared at an official reception as if nothing had happened. The man who had been branded the number two person in authority taking the capitalist road in the heady years of the Cultural Revolution was now reaffirmed as a key party leader, and with Zhou Enlai increasingly ill, Deng took on many of the Premiership duties until Zhou's death in 1976. When the party met at the 10th Party Congress in the summer of 1973, the rehabilitation process was confirmed as many more victims of the Cultural Revolution found their way back to power.

. . .

## NOTES

1. Although there is evidence to suggest that the story was written before Peng's dismissal.
2. Some sources say the fourth wife, counting the child marriage that Mao's father arranged for him. Whether this marriage ever formally took place is open to question, though the relationship was soon ended in any case by Mao's rebellion against his father's actions.
3. See Hollingworth, C. (1987) *Mao* (London: Triad Paladin) p. 44.
4. For more details of Jiang's life, see Witke, R. (1977) *Comrade Chiang Ching* (Boston: Little, Brown).
5. See Hollingworth, *Mao*, p. 61. Ironically, after 1949, the relationship between Mao and Jiang seems to have cooled.
6. Indeed, Wang's rise to the top was so rapid that he was referred to as a 'helicopter' because he went straight up.
7. The most notable of these officials was the Vice-Chairman of Beijing University, Lu Ping, who was dismissed following a student-led criticism of his actions.
8. Most of these were on short-term contracts, and received few or none of the welfare benefits (subsidised housing, food, medical care, education etc.) available in the state sector. Gray, J. (1990) *Rebellions and Revolutions: China from the 1800s to the 1980s* (Oxford: Oxford University Press) p. 351.
9. See Robinson, T. (1971) 'The Wuhan Incident: Local Strife and Provincial Rebellion During the Cultural Revolution', *China Quarterly* 47, pp. 413–38.
10. For more details on the radicalism of the Red Guards, see Granqvist, H. (1967) *The Red Guard: A Report on Mao's Revolution*

(London: Pall Mall Press). A more personal account of the era is provided by Jung Chang (1991) *Wild Swans: Three Daughters of China* (London: Flamingo/Harper Collins).

11. The official party line at the time is more or less repeated in Chen, J. (1975) *Inside The Cultural Revolution* (New York: Macmillan).

12. See Bridgham, P. (1968) 'The fall of Lin Biao' in *The China Quarterly* No. 34, pp. 1–35.

# Chapter 6

# MAO AND THE WORLD

The Lin Biao affair was yet another case where China's international relations became intertwined with not only domestic politics (that, after all, is only to be expected) but with inner party struggle. Mao's notions of China's place in the world were very much embedded in his revolutionary ideals, and his emphasis on the importance of maintaining the independence of the Chinese revolution. For Mao, the lessons of the revolution before 1949 were that Chinese conditions and experiences had to take precedence over revolutionary models developed in other places at other times. Mao had certainly not fought for years to rid China of one form of foreign colonial control simply to see the new revolutionary state fall under the influence of other foreign powers. And as we have seen, nor was he prepared to let others ignore the lessons of the Chinese revolution and follow erroneous 'foreign' development policies.

At first sight, China's foreign policy under Mao appears to be an area of continual U-turns and contradictions: from a close relationship with the Soviet Union in 1949, to open hostility and severe border clashes in 1969; from close support for the Vietnamese communists from the Yanan period (where key Vietnamese leaders including General Giap were trained), to hostility ultimately leading to the less than successful invasion of Vietnam after Mao's death; from open hostility to the United States (notably in the Korean War) to mutual trust (if not friendship) by 1971; from support for revolutionary movements in the third world to support for regimes which suppressed domestic communist parties.

Although specific policies did show remarkable degrees of change, there was a consistent logic that explains many of these policy changes. At the most basic level, we must return to the importance of the independence of the Chinese revolution, and the fact that for Mao, the communist revolution had a dual purpose. While building communism in China was an end in itself, it was also a means to the end of creating a strong China that could retake its rightful place of global pre-eminence. When the United States was considered the greatest obstacle to attaining these twin goals, then resisting the US was the key determinant of Mao's foreign policy. This not only shaped China's relations with the United States, but relations with all other states was contingent on their relationship with Washington – my enemy's friend is my enemy. Thus, when Mao decided that the Soviet Union, and not the United States, was the main danger, then Chinese foreign policy also changed. And again, this meant reappraising China's relations with all other states, depending on their relationship with Moscow. The constant was identifying the major threat to China's national interests and the Chinese revolution; the variable was identifying which superpower posed the greatest threat.

If we look more deeply at Mao's foreign policy initiatives, we see that domestic debates over ideology and notions of China's national interests and defence were inseparable from each other. And if we look more deeply at why Mao began to think that the Soviet Union provided the greatest threat to China's development, then we see that the Sino-Soviet alliance was built on shaky ground in the first place. Had it not been for US policy in Asia, then China would probably never have moved as close to the Soviet Union as it did in the early 1950s.

Finally, to understand fully Mao's motives and actions, we have to consider the importance of threat perceptions in Beijing. Rightly or wrongly, Mao and many of his colleagues thought that they faced the very real and immediate threat of attack from one or both of the superpowers for most of the 1949–76 period. Whilst a full-scale attack did not occur, Mao and his colleagues did have grounds to fear the worst. For example, when the American-led US forces in Korea crossed the 38th parallel into North Korea, Mao feared that they would not stop at the China–Korea border, but would push on over the Yalu River and invade China. Ironically, Mao's response to this perceived threat proved to be counter-productive. By supporting (if not originating) the anti-American campaign in the Korean War, Mao convinced American policy-makers of the need to maintain their presence in the region as a bulwark against the communist threat. In particular, American policy-makers had distanced themselves from the Guomindang in the later days of the Chinese civil war. But with the onset of the Korean War, Taiwan, which the Americans had previously designated as being 'strategically undefendable', was not only brought back into the American fold, but given extensive diplomatic, military and economic aid. For Mao, American support for the Guomindang on Taiwan proved that he had been right to fear American motives in Asia all along. Subsequent American intervention in Vietnam and elsewhere in east Asia (not to mention the anti-communist witch-hunts in America itself) did much to convince Mao that the US was determined to smash communism.

As for the Soviet Union, it too had a record of military intervention in the recalcitrant 'satellite' communist states of Hungary and Czechoslovakia. Furthermore, China did fight fierce border battles with the Soviet Union in 1969, and even for many western observers, some form of Sino-Soviet war seemed more likely than not.[1] As we shall see, the strength of these threat perceptions not only influenced the development of Chinese foreign policy, but also had a profound impact on domestic economic issues.

.   .   .

## MAO'S FOREIGN POLICY AND DOMESTIC POLITICAL CONFLICT

Mao was not a great diplomat. He was fortunate that he didn't need to be, as in the form of Zhou Enlai he had a man who was both willing and more than able to take on the mantle of Chinese diplomatic leadership. Zhou inspired confidence and trust in all of those that he met, perhaps because he spoke the language of diplomacy more eloquently than he spoke the language of revolution. It was Zhou, much more than Mao, who was the visible face of China's foreign policy. Other men also played important roles in defining bilateral relations with countries where they had special contacts or special knowledge. For example, Liao Chengzhi, who was only promoted to the Politburo in 1982 (and died before he could formally assume the position of Vice-President in 1983), was a key player in the normalisation of relations with Japan despite his lowly official status.[2]

Mao did not have much experience of the world beyond China's shores and boundaries. He only left China twice, and on both occasions this was to negotiate and barter with Soviet officials in Moscow. Other leaders such as Zhou Enlai, Liu Shaoqi and Deng Xiaoping spent at least some time away from China before 1949 being trained by the Comintern in either France or the Soviet Union (or both). Others, like Lin Biao, spent time in the Soviet Union receiving medical treatment during the revolutionary struggle. But while these men's vision of the world was at least in part being shaped by non-Chinese events and history, Mao remained in China being socialised and transformed by purely Chinese problems.

And here perhaps we see the root of Mao's foreign policy commitments and policies. While he was not a major figure in day-to-day foreign policy making, Mao was a crucial determinant of China's relations with the superpowers. And as Van Ness[3] and Ross[4] have shown, how China viewed each of the superpowers was the major determinant of China's relations with every other country.

What Mao lacked in knowledge of international affairs, he made up for, in his mind at least, in his knowledge of what China needed and wanted. Although he often talked of world revolution and international socialism, his primary commitment was to China. This is not to say that Mao did not support international revolution, far from it. But his commitment to international revolution was coloured by two considerations. First, if the needs of the international socialist revolution conflicted with China's own needs and requirements, then there was no argument: China's interests must come first. Second, his notions of what type of socialism the world should see differed considerably from those in the Comintern in Moscow. At the very least, Mao thought that the Soviets should not try and impose their view and model on other countries, as they had tried to do with China. Nor should they use other communist states as adjuncts to their own economy, or serving purely Soviet national interests, as he thought was the case in much of Eastern Europe. If socialist revolutions were going to work, then they had to be embedded in the specific historical, social, cultural and class context of each individual country.

At the end of Claire Hollingworth's work on Mao, she reprints a party document outlining the ten men who struggled and rose against Mao in the course of his political career. She notes that: 'It is most significant that the Soviet Union, the Comintern or the Russian Communist Party were intimately involved in nine out of the ten cases'.[5] If anything, Hollingworth underestimates the situation, as a strong case could be made for all ten men having a Moscow influence. This is not to say that all ten perceived of themselves as being pro-Moscow. Nor did they even necessarily perceive that they were anti-Mao. Men like Liu Shaoqi, Lin Biao and even Peng Dehuai were all very loyal to Mao for at least part of their political careers. But once they crossed Mao, then all that they had done previously was brought into question in Mao's mind.

Of these ten, the four men who crossed Mao after 1949 were Gao Gang, Peng Dehuai, Liu Shaoqi and Lin Biao. Whilst Gao Gang was indeed close to the Soviets, and even visited Moscow to establish his own quasi-independent relationship between north-east China and the Soviet Union, the case against the other three is harder to prove. While Peng Dehuai was in favour of remaining under the Soviet military umbrella and learning from the Soviet model, it takes a leap in faith to accept that he was working for the Soviets. Up until the SEM, Liu Shaoqi had been one of Mao's most loyal colleagues, and any assertions that Liu was 'China's Khrushchev', or indeed that he had tried to sell the revolution down the line to the Americans before 1949, have to be viewed in the atmosphere of radicalism and hyperbole of the Cultural Revolution. Liu's only crime, if a crime it was, was to look to the Leninist model as an example for China. As for Lin Biao, he did spend time in Moscow, but the notion that he was a rightist in disguise is bizarre in the extreme.

But it was not all a matter of political expedience. As we have seen throughout the preceding chapters, Mao held a deep-seated suspicion, not to say resentment, of those of his colleagues who looked outside China for their influences and inspirations. Furthermore, Mao spent much of his early career fighting to have his voice heard against those who were inspired by what they had learnt from reading Marx, or, more often, from their understanding of the Soviet revolution. Mao's long and at times bitter struggle to impose his views coloured his attitude towards both his Soviet-orientated colleagues and also the Soviet leadership in Moscow. The Comintern and Stalin had tried to push the importance of urban-based revolution; they had forced the CCP into an alliance with the nationalists

147

which cost them dear when Chiang Kai-shek purged the left in 1927; they had refused to acknowledge Mao's leadership after the Zunyi Conference, and maintained Wang Ming as China's communist leader in Moscow. The Soviets also remained loyal to the nationalists throughout the war against Japan. Stalin was far from convinced that the CCP could win a rural-based revolution, and in his negotiations with the allies, Stalin argued that the communists could not unite China, and committed the Soviet Union to returning Chiang Kai-shek to power after the defeat of the Japanese.

.   .   .

## FROM SINO-SOVIET ALLIANCE TO SINO-SOVIET SPLIT

If the relationship between Mao and Moscow before 1949 col-oured Mao's views of Stalin and the Soviet Union, the negotia-tions leading to the signing of the 1950 Treaty of Alliance and Mutual Assistance did not exactly place the relationship on firm ground. Mao left Beijing for Moscow as a hero, a man who had led a successful communist revolution against the twin evils of feudalism and colonialism. But when he arrived in Moscow, it was a different story. Stalin kept Mao waiting while he dealt with more important business, and when he did meet Mao, it was in the chamber reserved for leaders of communist parties, not the chamber for heads of state.

This might seem a trivial point, but it is in many ways indicat-ive of how the two sides viewed the relationship. For Stalin, here was another communist party leader who would (or at least should) accept Moscow's leadership in the international communist brotherhood. China and Mao were minor and dependent partners in the relationship. But Mao wanted China to be treated as an equal partner. The CCP had not simply been put into power by the Soviet Red Army as had been the case in Eastern Europe and North Korea, it had won its own independent revolution. Whilst Mao might have been prepared to accept that Stalin was the leading figure in the communist world, he wanted his and China's record to stand for itself. China was an independent communist state and it was not going to subvert its interests for anybody.

Despite their shared communist roots, the CCP had held out olive branches to the United States during the war against Japan. These overtures were largely ignored by the Americans, partly because they didn't think the communists could win, and partly because of existing anti-communist sentiment in the United States. When American Ambassador Hurley visited Yanan to talk to the communists, he greeted Mao and the communist leadership with a Cherokee war cry, thinking that this was the sort of salutation that the bandits would recognise. Hurley was unimpressed by the barren conditions in Yanan, and the simple uniforms and accommodation of the communist leadership. The nationalists in Chongqing just *felt* like a proper government and leadership.

But notwithstanding the history of Sino-US hostility before 1949, Khrushchev argued in 1959 that Mao was so annoyed with Stalin that he would have been prepared to draw back from Stalin in the summer of 1950 if the Americans had been prepared to deal with the CCP. The Sino-Soviet treaty signed in 1950 fell far short of what Mao wanted. The main benefit for the Chinese was the agreement that the Soviet Union would support China in any future conflict with Japan, or any state allied with Japan (i.e. the US). The Soviets also gave credits of US$300 million over five years – far less than even the smallest east Asian states were getting from the Americans, and at higher repayment terms.

In return, the Soviets retained control over the China Eastern Railway, which they had taken when the Japanese occupation of north-east China came to an end in 1945. They also retained control of Port Arthur-Dalian until 1952 and then refused to give it back to the Chinese until October 1954, established joint stock companies in Manchuria and north-west China to exploit mineral resources, and forced the Chinese to accept the independence of Outer Mongolia, perceived by many Chinese to be an integral part of Chinese territory.[6] In short, the treaty bore some of the hallmarks of the unequal treaties forced on China by the colonial powers in the late nineteenth century.

There is a monument in the city of Changchun in north-east China which thanks the Soviet people and army for the heroic help provided in liberating Manchuria from Japanese control. Yet the truth is that the Soviets only joined the war against Japan on 8 August 1945, a mere six days before the Japanese surrender. For their trouble, the Soviets took US$858 million in reparations, most of which came from factories in Manchuria and not directly from the Japanese themselves. Such an action represents a Soviet Union more concerned with its own strategic and domestic interests than it does a communist regime striving to aid its communist brethren and the Chinese revolution – a feature that was to characterise much of Moscow's attitudes to China even after 1949.

Given the uneasy nature of relations between Mao on one side, and Stalin and the Comintern on the other; given the Soviets' only limited support for the Chinese communists before 1949; given the apparent conflicting views of the nature of the relationship after 1949; and given the none too fraternal nature of the 1950 treaty, why did Mao lean towards the Soviet Union at all in the 1950s?

The answer is quite simply that he felt that China had no choice. Jack Gray argues that Mao's first choice in 1950 would have been to follow a middle course of independence, but this was simply not possible.[7] The Americans were instigating a diplomatic embargo on China, including installing the nationalists on Taiwan in the Chinese seat on the United Nations Security Council. The nationalists, though defeated on the mainland, were rebuilding their forces on Taiwan and might launch a re-invasion at any time. The initial movements towards a more socialist Japan after 1945 had now been overturned. The American military had also established large bases on the southern Japanese Okinawa islands, and also in the Philippines. Anti-communist regimes with differing degrees of American support were also being imposed in the southern half of Korea and Vietnam.

In short, China was surrounded by American, or American-backed, anti-communist regimes and forces, and was diplomatically isolated from the non-communist world. With the perception of threat very high, and with internal stability not yet guaranteed, Mao felt that they just could not risk non-alignment, and had to lean towards one side. As the Americans appeared to be the biggest threat to China's national interests and the Chinese revolution, then this meant leaning towards the Soviet Union.

The uneasy nature of the relationship with the Soviet Union was soon brought into sharper focus with the outbreak of the Korean War. While many in the west at the time saw the Korean War as a Chinese initiative, as Hinton notes, 'in its origin, this was a Soviet–North Korean affair'.[8] Nevertheless, the Chinese had much to fear from an American-led invasion of North Korea, and much to gain if the Americans could be defeated and pushed off the Korean peninsula. As such, Mao was an enthusiastic proponent of confronting the Americans, and China prepared for war (both in terms of preparing its troops and preparing its people through a propaganda campaign) during the summer of 1950. Nevertheless, it is notable that Chinese forces only joined the fray on 25 October 1950 as the UN forces moved inexorably closer to the Chinese border. China's participation in the Korean War might have resulted in the consolidation of communist power in North Korea, but Mao's decision to engage the Americans stemmed much more from his concerns for China's territorial safety than it did from fraternal love for Kim Il Sung's Korean communist brethren.[9] The Korean War had a profound impact on Mao. On a personal level, Mao suffered as many other Chinese suffered, by losing his son in the conflict. On a political level, the first impact of the war was to force China even closer to the Soviet Union – for the time being at least.

On one level, the experiences of the Korean War convinced China's military leaders, and notably Peng Dehuai, that China was in no position to defend itself. Mobile guerrilla warfare was all well and good for winning a prolonged civil war, but modern international conflict was another matter altogether. As we have seen, Peng's notions that the Chinese had to modernise the military on Soviet lines, and to remain under the safety of Soviet military assurances, were to place him on a road to conflict with Mao at Lushan in 1959.

On another level, the Korean War increased China's isolation and enhanced the perception of invasion. One of the more immediate consequences of China's involvement in Korea was an American-backed trade embargo. With China now essentially cut-off from the non-communist world, there was little alternative but to move even closer to the Soviet bloc. In 1949 only 8 per cent of Chinese trade was with other communist states; by 1952, the figure had risen to 87 per cent. If the Americans took a hostile stance towards the Chinese because they thought China was part of an international socialist bloc, then their actions became a self-fulfilling prophecy.

The Korean War also led to a rethinking of American priorities in Asia. Increasingly dismayed by the nationalists under Chiang Kai-shek, the United States had much decreased its support for the nationalists before 1949, and many considered

Taiwan to be strategically undefendable. Yet with the Chinese involvement in Korea, the Americans renewed their close alliance with Taiwan, and provided more diplomatic and military support for Chiang. As such, the threat of counter-invasion from Taiwan was increased, which forced Mao and the communists closer to Moscow.

But if the Korean War increased the need to stay close to the Soviets, it also raised many more questions about the Soviets' need and desire to support the Chinese. Although the Soviet Union did send arms shipments to the Korean front, the Chinese were dismayed by the standard of the technology that they were sent. The Chinese were also left to fund their own considerable expenses in prosecuting the war. As such, the loans that the Soviet Union had provided for economic reconstruction in 1950 were all but expended on the military campaign in Korea. Finally, the Soviets were not prepared to commit themselves to the conflict in any meaningful way. They were simply not sufficiently prepared to face widespread conflict with the US, particularly if the Chinese were prepared to fight the war on their behalf.

And here we see perhaps the fundamental difference between the Soviets and the Chinese. By 1950, the Soviet Union was relatively safe from aggression. The division of Europe at Yalta and Potsdam had provided a comfortable cushion on the western front. With Germany defeated, and Britain preoccupied with domestic reconstruction, the threat to the Soviet Union from Western Europe was much diminished. With the Chinese revolution, Moscow also now had a considerable buffer zone on its eastern borders. The new socialist Eastern Europe also provided a large economic sphere for Moscow to exploit. The creation of the Council for Mutual Economic Assistance (COMECON) in 1949 was ostensibly intended to facilitate economic integration between socialist states. However, with countries like Hungary and Czechoslovakia more economically advanced than the Soviet Union, it was perceived in China (as well as in Albania and by some western academics[10]) as a means of using their resources to develop the Soviet Union, and of making other socialist states dependent on Moscow. It is notable that China never joined COMECON, reflecting Mao's own interpretation of what COMECON was designed to achieve.

We should remember that the Soviet Union had, like China, just come out of a devastating war in which 20 million of its citizens had died. Why risk more international conflict by provoking the Americans when Moscow's economic and national security seemed to be guaranteed? By contrast, the new Chinese state was in a vulnerable position. China faced a rival regime under American custody on Taiwan, and saw hostile American forces well entrenched in much of east Asia. While the Soviets were relatively happy with the status quo, the Chinese were anything but, and wanted to remove hostile forces from their borders. So while the Chinese wanted to sponsor conflict in order to feel more secure, the Soviets were unprepared to get involved in anything that might threaten their own security.

The Sino-Soviet alliance was therefore on rocky grounds from the beginning. By the time that the Soviets withdrew their technicians and advisers from China in the early 1960s, the relationship was on its way to outright hostility. The conflict that emerged is sometimes portrayed as an ideological conflict – a conflict between the revisionism of the Soviet Union and the true communism of Mao's approach. Certainly, pages and pages of official Chinese papers and journals were devoted to exposing Moscow's dangerous revisionism and lauding the virtues of Mao's approach.

However, we must be aware that criticism of Moscow's policies was as much part of the Maoists' attempts to criticise those in China following a more Soviet-oriented model as it was part of a wider Sino-Soviet conflict. Nevertheless, the ideological dimension cannot be denied here. Quite clearly, Mao felt that the Soviets were not pursuing a revolutionary strategy, and had become content to maintain their current system – to routinise and bureaucratise the revolution. Indeed, what happened in the Soviet Union, particularly once Khrushchev assumed the reins of power, provided a stark example for Mao of what could happen to a revolution if it was in the hands of the wrong people.

Mao's ideological conflicts with Khrushchev became embroiled in bitter personal hostility between the two men. While Mao had his problems with Stalin, he nevertheless respected him as a great leader. He did not have any respect for Khrushchev. There are perhaps three main reasons for the personal conflict between the two. First, when Stalin died, Mao was irked that Khrushchev felt that he could step into Stalin's shoes and assume the mantle of leader of the communist world.

What right did this bureaucrat have to impose himself above a man who had led a glorious and successful revolution in China? Second, when Khrushchev began the process of de-Stalinisation with his 'secret' speech at the 20th Congress of the Communist Party of the Soviet Union, Mao and his followers took Khrushchev's criticisms of Stalin's personality cult as a thinly veiled attack on Mao himself (and were probably correct in their interpretations). Third, Khrushchev consistently criticised Mao's economic and social policies after 1956. While this criticism in itself was unfounded for Mao, the fact that it gave succour to Mao's opponents within China only compounded the crime.

But the real root of the ideological conflict between Mao and Moscow lies in an understanding of the nationalist basis of Mao's ideology. Mao was committed to doing whatever he could to ensure China's resurgence, and if the Soviet Union threatened these Chinese interests, then the relationship with Moscow would have to go. To reiterate: for Mao, the fortunes of the Chinese revolution and China's national interests were one and the same thing. If Khrushchev was trying to block Mao's domestic policy initiatives, then this was not just a battle over the means for the Chinese revolution, but an attempt to prevent China from attaining its true potential.

The debate over conflicting national interests took on a new importance in 1957. When the Soviets launched the first sputnik rocket, this not only signalled that they were ahead in the space race, but it also meant that they now had the ability to deliver an intercontinental nuclear weapon. A pre-emptive nuclear strike was now feasible, and for Mao this was a cause for rejoicing. Proclaiming that 'the east wind prevails over the west wind', Mao now believed that the Soviet Union could and should give its unconditional support for revolutionary movements in the third world. The growth of revolution would spread the counter-communist forces thin on the ground, and remove the immediate threat to China. Furthermore, the Chinese could now act aggressively against their opponents in Asia, safe in the knowledge that the US could not risk provoking Moscow into a tactical nuclear strike.

But Khrushchev had a different view. He was not prepared to risk nuclear conflict to support China's national interests, and instead saw the Soviets' nuclear capacity as a means of ensuring peace. Nuclear war, he argued, would be a disaster for all. The new rocket technology meant that the Soviets now had the means to defend themselves, and this allowed a new era of peace, not a new era of global revolution. To say that this view dismayed Mao would be something of an understatement. And if proof were needed that the Soviets were not prepared to look out for China's interests, it came in 1958 when the communists began bombardments of the two small islands of Quemoy and Matsu which remained under Guomindang control. Mao announced that the communists would use the offshore islands as stepping stones to invade Taiwan, although in reality it appears more likely that the communists were testing the water to see how far the Soviets would go. The answer was that the Soviets were not prepared to get involved at all.

It is difficult to put a specific date on the end of the Sino-Soviet alliance, but for Robert North, the events of 1958 played a crucial role in convincing Mao that enough was enough:

> Khrushchev's refusal to support the Chinese People's Republic against the United States and against India, in terms of more extensive economic and nuclear aid, appears to have convinced Mao Tse-tung by 1958 or thereabouts that Soviet policies constituted a serious threat to China's legitimate and fundamental interests.[11]

If there was a specific end to the alliance, perhaps it came with the 1959 Chinese invasion of Tibet. The Chinese had gone into Tibet to quell an uprising by the Tibetans under the leadership of the Dalai Lama to establish an independent homeland. The Chinese suppression of the Tibetan uprising brought international condemnation, and in particular heightened existing Sino-Indian tensions over disputed borders. The Tibetans were supported by the United States, Taiwan and India. Khrushchev, however, was not prepared to offer the same support to the Chinese for fear of jeopardising Moscow's relationship with India. Indeed, while the Soviets continued to provide credits to India, they withdrew their assistance to China's nuclear programme. When the Soviets supported the Indians in their conflict with China in October 1962, after the PLA had occupied the disputed border area, the fear that the Soviets were establishing the Indians as an alternative power base in Asia was confirmed for Mao and the Chinese leadership.[12]

. . .

## THE THEORY OF THE THREE WORLDS

When the Soviets and the Americans negotiated the Nuclear Test Ban Treaty that essentially squeezed China out of the nuclear race, then the die was cast. By the time that the treaty was signed in 1963, China was on its own. More to the point, it was almost totally surrounded. To the north, it was faced by an increasingly hostile Soviet Union, and its satellite state, Outer Mongolia. To the east, it faced the American-backed regime in South Korea and the American-supported Japanese (including extensive American air bases on Okinawa). To the south, the American navy continued to support the rival nationalist regime on Taiwan. To the west were the Indians, who not only had their own conflicts with China, but were also now, in Mao's eyes at least, also agents of Soviet hegemony. In the south-west, things were even worse. US intervention in South Vietnam against the pro-Soviet North Vietnamese meant that whichever side won, China would have no friends in Vietnam.

By the early 1960s, Mao felt that China faced the real threat of invasion. If the US did attack, then there was no chance that the Soviets would defend them. On the contrary, Sino-Soviet relations were now at such a low ebb that the Soviets themselves might launch an attack. Worse still, China might face a concerted attack on two fronts by both of the superpowers. Faced with this perceived threat, the Chinese accelerated two policies that they had been following in more moderate forms since the 1950s. The first was the programme of 'third front' industrialisation. With the benefit of information that only came to light in the west in the 1980s, we now know that national defence considerations were a major factor in shaping China's regional investment strategy for much of the 1950s, 1960s and 1970s. Fearing that tactical nuclear strikes could quickly and easily destroy China's entire industrial capacity, factories in eastern China were dismantled brick by brick and, along with the workforce, moved to safer havens in the west to establish 'a strategic defence in the rear'.[13]

This relatively new evidence challenges many of the interpretations of Chinese developmental policy written before the 1980s. As Cannon comments: 'All analyses of the country's economy until fairly recently have had no knowledge of this factor and so are fundamentally flawed'.[14] For example, analysts who looked at the amount of government investment in China's less-developed provinces in the west assumed that this was a result of an ideological commitment to promoting even development.[15] But Naughton has shown that this investment in the interior was almost entirely a result of national security considerations rather than developmental concerns.[16] Indeed, moving these factories miles away from sources of raw materials and markets proved to be a massive financial drain on the economy. If anything, economic development was sacrificed to secure national security. The government also diverted economic resources to build massive underground nuclear bunkers beneath China's major cities. With the reduction of tension in the recent era, these bunkers have now been turned over to other uses. In Taiyuan in Shanxi province, they house a small market; in Huhehotte in Inner Mongolia, there is a night club; in Xidan in Beijing, the tunnels used to house a respectable Mongolian restaurant before the developers changed the architecture of that part of Beijing.[17]

The second major policy drive was to enhance China's diplomatic initiatives and claims to not only independence, but leadership of non-aligned third world states. In the latter days of the revolution, and immediately after the creation of the new People's Republic, China did take a leading role in promoting revolution beyond its borders. The Chinese were particularly influential in aiding revolutionary movements in neighbouring states, notably in Burma, India, Indonesia, Malaya and the Philippines. To some extent, Mao appears to be rather inconsistent in his attitude towards revolution. On one level he argued that revolution could not be dictated by the model, wishes, or ideas of one central communist organisation with its own clearly defined ideas of revolution, and reflecting its own rather narrow and national interests. But at the same time, Mao promoted his revolutionary strategy as *the* strategy to follow – don't follow their model, follow mine.

On a theoretical level, Mao was being consistent. His model was to adapt ideas to fit the concrete situation on the ground. As such, his model could be seen as a 'no model' model. But it is also true that one thing Mao did not lack was self-confidence in his own ideas. Revolutionary movements in south-east Asia, Latin America and Africa could do worse than study the Chinese revolution. Rather than wait for the proletariat to emerge and build their bases in the cities, instead build the revolution around the dispossessed rural populations. Mao's combination of a nationalist revolution against colonial exploiters and a communist revolution against domestic exploiting classes could provide a guide to action that others would have to manipulate to fit their own specific circumstances.

But even in the early 1950s, Mao began to drop his support for external revolutions (although the rhetoric was slower in disappearing than concrete policy). The origins of China's non-aligned stance can be traced back to the 1954 conference in Geneva on France's position in south-east Asia. The following year, leaders from Asian and African states met at Bandung in Indonesia at a conference that owed much to Chinese initiatives. For the Chinese, Bandung was the opportunity to allay the fears of many in the third world that China was a major promoter and supporter of international revolution. Instead, Zhou Enlai portrayed China as a force for stability and peace.

This transformation from revolutionary foreign policy to pragmatic stability appears to be another example of inconsistency in Mao's foreign policy initiatives. But again, while the policy changed, the objectives remained the same. Mao wanted to defend China's borders and China's interests. In the early period, this seemed to be best served by promoting the rise of revolutionary regimes in neighbouring states where possible. But by the mid-1950s, China's interests no longer seemed best served by promoting revolution. Far from ridding Asia of the old colonialists, revolutionary movements had stiffened the resolve and participation of, for example, the British in Malaya, the French (and later the Americans) in Indo-China, the Americans in the Philippines, and so on. Furthermore, as China faced isolation from the American-backed diplomatic and economic blockade, and was increasingly wary of Soviet intentions and commitments, it became increasingly important to establish friendships (or at least reduce hostility) with neighbouring states and leaders.

Finally, the prospects of establishing other communist regimes in Asia became increasingly less appealing. If those new regimes were seduced into the Soviet sphere, then this might be worse for China's interests than maintaining the status quo. Thus, as Sino-Soviet alliance became Sino-Soviet hostility, China began to reassess its relations with other communist parties. For example, as the Soviet Union increasingly became seen as the major threat, its ally, the North Vietnamese, changed in

Mao's eyes from China's ally to the ally of China's enemy. The North Vietnamese communists had not changed their domestic or international strategies, but had become China's enemy (or at least, no longer its friend) by default. Accordingly, anybody who opposed Vietnam was opposing China's enemy's friend, and was therefore China's friend. Thus, China found itself in a rather unlikely and unholy alliance with the Cambodian regime of Pol Pot, even though the Khmer Rouge's policy of massacring the middle classes in Cambodia had had a particularly strong impact on the ethnic Chinese minorities in Cambodia.

This attitude not only affected China's relations with other communist states, but also with regimes around the world facing problems with domestic communist parties or insurgencies. Thus, the Chinese supported the suppression of the pro-Soviet Bangladesh communist movement. Similarly, the Chinese were the first state to recognise the new Pinochet regime in Chile, even though Pinochet had only overthrown the pro-Soviet (ish) Salvadore Allende and come to power thanks to American support.

While Zhou Enlai was the main figurehead of policy here, the ideas of Mao Zedong were not hidden too far behind the scene. Zhou's diplomatic initiatives were something of a charm offensive, not just to persuade China's neighbours and other third world states that China could be trusted, but also to appeal to the west to change their stance towards China. In the early days of the revolution, Mao took a rather black and white view of the world. It is perhaps stretching the point too far to say that Mao perceived the west as a single coherent and cohesive bloc – but not too far. But by the mid-1950s, Mao was reassessing this view. The western world was not as monolithic as Mao had previously perceived it to be. In the negotiations at Geneva, Zhou's charm offensive clearly impressed some of the western diplomats present – here was a man with whom they could deal. Furthermore, in the course of the discussions, it became increasingly clear to the Chinese side that the west was not speaking with one voice. There might be a common anti-communist stance, but beneath that common view there were many wide varieties of opinions and interests. If the Chinese trod carefully, they might be able to exploit these differences – at the very least, it meant a reassessment of policy to take into account these varieties.

Thus, the Chinese move towards a more independent foreign policy began to take shape. It was aided by a move to recognise China in the international community. After 1949, many countries refused to recognise the communist regime in Beijing as being the legitimate government of China. Instead, they retained diplomatic contacts with the Guomindang in Taiwan, which remained, in their eyes, the legitimate government of all China. As noted above, this approach entailed the Guomindang taking the Chinese seat on the UN Security Council, a move which severely impaired China's ability to take diplomatic initiatives on a global scale.

The exceptions to this diplomatic blockade were the East European communist states, and the more non-aligned European states: Switzerland, Norway, Sweden, Finland and Denmark. In 1954 the first major breakthrough occurred with the establishment of diplomatic relations with the Netherlands and Britain. These relations were only at chargé d'affaire level (i.e. not full diplomatic relations at embassy level) and the British remained simultaneously close to the Taiwan government. Nevertheless, it was the first real evidence that western countries could and would break ranks with the United States. This impression was confirmed when the British took the first steps in ignoring the US-sponsored trade embargo on China. When the French took the initiative in establishing full diplomatic relations with China in 1964, any notion that there was a common western China policy was dead and buried.

Thus, Mao began to develop a new ideology to explain China's position in the world, and to establish the framework for its diplomatic initiatives. The 'Theory of the Three Worlds' was actually announced by Zhou Enlai, but the credit for developing the theory is given to Mao himself. Mao argued that the first world comprised the two nuclear superpowers, the Soviet Union and the United States. Although they had distinctly different political and economic systems, they were both essentially imperialists bent on imposing their world-view on everybody else. The second world consisted of the allies of the two superpowers: for example, the Western European states, Japan and Taiwan were allied to the US, the East European states, Outer Mongolia and the North Vietnamese were allied to the Soviet Union. The third world comprised the remaining non-aligned independent states. China was not only part of this third world, but its leader. It would fight for the interests of all those non-aligned states, and once it resumed the China seat on the UN (which it did in October 1971) China would act as the mouthpiece of the third world in the UN Security Council.

But leadership of the third world was only part of this approach. The diplomatic recognition of China by the Scandinavian states, Switzerland, Britain, the Netherlands and France suggested that China could also try and drive a wedge between the first and second worlds. In addition to developing its relations with Western European nations, a new somewhat softer stance towards Japan began to emerge in the early 1960s, with Zhou Enlai meeting advisers to the ruling Liberal Democratic Party in the autumn of 1962. In Eastern Europe, the Chinese also gave support to the notion of a Polish road to socialism, to Tito's independent socialism, and to the Albanians during their split with Moscow. China also retained fraternal relations with the North Koreans (who themselves were only too happy to play Soviet and Chinese interests off against each other).

.   .   .

## LEANING TOWARDS WASHINGTON

The advances that China had made in establishing its credentials as a responsible international player could easily have come to nothing with the onset of the Cultural Revolution. In itself, the explosion of revolutionary fervour in China would have been sufficient to generate considerable unease in other states. To make matters worse, the Cultural Revolution was part targeted against signs of evil western and capitalist decadence, and 'revisionist' behaviour. It was not surprising, then, that foreigners in China came under attack as representatives of erroneous views, or as foreign spies. Radicals also briefly seized control of the foreign ministry and tried to initiate a revolutionary coup in Indonesia.[18]

But despite the radicalism of the Cultural Revolution, the period also saw the first steps towards a new rapprochement between China and the US. At first sight, it seems bizarre that in this new age of radicalism, an era of fervent anti-foreign and anti-capitalist rhetoric and action, Mao should be encouraging warmer relations with Washington. At second sight, given the escalation of American activity in Indo-China, it seems even more bizarre.

This change in Chinese policy has to be viewed in the light of ever worsening Sino-Soviet relations. Indeed, in March 1969 the tensions turned into outright conflict with serious clashes over who owned the Zhenbao Island (the Damansky Island in Russian) in the Ussuri River which marked the Sino-Soviet border. This was followed by another clash along the Amur River in July, and further conflict at Yuming in Xinjiang in north-west China in August. If Richard Nixon is to be believed, then the Soviets actually asked what the United States would do if they were to launch an all-out attack on China. Nixon's reply, that he would have to support the Chinese, was all that stood between Sino-Soviet nuclear conflict.

Thus, during the height of the radicalism in China, the Americans and Chinese began secret talks through their diplomatic missions in Warsaw – possibly so secret that Lin Biao, China's military leader and Mao's supposed heir apparent, didn't even know about them. In 1969 the first visible signs of rapprochement appeared, as the United States first eased its restrictions on travels to China, and then in December began to loosen the trade embargo. The next big breakthrough came in the form of 'ping-pong' diplomacy. Whilst the situation was still not ripe for a formal announcement of the new relationship, a signal of the way events were moving came when an American table-tennis team visited China in April 1971. Although the Americans had been told not to engage in anything that might appear like a political act, they were rather hijacked by Zhou Enlai's insistence on shaking each by the hand – a rather insignificant event in itself, but a gesture laden with massive political significance.

Three months later, Henry Kissinger made a secret visit to China, laying the foundations for Beijing's resumption of the China seat on the United Nations at the end of the year, and President Nixon's historic week-long visit to Beijing and Shanghai in February 1972. For the first time, Mao was seen in the presence of a major – *the* major – western political figure. For the first time, America's President visited communist China and enjoyed the hospitality of the People's Republic. And for the first time, the Chinese and Americans signed a joint agreement recognising the fact that there was only one China, and presaging the gradual reduction of American assistance to Taiwan. From Sino-Soviet alliance and Sino-American hostility in the early 1950s, the wheel had now turned full circle.

This is not to say that the Chinese and Americans were in a close alliance after 1972. The Americans did not officially recognise the PRC at diplomatic level until after Mao's death. Nor did Washington abandon its allies on Taiwan, even after the restoration of diplomatic relations with Beijing in 1979. Conversely, the Chinese continued to shell the offshore Taiwanese islands until 1979. They also supported (with rhetoric at least) the Vietcong's offensives against the Americans just a month after Nixon's visit. But the new quasi-alliance did bring great benefits.

Diplomatically, China not only gained its UN seat, but following the American initiative, the Japanese Premier Tanaka also visited Beijing and announced the transfer of official diplomatic relations from Taibei to Beijing. The Japanese also moved swiftly to increase economic exchanges to China, and whilst the diplomatic gains were very welcome, the economic benefits were more welcome still.

The new relationship with the United States did not end the fear of invasion overnight. Indeed, Mao remained concerned that the Soviets were still intent on silencing China, or at least in teaching it a lesson. On New Year's Day 1973, Mao called on the Chinese people to store grain and build defences in preparation for conflict. But the conflict never came. Presidents Nixon, Ford and Carter were all happy to play the China card as part of their policy towards the Soviets. And the Chinese for their part were more than happy to play the American card in their own relations with Moscow. Whilst tensions remained, Mao felt bold enough and perhaps safe enough to ignore President Brezhnev's calls for a new peace treaty in 1973.

.   .   .

## UNDERSTANDING MAO AND THE WORLD

Mao's main objective in all of his foreign policy initiatives from 1949 to 1976 was to safeguard China's borders, and then to restore China to its rightful position on the world stage. Although Mao railed against traditional Chinese thought and practice, his notions of China and China's world-view owed much to traditional Chinese Sinocentrism: the notion that China is the central place in the world, and that only those who recognise and accept Chinese superiority can be considered to be civilised.

China had been ravaged by imperialist powers from 1840, and suffered massive indignation, hardship and humiliation. The communist revolution owed a great deal to the nationalist aspirations of the people, and Mao shared – at times embodied – these sentiments. After a century of foreign domination and control, China broke free from these shackles on 1 October 1949. The desire to restore China's territory to what Mao believed it should be remained incomplete on his death. It would be another 21 years before Hong Kong returned 'home' and the only possible silver lining on the cloud of continued Guomindang rule over Taiwan was that Mao outlived Chiang Kai-shek.

There was never any chance that Mao would allow the Chinese revolution to fall under Soviet control. He recognised the need to lean to one side in the early years because of China's domestic and international weakness. But while the US posed the greatest external challenge to Chinese security, Mao in many ways feared, and despised, the Soviet Union more than the United States. The US were capitalist imperialists – you could not expect anything more from them. But the Soviets had had a revolution and installed a communist party, but had then wasted the revolution by allowing it to become bureaucratised, routinised and stable. By the time that Mao came to power, the Soviet state was not a dictatorship of the proletariat, but a dictatorship of the party-state bureaucracy over the proletariat.

Mao would do whatever he had to do to protect China's national interests, which in his mind were best served by following his own principles and policies. It is impossible to separate Mao's views of the Soviet Union from his views of domestic politics, and in particular his views of those colleagues who were more prepared to follow the Soviet model. The Sino-Soviet relationship, then, was inextricably linked with Mao's confidence in the correctness of his ideas, and his desire and ability to push those ideas through in the face of not inconsiderable opposition.

When the Soviet Union proved unprepared to support Mao in his foreign policy initiatives, then the fact that communist parties ruled both countries was irrelevant. The Soviet Union became a challenge to China's national interests and the alliance had to go. And the fact that the Americans were the epitome of evil capitalism was also irrelevant – they could help China's interests and so allying with them was not only possible, but desirable. Mao would not be distracted, would not be side-tracked, by the priorities of international socialist brotherhood. Mao was a Marxist, but he was a Chinese Marxist, and whether it aided his Chinese Marxism or not was the bottom line in all of his foreign policy objectives.

. . .

## NOTES

1. For example, see Salisbury, H. (1969) *The Coming War Between Russia and China* (London: Pan).
2. See Radtke, K. (1990) *China's Relations With Japan, 1945–83* (Manchester: Manchester University Press).
3. Van Ness, P. (1970) *Revolution and Chinese Foreign Policy: Peking's Support for Wars of Liberation* (Berkeley: University of California Press).
4. Ross, R. (1988) *The Indochina Tangle: China's Vietnam Policy, 1975–1979* (New York: Columbia University Press).
5. Hollingworth, C. (1987) *Mao* (London: Triad) p. 338.
6. And is still not accepted as being independent by the Taiwanese authorities.
7. Gray, J. (1990) *Rebellions and Revolutions: China from the 1800s to the 1980s* (Oxford and New York: Oxford University Press).
8. Hinton, H. (1994) 'China as an Asian Power' in Robinson, T. and Shambaugh, D. (eds), *Chinese Foreign Policy: Theory and Practice* (Oxford: Clarendon Press), p. 364.
9. For more details on China's participation in the Korean War, see Whiting, A. (1960) *China Crosses the Yalu: The Decision to Enter the Korean War* (New York: Macmillan).
10. See White, S., Gardner, J. and Schopflin, G. (1982) *Communist Political Systems: An Introduction* (London: Macmillan) pp. 11–12.
11. North, R. (1978) *The Foreign Relations of China* (3rd edition) (North Scituate, Mass.: Duxbury).
12. Mao was also dismayed by Khrushchev's handling of the Cuban missile crisis. Mao first thought that it was a dangerous game to play for minimal benefit, but once he had pushed the issue, his final capitulation was embarrassing.
13. Liu Guoguang *et al.* (1987) *China's Economy in 2000* (Beijing: New World Press) p. 258.
14. Cannon, T. (1990) 'Regions: Spatial Inequality and Regional Policy' in Cannon, T. and Jenkins, A. (eds) *The Geography of Contemporary China: The Impact of Deng Xiaoping's Decade* (London: Routledge) p. 39.
15. For example, see Cheng, C.Y. (1982) *China's Economic Development: Growth and Structural Changes* (Boulder: Westview) and Lardy, N.

(1978) *Economic Growth and Distribution in China* (Cambridge: Cambridge University Press).

16.  Naughton, B. (1988) 'The Third Front. Defence Industrialization in the Chinese Interior', *China Quarterly* 115.

17.  Whilst a student in Beijing in 1984, I was taken on a guided tour of the main areas of the bunker, emerging above ground via a changing room in a major department store. Bizarre as it may seem now, these bunkers are tangible evidence of how seriously the Chinese leadership took the threat of invasion.

18.  For details on the role of the Red Guards in the occupation of the foreign ministry, see Gurtov, M. (1969) 'The Foreign Ministry and Foreign Affairs during the Cultural Revolution', *China Quarterly* 40, pp. 65–102.

# Chapter 7

# THE POLITICS OF DE-MAOISATION

By the end of 1973, many of those leaders who had been so recently purged during the Cultural Revolution, and who had survived the worst excesses of the radicals, had returned from internal exile. The wheel had not turned full circle. The events of the Cultural Revolution meant that this was impossible. On one level, key leaders, notably Liu Shaoqi, were now dead. On another, as victims were rehabilitated, many found themselves working alongside radicals who had assumed power during the Cultural Revolution, often the very individuals who had personally attacked and victimised them in the first place.

Nobody could forget what had happened. On a mass level, the population had been traumatised. The Cultural Revolution had unleashed neighbour against neighbour, friend against friend, children against parents, classmate against classmate. Even those radicals who had prosecuted the Cultural Revolution had now also become its victims with their enforced exile in the countryside. Despite a remarkable, almost superhuman degree of tolerance, the memories could not be erased.

The entire country had suffered in economic as well as personal terms. Universities had been closed down, leading to what the Chinese refer to as the lost generation. Schooling at all levels had been disrupted. Factories had been paralysed. The planning system had virtually collapsed. Economic growth had been knocked back again, just as the recovery from the Great Leap appeared to be succeeding.

The vast majority of Chinese – both leaders and masses – now rejected Mao's radical ideas. Even many of Mao's previous followers were dismayed by what had happened, and had tired of mass campaigns, political mobilisation and radicalism. Nevertheless, the Cultural Revolution was still not officially over; indeed, Chinese sources refer to the Cultural Revolution 'decade' which only ended with Mao's death in 1976. Furthermore, at the 10th Party Congress in August 1973, Wong Hongwen declared that the Cultural Revolution would be a recurring phenomenon – a concept that dismayed and scared many in China.

The radical left were now massively out of step with the rest of the country. While most in China wanted an end of radicalism and a return to 'normal' politics, Wang Hongwen and the other members of the Gang of Four wanted to return to radicalism. Perhaps they really believed that this was the best way forward for China, that the chaos of the previous years was a necessary hardship that all had to face to ensure the purity of the revolution. It is more plausible, however, to argue that their continued radicalism was motivated by personal considerations. They had risen to power during the Cultural Revolution and had crossed many people on the way. The retreat from radicalism not only challenged their ideological platform and claims to leadership, but also brought back to power many people whom the left had attacked during the Cultural Revolution. If they were to stay in power after Mao's death, then they had no choice other than to maintain radicalism and even renew the purges if possible.

Mao's impending death was an important component in Chinese politics in the 1970s. Mao was increasingly crippled with illness, including Parkinson's Disease, and was not a visible figure for much of the 1973–76 period. If his doctor's biography is to be believed, Mao spent much of these later years on various drugs (not all of them medicinal), and most of his time was spent in either a narcotic haze, or enjoying some of the aphrodisiac qualities which power is oft cited as generating.[1] We should be careful, then, not to imbue Mao with too much authority to shape the direction of events in these last years of his life. If he was active during this period, it was only behind the scenes.

Even though the Cultural Revolution had damaged his reputation and he was now terminally ill, Mao remained the central figure in Chinese politics. Even when he was not there, other leaders always tried to second guess Mao's reaction before making any move – he was the invisible hand in all negotiations and policy meetings. The people and many in the party might have wanted to move to end the radicalism once and for all, but they weren't prepared or able to act whilst Mao remained alive. If this was not cause enough for instability, Zhou Enlai was also terminally ill with cancer. Thus, from around 1973, Chinese politics revolved around preparations for death.

At the central level, the left and the right were in an uneasy balancing act. For example, if Deng Xiaoping held the top position on a committee, Yao Wenyuan or another representative of the left would be his deputy, and vice versa. It would be stretching the point too far to call this a coalition. Neither side was happy with the situation and they constantly sparred with each other for predominance. In particular, the left was in many ways on borrowed time. Leading radicals knew that Mao's position and prestige largely underwrote their position in the central authorities. Once he went, their claims to power would be severely diminished. Thus, they initiated a number of campaigns to try and remove their opponents, or at least to undermine their position. For example, in November 1973 they launched a campaign to criticise Confucius, intended to be an allegorical attack on Zhou Enlai's protection of rightists within the party. On this occasion, they were thwarted when the campaign was hijacked by their opponents and turned into a 'criticise Confucius, criticise Lin Biao' campaign, which threw the focus back on the activities of the left. In the summer of 1975 they again launched a campaign against Zhou and Deng in the form of a highly obscure and confusing criticism of the old Chinese novel *The Water Margin*.

But in many ways, the left was over-consumed with trying to win ideological and personal conflicts in the party-state central elites. The Cultural Revolution saw a considerable shift in the locus of power in China towards the provinces. And the leftists were ultimately to reap what they themselves had sown. As part of the leftist agenda, provincial authorities were encouraged to become as self-sufficient as possible in every area of economic activity. With rival factions fighting it out at the centre, the initiative moved even more towards the provinces. And below the central level, the rehabilitated victims of the Cultural Revolution were more heavily represented than at the centre. While left–right conflict did occur at provincial level, the left were more heavily represented at the centre than in the provinces, and even some of the beneficiaries of the Cultural Revolution at the provincial level were unprepared to risk more chaos by accepting a new radical post-Mao political agenda.

For Jurgen Domes, the Cultural Revolution turned the Chinese political system from one characterised by factional-isation, to one characterised by factionalism.[2] Under the old factionalised system, people came together in short-lived alliances, but did not come together and stay together to fight specific policy platforms. It was a highly fragmented and fluid situation. Under factionalism, groups coalesced together to fight specific corners, and stayed together in more stable and goal-oriented alliances. Table 2 is an attempt to show where these groups lay on a very rough left–right axis.

The balance of powers at the centre was blown apart in the space of 17 months, as mortality began to take its toll on China's revolutionary leaders. In April 1975 Dong Biwu died. More important, Premier Zhou Enlai died in January 1976. The left were notable by their absence from Zhou's funeral, at which Deng Xiaoping made the key speech in memory of his former patron. On the traditional holiday to remember revolutionary heroes,[3] thousands of Chinese flocked to Tiananmen Square to lay tributes at the monument to revolutionary martyrs – a monument which carried Zhou Enlai's own calligraphy. This act of popular remembrance soon became a political demonstration, with the praise of Zhou Enlai becoming an attack on the Gang of Four and leftist policies. The square was cleared by brute force, with possibly hundreds of demonstrators summarily executed. Deng Xiaoping was blamed for fomenting the counter-revolutionary turmoil, and a new campaign, thought to have Mao's approval, was established to vilify Deng. This time, however, Deng was not around to be purged for a second time by the left, and escaped to the safe haven of southern China where he was protected by the southern military leader, Wei Guoqing, until his subsequent re-rise to power.

With the initiative apparently with the left, death once again weakened the fragile balance at the centre. In June, the veteran military leader Zhu De died. And then, on 9 September, the unthinkable happened – Mao died. The country came to a standstill as the party organised a period of official mourning. But the mourning did not interrupt the functioning of political intrigue for long. Just as it seemed that the Gang of Four and the radical left had gained the ascendancy, Hua Guofeng, the head of the secret police, moved to arrest his former allies and colleagues and placed himself in power.

Table 2

## Central Military Leadership

Mao Zedong

Zhu De, Ye Jianying. Hate the extreme left, but wary of Deng Xiaoping *et al.*
For unity and stability above all else.

*Beneficiaries of the Cultural Revolution*

*Victims of the Cultural Revolution*

| | | |
|---|---|---|
| **The Cultural Revolution Left**<br>Jiang Qing, Yao Wenyuan, Wang Hongwen, Zhang Chunqiao. Want to maintain radicalism, to revive the political policies of the Cultural Revolution and the economic policies of the Great Leap Forward. | **Unpurged Long March Veterans**<br>Dong Biwu, Li Xiannian. Critical and fearful of the Gang of Four and a return to ultra-leftism on Mao's death. Wary of Deng Xiaoping and 'economics in command'. Believe in strong central planning on the Soviet model, and the maintenance of ideological orthodoxy. Zhou Enlai is one of the key figures in this group, but his intense opposition to the Gang of Four and his fears for the future push him to support the right, and to develop Deng Xiaoping as his client. | **Rehabilitated Purgees**<br>e.g. Deng Xiaoping. In favour of de-radicalising the political system and placing economics in command. Out with mass campaigns and in with material incentives, some private activity and limited international economic contacts combined with strong control of political freedoms etc. |

**Mass Organisation Left**
e.g. Chen Yonggui, head of Dazhai, Ni Zhifu, Head of All China Federation of Trade Unions (ACFTU). Want to maintain the emphasis on political activity and radicalism, primacy of red versus expert and suspicion of the party-state machinery. More moderate in economic and social policy than the Gang of Four. Emphasise self-sufficiency.

**Secret Police Left (the Whateverists)**
Hua Guofeng. Originally very close to the Gang of Four. Becomes more moderate when he sees the mood of the people (and the provinces). Devotion to Mao and moderated Great Leap Forward economic policies.

The arrest of the Gang of Four unleashed a wave of popular euphoria. The people at last had the chance to vent their anger about what had happened during the Cultural Revolution, and they could now do this without raising questions about Mao's role. Indeed, the party leadership tried to place all the blame on the evils of the Cultural Revolution on the Gang of Four, and their allies, Lin Biao and Chen Boda. In this way, they hoped to legitimate criticism of all the past evils without risking undermining their own position by explicitly criticising Mao.

In the event, the attempt to blame the Gang of Four was only partially successful. In a widely publicised show trial the old horrors of the Cultural Revolution were brought back into the open.[4] To make matters worse, the Gang refused to play the game and simply accept that it was all their fault. Instead, Mao's wife, Jiang Qing, argued that she had been acting according to Mao's wishes – she was Mao's little dog, and if he told her to bite somebody, then she went away and did it. After being found guilty and sentenced to death (later commuted to life imprisonment), Jiang had to be dragged from the court, defiant to the end, screaming 'geming wan sui' or 'long live the revolution').

The nervous laughter in the court that accompanied Jiang's accusations against Mao indicated that many of those watching knew too well where the real blame lay. But the party leadership faced a huge problem. They were increasingly aware that the population were tired of Maoist mobilisation and tired of the party. Unless they created a new polity, a new economic strategy, and accepted that the Cultural Revolution had been a huge mistake, then their tenure in power could not be ensured. But if they turned round and accepted that the Cultural Revolution, and indeed the Great Leap, had been a mistake, then why should the people continue to support them? It would have been an acceptance that most of what had happened after 1949 had been wrong.

Of all China's leaders, Hua Guofeng faced the biggest challenge in responding to the legacy of Mao. He had, after all, been a beneficiary of the Cultural Revolution – he owed his very position to radicalism. He had also been a close ally of the Gang of Four during his time. And his sole claim to leadership was that Mao had personally blessed his succession: the story goes that Mao placed his hand on Hua's shoulders and told him 'with you in charge, I am at ease'.[5] How could Hua criticise

Mao or the Cultural Revolution without undermining his own position? Even criticising the much despised Gang of Four was dangerous for Hua, given his own Cultural Revolution experiences.

Hua's position, then, was an inherently unstable one. Unwilling and unable to move away from the Maoist past, Hua instead turned to old tried (but not necessarily tested) means of cementing his position. Hua argued Mao had been a great leader, and that the horrors of the Cultural Revolution were all down to the Gang of Four who had distorted the Great Helmsman's ideas and policies for their own gain. Hua portrayed himself as the true inheritor of Mao's unsullied ideological and political programme, a programme that Hua could implement now that the Gang of Four had been removed from the scene. Throughout the country, new posters depicting the moment that Mao anointed Hua as his heir apparent sprang up alongside existing pictures of Mao. Hua even began to wear his hair like Mao, and, in official portraits at least, the two men almost began to blur into one. Although Hua modified some of Mao's policies and ideas to suit himself,[6] it was essentially a period of Maoism without Mao.

Hua's position was a difficult one to maintain. He had destroyed much of his own constituency of support by arresting the Gang of Four. His attacks on the left brought into question his own record, not only during the Cultural Revolution, but also in the suppression of the 1976 Tiananmen Incident. With Deng Xiaoping's star rising, Hua's economic strategy also ran into problems, as his dash for rapid growth to win popular support placed too much stress on China's badly neglected infrastructure. By the end of 1978, his position was untenable. Deng argued that the best way to follow Mao was not to adhere slavishly to his past policies; indeed, this ran counter to Mao's political ideas. Mao had always argued that 'practice was the sole criterion of truth', and rather than follow models and old policies, you had to 'seek truth from facts'. Times had changed from when Mao was developing his policies, and this meant that to be a true Maoist, policy had to be changed to reflect the new realities.[7]

Hua held on to his formal position of leadership until 1981. As a sign of the new political atmosphere, he was not so much purged as allowed to fade into obscurity, and he actually held on to his Central Committee position. But at the 3rd Plenum of the 11th Central Committee in December 1978, the Maoist period of China's history essentially came to an end. The new leadership under Deng Xiaoping set about overturning the very basics of Mao's notions of politics, economics and society. Economic development became the paramount goal, and as Deng had said before the Cultural Revolution, anything that helped the economy to move forward was now legitimate irrespective of its impact on the social and cultural revolution. In addition, two of Mao's fiercest opponents, Tao Zhu and Peng Dehuai, were posthumously rehabilitated, and the first steps were taken to rehabilitate the good name of Mao's number one enemy in the Cultural Revolution, Liu Shaoqi.

Nevertheless, it took another three years before the new leadership were either prepared, or able, to make a serious reassessment of Mao's role in the revolution. At the 6th Plenum of the 11th Central Committee in June 1981, the party issued a long document assessing party history, now usually referred to as 'the resolution on party history'.[8] Even with the Gang of Four arrested and Hua increasingly irrelevant, the question of how far Mao should be criticised was a difficult one. It was not that anybody wanted to return to the Maoist past – with the exception of a few remaining provincial leaders, the Maoist left was now defeated. Instead, the issue was how far the party should go – perhaps could go – to rebuild its legitimacy.

On one side, men like Lu Dingyi and Xue Muqiao wanted a very critical report that accepted that the failings of the past had largely been Mao's own failings. However, other leaders argued that this might actually work against the party and undermine their position; after all, they had spent much of the preceding 30 years telling the people that Mao was almost infallible and the people should be wholly grateful to him. In the end, the final document represented something of a compromise. Great attention was paid to the successes of the early years, and to Mao's contribution to bringing the CCP to power in the first place: 'Our party and people would have had to grope in the dark much longer had it not been for Comrade Mao Zedong, who more than once rescued the Chinese revolution from great danger'. The resolution was also careful to point out that his successes far outnumbered his errors, and even his errors were the errors of a great revolutionary.

Nevertheless, it is notable here that Mao is referred to as 'comrade' and not 'Chairman', and the resolution took great pains to point out that other leaders, and not just Mao, had done a huge amount for the revolution and the Chinese people. Indeed, although the resolution affirmed that Marxism-Leninism-Mao Zedong Thought remained the guiding principle of the party, Mao Zedong Thought was not necessarily what Mao Zedong thought. Somewhat confusingly, Mao Zedong Thought was now described as being the collective wisdom of the party leadership – it was as much the thought of Deng Xiaoping, Liu Shaoqi, Chen Yun and others as it was the thought of Mao himself. The party looked back to 1956 as the golden age of Chinese politics – a period of moderate economic reform and collective leadership built on the principles of democratic centralism. As Mao had actually broken the norms of democratic centralism in the way he launched the collectivisation drive, then Mao Zedong himself had rather bizarrely abrogated Mao Zedong Thought in 1956 and 1957.

The resolution had to be careful in its analysis of the events of 1957. Deng Xiaoping himself had been in the Maoist camp at this stage, and had taken a leading role in implementing the 1957 anti-rightist campaign. Perhaps not surprisingly, then, the anti-rightist campaign was designated as being correct in principle, but wrong in implementation. But the biggest criticisms were reserved for the events of the Great Leap Forward and, in particular, the Cultural Revolution. Mao was accused of having become 'smug' about his successes, and impatient for quick results in launching the Great Leap. He was also criticised for breaking the norms of inner party democracy in the purge of Peng Dehuai at Lushan in 1959. As for Mao's subsequent initiatives, 'his theoretical and practical mistakes . . . became increasingly serious, his personal arbitrariness gradually undermined democratic centralism in the party and the personality cult grew grave and graver'. And despite placing a large amount of blame for the excesses of the Cultural Revolution on the Gang of Four and Lin Biao, 'Chief responsibility for the grave left errors of the cultural revolution . . . does indeed lie with Mao Zedong'.

The façade of the infallibility of Mao was finally broken. Yet his profile has not totally disappeared. While most of the posters and statues have been torn down, Mao's face still rests on the Gate of Heavenly Peace at the top of Tiananmen Square, now lovingly restored after being sprayed with paint by a protester in 1989. Mao has also seen something of a comeback in the form of pendants in the millions of cars that clog Chinese streets. But in many ways he is now nothing more than a lucky talisman to protect drivers from harm; a Chinese St Christopher.

Mao is also still in residence in his mausoleum – the Maosoleum – in the centre of Tiananmen Square.[9] The queues to visit the Maosoleum to see the embalmed leader are still large and snake across the square. It is fair to say that some of the visitors are there merely out of curiosity (it is one of the few places that you don't have to pay to go into) – it is one of the things to do when you visit Beijing. But some are also there to pay homage for what Mao did for the Chinese people before 1956. It is somewhat ironic that as you leave the ordered reverence of the chamber, you emerge into a market selling Maorabilia and other tokens to commemorate your visit to Beijing. As you leave the stalls and re-enter the square, two of the first things that catch your eye are the Kentucky Fried Chicken and Mc-Donalds restaurants to the south of the square.

In itself, the contrasts between the inside and outside of the Maosoleum are indicative of what has happened to China since Mao's death. But perhaps the final word should go to Chen Yun, a man who had more than his fair share of conflict with Mao after 1949, and whose assessment of Mao's legacy sums it all up perfectly. Chen argued that if Mao had died in 1949, he would have been remembered as a great revolutionary hero who had led the Chinese people to a remarkable victory. Had he died after the Great Leap, his record would have been somewhat tarnished, but he would have still been remembered with fondness. But as he had only died in 1976, 'there is nothing we can do about it'![10]

.   .   .

## NOTES

1. Indeed, some would question the extent to which Mao's pre-occupation with mind-enhancing drugs and physical recreation affected his view of politics and revolution from a much earlier period.
2. Domes, J. (1977) *China After the Cultural Revolution: Politics Between Two Party Congresses* (Berkeley: University of California Press).
3. The holiday was grafted onto the traditional Confucian *qing ming* or the sweeping of graves festival.
4. The transcript is available in the 1981 publication *A Great Trial in Chinese History: The Trial of the Lin Biao and Jiang Quing Counter-Revolutionary Cliques* (Beijing: New World).

5.  It is likely that Mao was only referring to Hua's leadership of the campaign to vilify Deng Xiaoping after April 1976.

6.  For example, he tried to re-centralise power away from the generally more sceptic provincial leaders.

7.  Deng Xiaoping (1984) 'Hold High the Banner of Mao Zedong Thought and Adhere to the Principle of Seeking Truth From Facts (16 Sep 1978)' in *The Selected Works of Deng Xiaoping* (Beijing: Foreign Languages Press) pp. 141–4.

8.  The following quotes from the resolution are taken from Goodman's assessment of the 6th Plenum. Goodman, D. (1981) 'The Sixth Plenum of the 11th Central Committee of the CCP: Look Back in Anger?', *China Quarterly* 87, pp. 518–27.

9.  Various stories suggest that the Maosoleum was built to withstand a nuclear attack, and that bits of Mao's body have fallen off at various times.

10. Lieberthal, K. and Lardy, N. (1983) *Chen Yun's Strategy for China's Development: A Non-Maoist Alternative* (Armonk, N.Y.: M.E. Sharpe).

# CHRONOLOGY

| | |
|---|---|
| 1893 Dec. 26 | Mao born in Shaoshan in Hunan province. |
| 1895 Oct. | Sun Yatsen fails to organise a rebellion in Guangzhou. |
| 1896 Oct. | Sun Yatsen kidnapped by Chinese legation in London. |
| 1898 Summer | Hundred Days of Reform. |
| Sep. | Reform period ends with the arrest of the Emperor Guang Xu. |
| 1900 Aug. | Foreign troops enter Beijing and put down the Boxer Rebellion. |
| Oct. | Sun Yatsen organises an unsuccessful uprising in Guangdong province. |
| 1905 Aug. | Sun Yatsen forms the Chinese Revolutionary Alliance in Japan. |
| Sept. | Japan takes control of much of north-east China. |
| 1908 Aug. | Plans published for a new constitution – but not to be implemented until 1916. |
| Nov. | Emperor Guang Xu and Empress Dowager Cixi die. Puyi becomes new (and last) emperor. |
| 1911 Oct. | Rebellion in Wuhan marks the start of the 1911 revolution. |
| Dec. | Sun Yatsen elected President of the new Republic of China. |
| 1912 Jan. | Formal proclamation of the new Republic of China. |
| Feb. | Formal abdication of Emperor Puyi. Yuan Shikai assumes Presidency in place of Sun Yatsen and declares national elections null and void. |

| | |
|---|---|
| Aug. | Formation of the Guomindang (Nationalist) Party. |
| 1913 July | Start of the collapse of the Republican government as military leaders declare independence from Yuan Shikai's regime. |
| 1914 Autumn | Japan seizes Shandong province. |
| 1916 June | Yuan Shikai dies and is replaced as President by Li Yuanhong. |
| 1917 July | Abortive attempt to restore Puyi and the imperial system. |
| Autumn | China descends into civil war. |
| 1918 Apr. | Mao and friends establish Study Society in Changsha. |
| Autumn | Mao goes to Beijing and works in the library at Beijing University. |
| 1919 | Mao returns to Changsha and establishes new study groups. |
| Apr. | Paris peace conference hands German territory in China to Japan. China refuses to sign Treaty of Versailles. |
| | Communist Manifesto published in Chinese. |
| May | Mass demonstrations against the Treaty of Versailles in Beijing in May Fourth demonstrations. |
| Dec. | Mao forced to leave Changsha because of his political activities and moves to Shanghai. |
| 1920 | Mao returns to Changsha and marries Yang Kaihui; becomes headmaster of Changsha Normal School and establishes communist discussion group. |
| 1921 July | CCP established in Shanghai with Mao as a founder member. |
| 1923 May | CCP decides to cooperate with the Guomindang. Mao subsequently works in the Guomindang Propaganda Department and the Peasant Training Centre. |
| June | Mao becomes member of the CCP Central Committee. |
| 1925 Mar. | Death of Sun Yatsen – later succeeded by Chiang Kai-shek. |
| July | Chiang Kai-shek launches Northern Expedition to reunify China under Guomindang control. |

| | | |
|---|---|---|
| 1927 | Spring | Mao writes and publishes his report on the revolutionary potential of peasants in Hunan – later rejected by the rest of the communist leadership. |
| | Apr. | Chiang Kai-shek forms new national government in Nanjing. |
| | | Guomindang initiate campaign to wipe out the CCP. |
| | Aug. | Failed Nanchang uprising by the CCP on 1 August – later becomes known as the birth of the communist Red Army. |
| | Sept. | Mao leads failed 'Autumn Harvest' uprising in Changsha. |
| | Dec. | Failed communist armed uprising in Guangzhou. |
| | Winter | Mao escapes capture by the Guomindang and establishes a new base in Jinggangshan in Jiangxi province – the start of the Jiangxi Soviet. |
| 1928 | June | Nationalist troops take Beijing. |
| | Dec. | Northern Warlord Zhang Xueliang allies with the Guomindang, signalling the full unification of the country under Guomindang rule. |
| 1930 | Jan.–Feb. | Failure of communist uprising in Changsha. |
| | Nov. | Mao's wife, Yang Kaihui, executed by the Guomindang. Mao already living with He Zhizhen. |
| 1931 | Sept. | Japanese troops begin to occupy north-east China – Manchuria under total Japanese control by the end of the year. |
| | Nov. | Formal establishment of the Jiangxi Soviet in Ruijin. Mao criticised by pro-Moscow leaders, but is elected chairman of the Jiangxi Soviet. |
| 1932 | Mar. | Japan establishes a new independent state in north-east China, and installs the former Emperor Puyi as its puppet leader. |
| 1934 | Oct. | Communists leave Jiangxi Soviet and set off on the Long March. |
| 1935 | Jan. | Mao becomes *de facto* head of the CCP at the Zunyi Conference during the Long March. |

| | | |
|---|---|---|
| | Oct. | End of Long March as communist troops settle in northern Shaanxi province. |
| 1936 | Dec. | Chiang Kai-shek kidnapped in Xian and forced to abandon his campaign against the communists and create a new united front to resist Japan. |
| | | Communists move to Yan'an. |
| 1937 | July | Japanese troops enter Beijing, signalling the start of the Sino-Japanese War. |
| | Aug. | Communist forces renamed 'Eighth Route Army' as part of new CCP-Guomindang alliance against Japan. |
| | Nov. | Nationalist government moves to Chongqing in Sichuan province in the face of Japanese military onslaught. |
| | Dec. | The 'Rape of Nanjing' by Japanese troops. |
| 1940 | Mar. | Former Nationalist leader Wang Jingwei installed as head of a puppet regime by the Japanese in Nanjing. |
| 1941 | Jan. | Guomindang troops attack their supposed communist allies in South Anhui signalling the *de facto* end of the United Front. |
| | Dec. | Japanese attack on Pearl Harbour brings the United States into the war against Japan. |
| 1942 | Spring | Mao launches a 'rectification' campaign in Yan'an to promote his ideas and ideology. |
| | | CCP holds forum on art and literature in Yan'an. |
| 1943 | Mar. | Mao formally elected as Chairman of the CCP Politburo. |
| | Sept. | Mao's younger brother executed in Xinjiang in north-west China. |
| 1945 | Aug. | Soviet Union declares war on Japan and invades Manchuria. |
| | Sept. 9 | Japan formally surrenders. |
| | | Mao travels to Chongqing to negotiate a post-war settlement with Chiang Kai-shek. |
| 1946 | May | CCP armed forces renamed the People's Liberation Army. |
| | | Guomindang formally re-establishes Nanjing as the national capital. |

| | | |
|---|---|---|
| | June | Guomindang launches offensive against the CCP. |
| 1947 | Mar. | Guomindang forces take Yan'an. |
| 1948 | Autumn | CCP forces win major battles in north-east China. |
| 1949 | Jan. | CCP forces take Tianjin and Beijing. |
| | | Chiang Kai-shek resigns as head of Guomindang. |
| | Apr. | Nanjing falls to the communists. |
| | May | Shanghai falls to the communists. |
| | Oct. | Formal declaration of the new People's Republic of China. |
| | Dec. | Mao flies to Moscow to negotiate with Stalin – Mao's first trip outside China. |
| | | Chiang Kai-shek arrives in Taiwan. |
| 1950 | Feb. 14 | China and the Soviet Union sign Treaty of Friendship and Mutual Alliance. |
| | Oct. | Chinese forces enter Korea. |
| 1951 | May | Mao's son killed in Korea. |
| 1952 | Jan. | Three Antis campaign launched against corruption, waste and bureaucratism. |
| | Feb. | Five Antis campaign launched against corruption. |
| | July | Land reform completed in most areas. |
| 1953 | July | Signing of armistice in Korean War. |
| 1954 | Mar. | Gao Gang and Rao Shushi become first CCP officials to be purged. |
| 1955 | Apr. | Zhou Enlai attends Bandung Conference. |
| | July | First Five Year Plan (1953–57) formally adopted. |
| 1956 | Feb. | Khrushchev denounces Stalin. |
| | May | Mao calls for more criticism – the start of the Hundred Flowers campaign. |
| | Sep. | CCP holds Party Congress in Beijing. |
| | | Second Five Year Plan accepted. |
| 1957 | Feb. | Mao's speech 'On the Correct Handling of Contradictions among the People' appears to sanction criticism of the party. |
| | Spring | Wide-scale criticism of the party. |
| | June | *People's Daily* criticises rightists and counter-revolutionaries – the start of the anti-rightist campaign. |

|            |       |                                                                                                                                              |
|------------|-------|----------------------------------------------------------------------------------------------------------------------------------------------|
|            | Dec.  | National conference adopts Mao's twelve year plan for agriculture – China plans to overtake Britain in 15 years.                              |
| 1958       | Apr.  | First commune established in Henan province.                                                                                                  |
|            | May   | Central Committee supports Mao's communisation strategy and endorses the Great Leap Forward, essentially overturning the second Five Year Plan. |
|            | Aug.  | Politburo affirms the communisation policy.                                                                                                   |
|            | Nov.  | Partial retreat from the Great Leap.                                                                                                          |
| 1959       | Mar.  | Uprising in Tibet against Chinese rule suppressed.                                                                                            |
|            | Apr.  | Liu Shaoqi replaces Mao as State Chairman (Mao remains Party Chairman).                                                                       |
|            | Aug.  | Peng Dehuai dismissed after criticising Mao at Lushan.                                                                                        |
|            | Sept. | Lin Biao replaces Peng as Minister of National Defence.                                                                                       |
|            | Oct.  | Sino-Indian border clash.                                                                                                                     |
| 1960       | July  | Soviet Union decides to withdraw all experts from China.                                                                                      |
| 1961       |       | Wu Han publishes his play *Hui Rui Dismissed from Office* – later criticised as an attack on Mao.                                             |
| 1962       | Sept. | Mao launches Socialist Education Movement.                                                                                                    |
|            | Oct.  | Sino-Indian Border War.                                                                                                                       |
| 1963       | May   | A conference in Hangzhou endorses Mao's Socialist Education Movement.                                                                         |
|            |       | Learn from Lei Feng campaign launched.                                                                                                        |
|            | Sept. | The Central Committee issues new instructions for the Socialist Education Movement which contradict Mao's original directive.                 |
| 1964       | Feb.  | *People's Daily* calls for people to 'Learn from the PLA'.                                                                                    |
|            | Sept. | Socialist Education Movement essentially killed off.                                                                                          |
| 1965       | Nov.  | Yao Wenyuan criticises Wu Han and anti-party elements.                                                                                        |
| 1966       | May   | Central Committee establishes Cultural Revolution Small Group.                                                                                |
|            |       | Luo Ruiqing formally dismissed as PLA Chief of General Staff.                                                                                 |

| | |
|---|---|
| June | Peng Zhen removed as Mayor of Beijing. |
| | Liu Shaoqi sends work-teams into schools and colleges to prevent the spread of radicalism. |
| July | Chen Boda takes control of the Cultural Revolution Small Group. |
| | Mao swims across the Yangtze River to prove his good health. |
| Aug. | Mao Zedong issues poster encouraging young people to 'Bombard the Headquarters'. |
| | Central Committee endorses the Cultural Revolution. |
| | First mass rally in Beijing. |
| | Red Guards in Beijing start to attack feudal and counter-revolutionary elements. |
| | Writer Lao She killed while escaping a Red Guard mob. |
| Oct. | Liu Shaoqi and Deng Xiaoping write self-criticisms. |
| 1967 Jan. | First Revolutionary Committee established in Heilongjiang. |
| | Military ordered to 'support the left'. |
| Feb. | Short-lived 'Shanghai Commune' established. |
| Mar. | First public attack on Liu Shaoqi – but still only referred to as 'number one person in authority taking the capitalist road'. |
| Aug. | British quasi-Embassy in Beijing burnt down. |
| | Virtual civil war in Wuhan as rival military groups clash – the Wuhan incident. |
| Sept. | Zhou Enlai calls on Red Guards to stop the violence and return home. |
| 1968 Feb. | Campaign launched against 'anarchism' (i.e. excessive Red Guard radicalism). |
| June | Arms on route from the Soviet Union to Vietnam are seized by Red Guards – violent clashes between rival groups in Guangxi. |
| July | Mao criticises Red Guard leaders for their actions in the Cultural Revolution – the start of the de-radicalisation of the Cultural Revolution. |
| Sep. | New Revolutionary Committees established across China – order restored in most places. |

| | | |
|---|---|---|
| | Oct. | Liu Shaoqi formally dismissed from all positions. Campaign started to 'rebuild the party'. |
| | Dec. | Mao calls for Red Guards to be sent down to the countryside. |
| 1969 | Feb. | Mao calls for 'reasonable targets' in all planning. |
| | Mar. | Two serious Sino-Soviet border classes along the Ussuri River. |
| | June | Sino-Soviet border clash at Yumin. |
| | Nov. | Liu Shaoqi dies in jail. |
| 1970 | Aug. | Lin Biao angers Mao by calling for the post of Vice-Chairman of the party to be re-established. |
| | | Mao calls for criticism of his previous close ally, Chen Boda. |
| 1971 | Apr. | American table-tennis team visits China. |
| | July | Kissinger visits Beijing. |
| | Sept. | Lin Biao's plot to assassinate Mao is discovered – Lin dies in a plane crash trying to flee to Moscow. |
| | Oct. | China joins the United Nations leading to the expulsion of Taiwan. |
| 1972 | Jan. | Death of former Foreign Minister Chen Yi. |
| | Feb. | President Nixon visits China. |
| | Sept. | Japanese Premier Tanaka Kakuei visits China. |
| 1973 | Apr. | Deng Xiaoping returns as Vice-Premier. |
| | Aug. | Wang Hongwen argues that the Cultural Revolution will be a recurring phenomenon. |
| 1974 | Apr. | Deng Xiaoping promotes China as leader of the Third World in opposition to American and Soviet hegemony in a speech at the United Nations. |
| 1975 | Apr. | Death of Dong Biwu. |
| | | Death of Chiang Kai-shek in Taiwan. |
| | Dec. | President Ford visits China. |
| | | Death of Kang Sheng. |
| 1976 | Jan. | Death of Zhou Enlai. |
| | Feb. | Hua Guofeng named as new Premier. |
| | | Poster campaign against Deng Xiaoping at Beijing University. |
| | Apr. | Mass demonstration in support of Zhou Enlai in Tiananmen Square suppressed by military force. |

|        | Tiananmen protest designated as 'counter-revolutionary'. |
|--------|--------|
|        | Deng Xiaoping dismissed from all posts. |
| July   | Death of Zhu De. |
| Sept.  | Death of Mao Zedong. |
| Oct.   | Gang of Four arrested – Hua Guofeng becomes head of state, head of the party, and head of military affairs. |

# GLOSSARY

*Beijing*
China's capital before 1911 and after 1949, Beijing literally means 'North Capital'. Often spelt Peking in keeping with the old post-office style of transliteration. Just to confuse things even more, it was known as Beiping (Peip'ing), meaning Northern Peace, in 1911–49 when the national capital was in Nanjing (Nanking), the 'South Capital'. See the map on pp. 216–17.

*Boxer Rebellion*
An anti-foreign uprising that enjoyed much popular support between 1898 and 1900. The rebels slaughtered Christian missionaries throughout China, and by June 1900 large numbers of Boxers had converged in Beijing. Western powers responded with concerted and fierce military action that destroyed the rebellion. The Boxer Protocol of September 1901 forced the Chinese to pay massive indemnities that equated to something in the region of 12 times the total annual revenue at the time.

*Bo Yibo (Po I-po)*
Veteran Chinese leader from Shanxi province. Active in the party from the 1920s, Bo became a key central planner in the early 1950s, later reaching the heights of Vice-Premier. Became a loud and constant critic of market reforms in the 1980s, although he himself was criticised by students in 1989 for sending his children to be educated abroad.

*Cadres*
The term used to describe officials working within the party and state administration.

## Central Committee (CC)

An elected body of leading party members that is the theoretical decision-making body in the PRC. Meets a couple of times a year in full or plenary session, where it essentially rubber stamps Politburo decisions. The CC elects leaders and other committees to act on its behalf in the meantime. Each Central Committee is known by the number of the national conference that elects it. Thus, the 3rd plenum of the 11th CC which started the post-Mao reforms was the third time that the CC elected at the 11th National Party Conference met in full session.

## Central Military Commission

The main decision-making organ for military affairs, and one of the major tools for ensuring that 'the Party Commands the Gun'.

## Chen Boda (Ch'en Pota)

One of the party's main theoreticians, Chen was a very close ally of Mao Zedong. He was thought to have helped Mao draft many of his major theoretical articles, and was a mouth-piece for Maoism in the 1950s and 1960s. He played a leading role in launching the Cultural Revolution, and was a member of the Cultural Revolution Small Group charged with attacking revisionism. When Mao de-radicalised the Cultural Revolution, Chen Boda found himself in conflict with his patron, and he was purged in 1970 and disappeared for supposedly plotting against Mao.

## Chen Duxiu (Ch'en Tu-hsiu)

One of the early CCP leaders, Chen played a crucial role in developing Marxist ideas in China, and was an honorary founder member of the CCP. Later became officially designated as one of the ten men who plotted against Mao for being too dependent on the Soviets.

## Chen Yun (Ch'en Yun)

Chen Yun is perhaps one of the least well known, but one of the most influential of China's first generation of communist leaders. Born in Jiangsu province (some sources say in 1900, others in 1905), he was one of the few post-1949 leaders who had a 'Soviet' style background in the urban trade union movement whilst working as a typesetter for Commercial Press in

Shanghai in the 1920s. Having joined the party in 1924, he was involved in the early part of the Long March, but then left for Moscow for ideological and organisational training. On his return to China, he led the Party Organisation Department but increasingly turned his attentions towards economic affairs during the 1940s.

From 1949 to 1954, Chen Yun led the committee in charge of financial and economic work which successfully managed the first stage of industrialisation and economic recovery. After the collapse of the Great Leap, he once more took control of the economy, gradually generating economic recovery, only for his policies to be overthrown by Mao for a second time in 1966 with the onset of the Cultural Revolution.

Whilst disappearing politically, Chen did not personally bear the brunt of Mao's hostilities during the Cultural Revolution, and in 1978 the party turned to Chen Yun once again to regenerate the economy. However, he became concerned that the party let market forces become too dominant in the 1980s, and by his death in 1995 he had become one of the fiercest and loudest critics of the direction of the reform process.

*Chiang Kai-shek* (Jiang Jieshi)
Born in Ningbo in Zhejiang province in either 1887 or 1888. Despite many years as leader of the Guomindang, Chiang was primarily a military man. Initially sent to Japan to study military affairs, he joined Sun Yatsen's Revolutionary Alliance. Returning to China in 1910, he spent a number of years on the fringes of the Shanghai underworld, before reviving his military/political career in Guangzhou in the early 1920s. Chiang gained Sun's patronage, and was sent for military training in the Soviet Union in 1923, returning to lead the important Whampoa military academy.

Chiang's military and underworld connections played a crucial role in winning the leadership of the Guomindang on Sun Yatsen's death in 1925. But this victory was achieved at the expense of considerable damage to party unity that dogged his leadership until 1949. With the support of a number of allied warlords, the Northern Expedition successfully reunited China under Guomindang rule, and Chiang established a new national government in first Wuhan and then Nanjing in 1927.

Once in power, Chiang abandoned the united front with the communists which had been forced on both parties by their mutual backers, the Soviet Union. The purge of communist elements was followed in December by his marriage to Soong Meiling, the younger sister of Sun Yatsen's widow, Soong Qingling. As another sister was married to the wealthy and influential financier, H.H. Kung, the marriage combined Chiang's formal leadership with the informal connections that remained an important element of political leadership in nationalist China.

The Nanjing rule of the Guomindang collapsed in 1937 under an extreme and brutal Japanese onslaught. Chiang moved the capital to Chongqing, where the nationalists sat out the war in relative comfort. There was considerable scepticism amongst American advisers in Chongqing regarding Chiang's beliefs and loyalties, and a widely held belief that he diverted American aid for his own use, and stored up weapons for use in the coming civil war with the communists. Nevertheless, the Americans and indeed the Soviets remained committed to restoring him to power throughout the war years.

Despite defeat in the civil war, Chiang escaped to the island of Taiwan and refused to relinquish his claim to be the legitimate ruler of all China. To this end, he was supported by the Americans, who installed the Taiwan regime in the Chinese seat at the United Nations (prompting a Soviet walk-out which enabled the Americans to pass a resolution sending UN troops to Korea) which they held until 1972. Chiang consolidated power under martial rule and by linking closely with the American and later the emerging Japanese economies, facilitated the economic modernisation that had eluded the Guomindang in Nanjing, a process continued after his death in April 1975 by his son, Chiang Ching-kuo (Jiang Jingguo). Nevertheless, he will be first and foremost remembered as 'the man who lost China'.

*Chongqing (Chungking)*
City in western Sichuan province that became the Guomindang's home and China's capital in exile during the war with Japan.

*Cixi (Tzu-hsi)*
The Empress Dowager, the official concubine of the Emperor Xian Feng. The real power behind the throne in the declining years of the Qing dynasty, mother of Zai Chun and aunt of

Guang Xu, she did more than most to bring the empire to its knees by blocking essential reforms in the nineteenth century. Her mishandling of the Boxer Rebellion gave the foreign powers the excuse they needed to occupy Beijing, launching the imperial system into a crisis from which it never recovered.

*Communes*
A basic level of administration in the countryside designed to facilitate economic and political revolution. The Chinese term *gong she* refers to a number of basic-level agricultural organisations, but we tend to use it to refer to the radical experiments in communal living during the Great Leap.

*Communist International (Comintern)*
Established by the Soviets to promote international revolution, the Comintern supported both the nationalists and the communists throughout the civil war between the two. The Comintern's insistence on following the path of proletarian revolution forced the CCP into instigating disastrous urban uprisings that all but destroyed the party. The Comintern came into almost continual conflict with Mao after the Long March, refusing to accept him as leader of the CCP.

| *Leading Comintern figures* | *CCP Comintern supporters* |
|---|---|
| Borodin | Xiang Zhongfa (Hsiang Chong-fa) |
| Maring (Snievlet) | Li Lisan (Li Li-san) |
| | Wang Ming (Wang Ming) |
| | Bo Gu (Po Ku) |

*Confucianism*
The state ideology of the imperial system. The ideas of Confucius were adapted (some would say distorted) by subsequent thinkers (notably Mencius). These ideas were often in themselves adapted by new regimes which sought to place their legitimacy to rule in a historical context. For example, the theory of the mandate of heaven which justified rebellion against a bad ruler was not in Confucius's own writings, but adopted by a new dynasty to vindicate its successful rebellion against the old regime. Over the centuries, Confucianism absorbed some of the ideas of Daoism, Legalism, and other schools of thought, to become a distinct state ideology. Note that Confucianism as we refer to it in China is not identical to the Confucian ideologies that emerged in Korea and Japan.

*Danwei*

The 'work unit' in urban China. The danwei was a unit of social and political organisation as well as a workplace. Workers lived in the danwei, their children were educated there, it provided health care and welfare in retirement, and so on. In addition, the workplace was the focal point of local political organisation, and a means of controlling the workforce. It was, in essence, a mini-state.

*Democracy Wall*

A spontaneous intellectual movement to vilify the Cultural Revolution and the Gang of Four after 1976. The wall itself was at Xidan, one of the main shopping streets in Beijing at the time. It became covered with posters and pamphlets, and the unofficial meeting place for young Chinese dissidents. Whilst the movement was useful for Deng Xiaoping in his struggle against the residual left, he suppressed it almost as soon as he took power in 1978.

*Deng Xiaoping* (Teng Hsiao-p'ing)

Born in Guangan in Sichuan province in 1904, Deng's political career was one of remarkable ups and downs. He was the youngest of a small group of young communists who were sent on a work-study programme in France by the Communist International. Returning to China, he supported Mao's view that the peasantry were a positive revolutionary force, and was subsequently heavily criticised by Li Lisan – the first and mildest of his official condemnations. A veteran of the Long March, Deng also served as a political commissar in the Second Field Army in his native south-west China.

After a brief period in charge of the south-west region after 1949, he was brought into the central political apparatus where he served as party secretary general. Despite his impressive leadership credentials, his rapid promotion to central leadership owed much to Mao's patronage. It is sometimes forgotten that Deng was once a very strong supporter of Mao, particularly during the formative years of the Great Leap Forward. However, when the Great Leap collapsed into the great famine, he changed his view, or at least changed his allegiances.

Deng suffered massive humiliation and hardship during the Cultural Revolution, as did the rest of his family (his son, Deng Pufang, was paralysed by a 'fall' from a window). However, his treatment was partly tempered by Zhou Enlai's intervention, and Zhou played a leading role in ensuring Deng's rehabilitation in 1973. Deng worked as Zhou's deputy until his death in January 1976. When a spontaneous mass demonstration occurred in Tiananmen Square in April in support of Zhou (and by implication Deng), Deng was accused of orchestrating a counter-revolutionary movement, and he was purged again.

Deng found a safe haven in the south under the protection of the military leader, Wei Guoqing, and returned once more to power in December 1978. He oversaw the radical reform of the Chinese economy, and initiated a reappraisal of Mao's revolutionary role. However, it is questionable whether he will be remembered more for instigating the reform process, or ordering the suppression of student demonstrators in Tiananmen Square on 4 June 1989.

### Gang of Four

Group of radical Maoists in Shanghai and eastern China who either used Mao or who were used by Mao to start the Cultural Revolution. They were: Jiang Qing (Chiang Ch'ing), Wang Hongwen, Zhang Chunqiao (Chang Ch'un-chiao) and Yao Wenyuan. Rose to power and prominence during the Cultural Revolution, but were quickly arrested and jailed by their former ally, Hua Guofeng, after Mao's death.

### Guomindang (GMD) (Kuomintang) (KMT)

The Chinese nationalist party, established in 1912 as the political successor to the Revolutionary Alliance. Received aid and support from Moscow despite its often bloody conflict with the CCP. Nominally unified China during the Northern Expedition of 1927, but failed to establish an effective national regime from the new capital in Nanjing. Forced to abandon Nanjing after the Japanese invasion of 1937, it briefly established a capital in Wuhan before moving on to sit out the war in Chongqing. Despite vastly superior forces and armaments, it was defeated by the CCP in the 1945–49 civil war. The rump of the GMD escaped to Taiwan where they remain to this day.

### Leading figures

Chiang Kai-shek (Jiang Jieshi) – succeeded Sun as head of GMD in 1925.
Soong Ching Ling (Song Qingling) – Chiang's wife.

Wang Jingwei (Wang Ching-wei) – lost out to Chiang in post-Sun power struggle. Stayed in Guangzhou to lead a rebel GMD faction. Installed as puppet leader of China by Japanese after the 1937 revolution.
Hu Hanming (Hu Han-ming)
Chen Guofu (Ch'en Kuo-fu)
Chen Lifu (Ch'en Li-fu)

### Hong Xiuquan (Hung Hsiu-chuan)

Leader of the Taiping Rebellion. Hong thought that he was Jesus's younger brother, but was also a relatively pragmatic and, for a while, successful revolutionary.

### Hua Guofeng (Hua Kuo-feng)

One of the (relatively) younger political figures in Mao's China, Hua was born in 1921 in Shanxi province. Originally a successful local leader in Mao's native Hunan province, he rose to prominence during the Cultural Revolution, and through his position within the secret police in Beijing became an important power-broker. Hua abandoned his colleagues in the left, and having arrested the Gang of Four, installed himself in power after Mao's death. Although he held all of the major positions in the Chinese party, state and army, he lost power in less than two years to the resurgent Deng Xiaoping.

### Hundred Days of Reform 1898

A last attempt to save the dynasty from collapse by fundamentally reforming all aspects of politics and power. Despite being sanctioned by the Emperor, the reforms were crushed by a combination of elite resistance, opposition from Cixi and military intervention by Yuan Shikai's troops.

| The reformers | The opponents |
|---|---|
| Emperor Guang Xu (Kuang Hsu) | Cixi (Tz'u-hsi) |
| Kang Youwei (K'ang Yu-wei) | Yuan Shikai (Yuan Shih-k'ai) |
| Liang Qichao (Liang Ch'i-ch'ao) | |

### Hundred Flowers

When they were told to give their opinion of the Chinese revolution, many intellectuals did. Those who made criticisms were subsequently purged. Either a skilful ploy by Mao to weed out his enemies, or a shocked response by a hurt Mao, depending on your point of view. Whichever the case, a key event in the evolution of Mao's political ideas and strategies.

## Jiang Qing (Chiang Ch'ing)
Mao's third wife. A former film star and socialite in Shanghai, Jiang was detested by Mao's colleagues in the party. She developed a clique of radical communists, the Gang of Four, who were the spark behind the Cultural Revolution. During the Cultural Revolution, Jiang re-wrote a number of 'revolutionary operas' which became the main (and, for a time, only) source of 'entertainment' in China. She was arrested after Mao's death, and charged with having distorted Mao's policies and committing many crimes under the guise of the Cultural Revolution. She refused to accept the blame, claiming to the end that she was simply following Mao's orders. Died in jail after her original death sentence was commuted to life imprisonment.

## Jiangxi (Kiangsi) Soviet
The mountainous area in south-eastern China that became the home of the CCP after the failure of urban uprisings sponsored by the Comintern in 1927 and 1930. The CCP were forced out of Jiangxi by GMD military campaigns in 1934 – the start of the Long March.

## Kang Sheng (K'ang Sheng)
Born in Shandong province in 1898, Kang is remembered in China as being one of the most brutal of Chinese leaders. A major figure in the Cultural Revolution left, Kang was very close to both Mao and the Gang of Four. Whilst Kang helped Mao develop his theoretical principles, he is best know as Mao's henchman, and for his ruthless treatment of Mao's opponents in the Cultural Revolution.

## Li Dazhao (Li Ta-chao)
One of the original communist thinkers and theoreticians in China, and an honorary founder member of the CCP.

## Lin Biao (Lin Piao)
Born in Hubei province in 1907, Lin was a leading military figure during the revolution, leading communist troops in a number of significant victories. Spent various periods in Moscow receiving medical treatment, Lin later became an idol of

the radical left. As Minister of National Defence in the 1960s, he was responsible for publishing 'the little red book' and promoting loyalty to Mao within the army. A crucial player in launching the Cultural Revolution, he was Mao's chosen heir and successor, but became increasingly isolated from his patron as Mao moved away from radicalism in 1969 and 1970. Supposedly died in a plane crash after trying to assassinate Mao in 1971.

## Li Lisan Line

The policy of sponsoring urban proletarian revolution and ignoring the revolutionary potential of the peasantry. Mao's opposition to this policy got him in trouble with the party authorities, and annoyed the Comintern in Moscow.

## Liu Shaoqi (Liu Shao-ch'i)

Born in 1898 in Hunan province, Liu became an active communist at an early age and was taken to Moscow for ideological training by the Comintern. On his return to China, Liu was a voice of Moscow in China. Nevertheless, he was very loyal to Mao after 1949, and was assumed to be Mao's chosen successor in the 1950s. The relationship between Mao and Liu became more and more uneasy during the Hundred Flowers Movement and the Great Leap. With Deng Xiaoping and Chen Yun, Liu played a leading role in moving China back to a more Leninist model of development after the Great Leap, and crucially blocked Mao's attempts to instigate a mass Socialist Education Movement in 1962. Designated by Mao as the 'number one person in authority taking the capitalist road' and 'China's Khrushchev', Liu was the primary target of the Cultural Revolution. He was purged, and died in prison in 1969 from a combination of physical and psychological abuse.

## May Fourth Movement (New Culture Movement)

Named after a demonstration in Tiananmen Square on 4 May 1919 after German territories in China had been handed over to the Japanese by the allies. The period saw an influx of western ideas into China, and sparked an increasing fascination with democracy, anarchism, Marxism and other western philosophies. It was the spark that ignited the young generation into political activity.

*Nanjing (Nanking) Decade*
The period of nationalist rule from Nanjing, 1927–37.

*1911 Revolution*
The overthrow of the imperial system. Started in Wuhan in central China when the local military rose up against the empire. This was not so much a revolution as a formal recognition that the Qing had long since lost control. One by one, the provinces of China declared independence from Beijing. A largely bloodless affair, the Qing's attempts to save itself backfired when their leading military figure, Yuan Shikai, joined the revolution. Puyi, the last Emperor, formally abdicated on 12 February 1912.

*Nomenklatura*
The system by which a person must get on the 'name list' in order to be considered for any post of importance in not only government and administration, but in education, finance, and all levels of business. A crucial means for the party indirectly to control all spheres of life.

*Northern Expedition*
The military activity that brought the Guomindang to power in 1927. Often carried out in proxy by warlord armies.

*Opium Wars*
The CCP regards the outbreak of the first Opium War in 1840 as the beginning of modern Chinese history. Britain had been involved in one of the biggest drug-running campaigns in history. Opium grown in northern India was transported to China and sold to a growing number of addicts. When the Chinese tried to ban the trade, superior British military technology was utilised to force the Chinese into a humiliating retreat. The resulting treaty forced China to lease Hong Kong to the British until 1997. The Second Opium War, sometimes called the Arrow War (1856–60), was essentially a case of the British (and now the French) bullying the Chinese into granting more and more concessions to the western powers. The Opium Wars marked the beginning of the end of the imperial system in China. The Middle Kingdom had been shown to be inferior to the western barbarians, but proved unable to reform itself in the face of this challenge. *See Unequal Treaties.*

*Peng Dehuai (P'eng Teh-huai)*
Born in Hunan province in 1898, Peng was a leading military figure during and after the revolution. Originally a loyal follower of Mao, the two began to split after 1949. Peng argued that China should follow the Soviet model of development, and criticised Mao's Great Leap strategy. Having led Chinese troops in the Korean War, Peng believed that China could not fight the US on its own, and thus needed to remain close to the Soviet Union diplomatically and militarily. He retained close personal relations with Khrushchev, and when he criticised Mao's policies at the Lushan party meeting in 1959, his subsequent purge owed as much to his relations with Moscow as it did to his criticisms of Mao. He died in disgrace in 1974, and was only officially posthumously rehabilitated after Mao's death.

*Peng Zhen (P'eng Chen)*
Peng was born in Shanxi province in 1900 or 1902. He combined both local and national level leadership, serving on the party Politburo as well as being Mayor of Beijing. He was a long-time opponent of Mao's development strategy and isolated the left in Beijing in the 1960s. When Peng's deputy, Wu Han, was accused of attacking Mao at the onset of the Cultural Revolution, Peng Zhen was put in charge of the committee to investigate cultural affairs (the Cultural Revolution Small Group). This move, intended to limit the Cultural Revolution, only served to increase the left's hatred of Peng, and he became one of the first major casualties of the Cultural Revolution, only returning to power after Mao's death.

*People's Liberation Army (PLA)*
Refers to all units of the armed forces in China. A crucial component in the power configuration in post-1949 China.

*Politburo*
Short for political bureau. Elected by the CC, this (perhaps more correctly, the Standing Committee of the Politburo) is the party's major decision-making organ.

*Proletariat*
The Chinese for proletariat is *wu chan jie ji* – literally, the classes without property. This means that in Chinese terms, the proletariat is not just the industrial working class, but soldiers, party-state employees, and crucially the peasantry.

*Puyi (P'u I)*
China's last emperor was only a boy when the imperial system collapsed. He was later seduced (in more ways than one) by the Japanese to become Emperor of the puppet kingdom of Manchuko after the Japanese annexed northern China. Later a gardener in Beijing.

*Qing (Ch'ing) Dynasty*
The imperial family or dynasty that ruled China from 1644 to the abolition of the royal family and the creation of a republic in 1911. The Qing were from the Man ethnic minority (Manchu) and this became a focus for opposition from the majority Chinese (Han) population during the later years of their rule.
*Leading figures*
Emperors   Xian Feng (Hsien Feng) (r. 1851–61)
           Zai Chun (Tsai Ch'un) aka Tong Zhi (T'ung Chih)
               (r. 1861–75)
           Guang Xu (Kuang Hsu) (r. 1875–1908)
           Puyi (P'u I or P'u Yi) (r. 1908–11)
Empress Dowager Cixi (Tzu Hsi) (1835–1908).

*Red Book*
Initially collected by Lin Biao to instil revolutionary consciousness into the people, this became the bible of the Maoist left. It is a collection of bits and pieces of Mao's speeches.

*Red Guards*
The student and worker groupings that formed during the Cultural Revolution to prosecute the revolution. Degenerated into internecine conflict and virtual civil war during 1967–68.

*Revolutionary Alliance*
Formed in exile in Tokyo in 1905 under the leadership of Sun Yatsen (1866–1925), the first political grouping to organise on a national level. The aim of creating a Chinese republic appeared to have been fulfilled by the 1911 revolution which overthrew the Qing and installed Sun Yatsen as President. The Alliance transformed itself into the Guomindang, but the revolution was usurped by Yuan Shikai and the warlords.

*Ruijin*
The capital of the Jiangxi Soviet.

*Sinocentrism*

Refers to the belief that China is the centre of the universe, and that Chinese civilisation is superior to any other.

*Sun Yatsen*

Sun Yatsen, who is widely regarded as being the father of modern Chinese nationalism, was originally named Sun Wen, and is known throughout the mandarin speaking world as Sun Zhongshan. He was born in Xiangshan (now called Zhongshan in his honour) in the southern Chinese province of Guangdong on 12 November 1866. He converted to Christianity and received a western education, studying medicine in Hong Kong. Whilst his revolutionary influence was enormous, Sun was not a particularly good revolutionary himself. His two attempts to lead anti-imperial uprisings in southern China in October 1895 and October 1901 were abject failures. After the first occasion, he was forced into exile in America and later Britain, where he was kidnapped by the Chinese legation, and only released after the British government threatened to impose sanctions on China.

Sun developed an ideology known as 'The Three Principles of the People', which advocated the end of imperial rule and the promotion of nationalism, democracy and people's livelihood (*min sheng*) (the Three Principles remain the ideological basis of the Chinese nationalists in Taiwan). He also established the Chinese Revolutionary Alliance (*tongmenghui*) in July 1905 in exile in Japan, which nominally carried out the revolution in 1911 that overthrew the old imperial order. Sun returned to China where he was elected as the first provisional President of the new republic based in Nanjing, but fled to Guangdong when the military leader, Yuan Shikai, took power into his own hands. From 1913 to his death in 1925, Sun spent the remainder of his life fighting ever more divisive and destructive internecine warfare with various fragments of the Guomindang as China slid into a period of warlordism where might, and not ideas, held sway.

*Taiping (T'ai-p'ing) Rebellion (1851–64)*

An attempt to overthrow the imperial system and set up a 'heavenly kingdom' in China. The rebels took huge areas of land across southern China, and set up a new capital in Nanjing. Defeated by a combination of internal fighting and imperial aggression. The empire's forces were aided by the intervention of foreign powers, who perceived that the rebels were threatening their interests in China.

| *The rebels* | *The empire* |
|---|---|
| Hong Xiuquan (Hung Hsiu-ch'uan) | Emperor Xian Feng (Hsien Feng) |
| Yang Xiuqing (Yang Hsiu-ch'ing) | Zeng Guofan (Tseng Kuo-fan) |
| Wei Changhui (Wei Ch'ang-hui) | Li Hongzhang (Li Hung-chang) |
| Shi Dakai (Shih Ta-k'ai) | Frederick Townsend Ward |
| | Charles George Gordon |

*Tiananmen Square Incident*

Although we now generally refer to the events of 1989 as the Tiananmen Square Incident, it was, in fact, the second major protest (and massacre) in recent Chinese history. The first incident, and the one which is relevant for this study, occurred in April 1976. Some 200–400 students and intellectuals were executed for protesting in favour of the recently dead Zhou Enlai (and by implication for Deng Xiaoping) against the Gang of Four (and by implication Mao Zedong). This event marked the second purge of Deng Xiaoping, although the once-bitten Deng did not wait to be purged, and escaped to the south where he was protected by sympathetic local military leaders.

*Tongzhi (T'ung-chih) Restoration*

An attempt to reform China's foreign relations and restore the dynasty to power in the face of internal rebellion. Begun in 1861, the reforms had petered out due to a mixture of continued foreign aggression and internal opposition by about 1895.

*The reformers*

Zeng Guofan (Tseng Kuo-fan)
Li Hongzhang (Li Hung-chang)
Shen Guifen (Shen Kui-fen)
Wen Xiang (Wen Hsiang)

*Unequal Treaties*

From 1840 onwards, China fought – and lost – a series of wars with western powers (and later Japan). On each occasion, the victors forced China to sign humiliating treaties. These entailed ceding control over virtually the entire coast and paying massive indemnities that bankrupted the state. In addition, foreigners were granted extraterritorial rights, which granted them immunity from Chinese laws.

## United Front

The periods of collaboration between the GMD and CCP. The crucial period was the alliance against the Japanese invaders after 1937. The united front was always a fragile alliance. Chiang Kai-shek was only forced to abandon his attacks on the CCP by the intervention of the northern warlords who kidnapped him in Xian in December 1931 and forced the GMD to turn their attentions to the Japanese. GMD aggression towards the CCP continued throughout the war against Japan, and a renewed civil war after the defeat of the Japanese was all but inevitable.

## Wang Ming

Probably the man most hated by Mao. Wang was very close to the Soviets, and stayed in Moscow where he issued proclamations and policy on behalf of the CCP whilst Mao was leading the remnants of the party on the Long March. Recognised as CCP leader by Stalin until as late as 1942.

## Warlords

Powerful provincial leaders who built up their own armed forces and created local power bases during and after the collapse of the dynasty. Although many declared allegiance to the GMD in Nanjing, they in fact ruled their territories as independent kingdoms. Indeed, the relationship between Chiang Kai-shek and the warlords was a crucial determinant of politics in the Nanjing era and after. Despite the establishment of the GMD regime, they remained major power-brokers within the political system until the end of the civil war in 1949.

### Leading warlords

Li Zongren (Li Tsung-jen)
Li Jichen (Li Chi-ch'en)
Feng Yuxiang (Feng Yu-hsiang)
Zhang Xueliang (Chang Hsueh-liang)
Zhang Zuolin (Chang Tso-lin)
Yan Xishan (Yen Hsi-shan)
Wu Peifu (Wu P'ei-fu)

## Worker-Peasant Study Tours

A supposed way of taking young Chinese socialists to France where they could learn more about Marxism. In reality, many of the young men ended up working in armaments factories. Zhou Enlai and Deng Xiaoping both went to France and joined the French Communist Party.

*Yanan (Yenan)*
The area in Shaanxi province in northern China that became the CCP's home after 1935. Yanan became a symbol of anti-Japanese activity as well as the base of Chinese communism, and was the cornerstone of the successful revolutionary movement that was to follow.

*Yuan Shikai (Yuan Shih-k'ai)*
Former leader of the Northern (Beiyang) Army. Yuan played a leading role in the collapse of national government in China. Brought to Beijing to support the 100 Days of Reform, he instead threw his lot in with Cixi and stopped the reforms. Sent to put down the nascent 1911 revolution, he instead threw his lot in with the revolutionaries. When the GMD won the first national elections in China in 1912, he declared them null and void and outlawed the GMD. Yuan declared himself leader, and even tried to crown himself Emperor! In reality, power had already slipped into the hands of the warlords.

*Zhang Guotao*
Communist military leader who fell out with Mao over where the Long March should go. Tried to head off towards the Soviet Union, but forced back by a hostile terrain and even more hostile national minorities. The only major CCP leader to defect to the nationalists.

*Zhou Enlai*
Zhou Enlai was born in March 1898 in Huaian in Jiangsu province into a family of imperial officials. Educated at the prestigious Nankai Middle School in Tianjin, Zhou first became interested in Marxism in 1917. He returned to China in 1919, and became a leading student activist in Tianjin, where he met his future wife, Deng Yingchao, who became an important post-1949 political leader in her own right. His political activity brought him to the attention of the Communist International, who sent him on a work-study tour to France in 1920, where Zhou organised Marxist study groups amongst Chinese students and workers in France and Germany.

Despite initially opposing Mao Zedong's revolutionary strategy, Zhou's decision to support Mao at the Zunyi Conference in January 1935 was crucial in assuring Mao's ascension to party leadership. Zhou spent much of the 1937–45 period in Chongqing as the communists' representative in the exiled nationalist government, and held a number of talks with American and other foreign delegations. After the breakdown of talks with the Guomindang in 1946, he returned to the communist base area in Yanan, where he helped formulate the successful revolutionary strategy, and laid the foundations for the post-revolutionary structure of political power.

After 1949, Zhou served as China's Premier, and also took charge of China's international relations, spending much of the 1950s and 1960s travelling the world in pursuit of his diplomatic initiatives. He was a regular visitor to third world capitals, and also spent more time in Moscow than any other Chinese leader as Sino-Soviet relations declined to the point of a short border war (officially skirmishes) in 1969. Zhou is also credited with paving the way for President Nixon's visit to China in February 1972 and the resulting Sino-US rapprochement. In domestic politics, he was credited for being a voice of reason and pragmatism, for defending the victims of the Cultural Revolution where possible, and for persuading Mao to make a partial retreat from extreme radicalism between 1969 and 1971. His popular reputation was even further improved by his actions between 1973 (when he played a crucial role in rehabilitating Deng Xiaoping) and his death in January 1976. Zhou shared the popular mistrust and hatred of the radical leftist Gang of Four who had risen to power during the Cultural Revolution. He was determined to block their influence (not least because of its potential damage to China's new-found international respectability) and continued to control state affairs with his deputy Deng Xiaoping even after being hospitalised with terminal cancer in 1974.

*Zhu De (Chu Teh)*

Zhu was born in 1886 in Sichuan province. Originally active in southern China, Zhu De joined up with Mao in the Jiangxi Soviet after the failure of armed uprisings in 1927. The alliance between Zhu and Mao was an essential component in building the communists' revolutionary strategy, and Zhu did more than most to build the Red Army, and to develop guerrilla tactics. Zhu stood alongside Mao throughout the revolution, and was rewarded by a position on the Politburo after 1949 until his death in 1976. However, he was not politically active after 1949, and served more as an icon of the party's glorious revolutionary past.

*Zunyi (Tsun-I or Tsun-Yi) Conference*
The unofficial conference during the Long March in January 1935 where Mao assumed power from the Comintern-backed wing of the CCP.

# BIBLIOGRAPHICAL ESSAY

Numerous books and articles have been written over the years on Chinese communist politics. The details of those sources used in the preparation of this book are provided in the full bibliography on page 210. Readers should also consult the footnotes within the chapters for guides to further reading on specific issues. The following list of suggested further reading is merely a small selection of works that provide good general introductions to politics in Mao's China.

*General Introductions*

Perhaps the most accessible way of finding out more about China is to start with literary approaches. A good starting point is Jung Chang's (1991) *Wild Swans* (London: Harper Collins), which has received wide literary acclaim over recent years. Anchee Min's (1996) *Red Azalea* (London: Cassell/Gollancz) is a similar account, but with more emphasis on the personal than the political. On a different level, Edgar Snow's (1968) classic *Red Star Over China* (London: Gollancz) is a fascinating and unique account of a non-Chinese participant in the Chinese revolution.

Pa Chin's (1978) *The Family* (Peking: Foreign Languages Press) and Lao She's (1982) unfinished *Beneath the Red Banner* (Beijing: China Publications Centre) are both excellent and very readable insights into urban life in China at the end of the Empire. On a different tack, Tu Peng-cheng's (1983) *Defend Yanan* (Beijing: Foreign Languages Press) is a classic example of the blending of art and propaganda in Chinese communist literature.

There are a number of works which cross the popular–academic divide. For example, Elizabeth Wright's (1989) *The Chinese People Stand Up* (London: BBC Books) was written as a companion to a BBC radio series on China, and is useful for both undergraduate students and general readers. Other major works that provide comprehensive and accessible introductions to twentieth-century China include Spence (1990) *The Search for Modern China* (London: Hutchinson), Hsu (1995) *The Rise Of Modern China* (New York: Oxford University Press) and Fairbank and Reischauer (1989) *China: Tradition and Transformation* (London: Allen & Unwin). Hinton (1966) *Fanshen: A Documentary of Revolution in a Chinese Village* (New York: Vintage Books), Hinton (1983) *Shenfan* (London: Secker and Warburg) and Endicott (1988) *Red Earth: Revolution in a Sichuan Village* (London: I.B. Tauris) all rely heavily on the reminiscences of Chinese villagers to portray life in two parts of rural China.

*Introductory Texts for Students*

There are a number of general texts on Chinese politics. For undergraduate students, one of the best texts is Gray (1990) *Rebellions and Revolutions: China from the 1800s to the 1980s* (Oxford and New York: Oxford University Press), which covers a long time span in great detail. Amongst the many other texts on this period, Brugger's two volumes (both 1981), *China, Liberation and Transformation, 1942–1962* and *China, Radicalism to Revisionism, 1962–1979* (London: Croom Helm) are both good introductions. A more detailed account is provided by MacFarquhar's (1973, 1983 and 1997) three volume account on 'The Origins of the Cultural Revolution'; *Contradictions among the People, 1956–1957, The Great Leap Forward, 1958–1960,* and *The Coming of the Cataclysm: 1961–1966* (all Oxford: Oxford University Press).

The more recent publications obviously focus more on the contemporary situation than on the Maoist era, though all carry analyses of pre-reform China to set the historical context of contemporary reform. One exception is MacFarquhar (1993) *The Politics of China 1949–1989* (Cambridge: Cambridge University Press), which contains detailed accounts of Mao's China as well as an appraisal of more recent affairs.

For more detailed accounts of the machinations of Chinese politics, particularly amongst the central elites, Chang (1975)

*Power and Policy in China* (University Park: Pennsylvania State University Press), and Teiwes (1979) *Politics and Purges in China: Rectification and the Decline of Party Norms, 1950–1965* (New York: M.E. Sharpe) are both particularly good accounts. Schurmann (1968) *Ideology and Organization in Communist China* (Berkeley: University of California Press) was first written in 1965, yet remains the most comprehensive introduction to the organisation and structure of the Chinese communist party state.

## Maoism

For those who want to read Mao's many words for themselves, his major speeches and articles are collected in five volumes in English translation published by the Foreign Languages Press in Beijing. Of these, the first four concentrate on Mao's works before 1949. The Foreign Languages Press has also grouped Mao's works together by themes, like the 1966 collection on military writing, and the 1976 collection of Mao's poems. Alternatively, Schram (1974) has edited a collection of Mao's more important talks and letters in *Mao Tse-tung Unrehearsed* (Harmondsworth: Penguin). Hinton (1980) *The People's Republic of China, 1949–1979: A Documentary Survey* (Wilmington, Del.: Scholarly Resources) is also a good collection for those who prefer to study China by reading primary sources.

Of the various academic interpretations of Mao's ideas, Schram (1988) *The Thought of Mao Tse-tung* (Cambridge: Cambridge University Press) is one of the most comprehensive. There has been considerable academic debate over whether Mao's ideas represent a strand of Marxism, or a new and different ideology. Starr (1986) provides an excellent overview of these debates in ' "Good Mao", "Bad Mao": Mao Studies and the Re-Evaluation of Mao's Political Thought' in *The Australian Journal of Chinese Affairs* 16, pp. 1–22. See also Knight (1983) 'The Form of Mao Zedong's "Sinification of Marxism" ' in *The Australian Journal of Chinese Affairs* 9, pp. 17–33.

## Other Chinese Communist Leaders

While this book has concentrated on Mao's role in the Chinese revolution, the role of other leaders should not be ignored. For the role of Liu Shaoqi, and particularly his treatment in the Cultural Revolution, see Dittmer (1974) *Liu Shao-ch'i and the*

*Chinese Cultural Revolution: The Politics of Mass Criticism* (Berkeley: University of California Press). Of the numerous books on Deng Xiaoping, one of the best is Goodman (1994) *Deng Xiaoping and the Chinese Revolution: A Political Biography* (London: Routledge). Lieberthal and Lardy (1983) *Chen Yun's Strategy for China's Development: A Non-Maoist Alternative* (Armonk, N.Y.: M.E. Sharpe) contains an excellent introduction to Chen Yun's ideas as well as a selection of his major speeches. Wilson (1984) *Zhou Enlai: a Biography* (New York: Viking) is a good starting point for the role and impact of Zhou Enlai, while Han Suyin (1994) *Eldest Son: Zhou Enlai and the Making of Modern China, 1898–1976* (New York: Hill and Wang) is an interesting account from a writer who has remained close to the official Chinese government line even when that line has changed.

## Bibliographical Sources

Over a number of years, the Cambridge University Press has developed a comprehensive account of China from the earliest dynasties to the present day in the *Cambridge History of China* series under the general editorship of Twitchett and Fairbank. Volumes 14 and 15 both deal with the Maoist period, the former dealing with the period from 1949 to 1965, and the latter from 1965 to 1982. In addition to excellent chapters covering all areas of politics and society, these volumes contain detailed bibliographical essays which will guide the reader through one of the most extensive lists of sources on Chinese politics in print today.

# BIBLIOGRAPHY OF ALL WORKS CITED IN THE TEXT

Blecher, M. (1986) *China* (London: Pinter).

Bridgham, P. (1968) 'The Fall of Lin Piao' in *The China Quarterly* 34, pp. 1–35.

Cannon, T. (1990) 'Regions: Spatial Inequality and Regional Policy' in Cannon, T. and Jenkins, A. (eds) *The Geography of Contemporary China: The Impact of Deng Xiaoping's Decade* (London: Routledge) pp. 28–60.

Chan, A (1985) *Children of Mao: Personality Development and Political Activism in the Red Guard Generation* (Seattle: University of Washington Press).

Chang, J. (1991) *Wild Swans: Three Daughters of China* (London: Flamingo/Harper Collins).

Chang, P. (1975) *Power and Policy in China* (University Park: Pennsylvania State University Press).

Chen, J. (1975) *Inside The Cultural Revolution* (New York: Macmillan).

Cheng, C.Y. (1982) *China's Economic Development: Growth and Structural Changes* (Boulder: Westview).

Chow, T. (1960) *The May Fourth Movement: Intellectual Revolution In Modern China* (Cambridge, Mass.: Harvard University Press).

Deng Xiaoping (1984) *The Selected Works of Deng Xiaoping* (Beijing: Foreign Languages Press).

Dirlik, A. (1989) *The Origins of Chinese Communism* (New York and Oxford: Oxford University Press).

Djilas, M. (1957) *The New Class; an Analysis of the Communist System* (New York: Praeger).

Domes, J. (1977) *China After the Cultural Revolution: Politics Between Two Party Congresses* (Berkeley: University of California Press).

Donnithorne, A. (1972) 'China's Cellular Economy: Some Economic Trends Since the Cultural Revolution' in *The China Quarterly* 52, pp. 605–19.

Eastman, L. (1984) *Seeds of Destruction: Nationalist China in War and Revolution 1937–1949* (Stanford: Stanford University Press).

Endicott, S. (1988) *Red Earth: Revolution in a Sichuan Village* (London: I.B. Tauris).

Forster, K. (1990) *Rebellion and Factionalism in a Chinese Province: Zhejiang, 1966–1976* (Armonk, N.Y.: M.E. Sharpe).

Gillin, D. (1964) 'Peasant Nationalism in the History of Chinese Communism' in *Journal of Asian Studies* 23 (2).

Goodman, D. (1981) 'The Sixth Plenum of the 11th Central Committee of the CCP: Look Back in Anger?' in *The China Quarterly* 87, pp. 518–27.

Goodman, D. (1986) *Centre and Province in the People's Republic of China: Sichuan and Guizhou 1955–1965* (London: Cambridge University Press).

Granqvist, H. (1967) *The Red Guard: A Report on Mao's Revolution* (London: Pall Mall Press).

Gray, J. (1990) *Rebellions and Revolutions: China from the 1800s to the 1980s* (Oxford and New York: Oxford University Press).

Gregor, A.J. (1995) *Marxism, China and Development* (New Brunswick: Transaction Books).

Gurtov, M. (1969) 'The Foreign Ministry and Foreign Affairs during the Cultural Revolution' in *The China Quarterly* 40, pp. 65–102.

Han Suyin (1976) *Wind in the Tower: Mao Tsetung and the Chinese Revolution, 1949–1975* (London: Cape).

Hinton, H. (1994) 'China as an Asian power' in Robinson, T. and Shambaugh, D. (eds) *Chinese Foreign Policy: Theory and Practice* (Oxford: Clarendon Press).

Hinton, W. (1966) *Fanshen: A Documentary of Revolution in a Chinese Village* (New York: Vintage Books).

Hollingworth, C. (1987) *Mao* (London: Triad Paladin).

Johnson, C. (1962) *Peasant Nationalism and Communist Power: The Emergence of Revolutionary China, 1937–1945* (Stanford: Stanford University Press).

Kane, P. (1988) *Famine in China, 1959–61: Demographic and Social Implications* (London: Macmillan).

Knight, N. (1983) 'The Form of Mao Zedong's "Sinification of Marxism" ' in *The Australian Journal of Chinese Affairs* 9, pp. 17–33.

Lardy, N. (1978) *Economic Growth and Distribution in China* (Cambridge: Cambridge University Press).

Levine, S. (1987) *Anvil of Victory: The Communist Revolution in Manchuria* (New York: Columbia University Press).

Leys, S. (1977) *The Chairman's New Clothes: Mao and the Cultural Revolution* (London: Allison and Busby).

Lieberthal, K. (1993) 'The Great Leap Forward and the Split in the Yan'an Leadership 1958–65' in MacFarquhar, R. (ed.) *The Politics of China 1949–1989* (Cambridge: Cambridge University Press) pp. 87–147.

Lieberthal, K. and Lardy, N. (1983) *Chen Yun's Strategy for China's Development: a Non-Maoist Alternative* (Armonk, N.Y.: M.E. Sharpe).

Liu Guoguang *et al.* (1987) *China's Economy in 2000* (Beijing: New World Press).

MacFarquhar, R. (1973) *Origins of the Cultural Revolution Vol I: Contradictions Among the People, 1956–1957* (Oxford: Oxford University Press).

MacFarquhar, R. (1983) *Origins of the Cultural Revolution Vol II: The Great Leap Forward, 1958–1960* (Oxford: Oxford University Press).

Mao Tsetung (1976) *Poems* (Beijing: Foreign Languages Press).

Mao Zedong (1977) *Mao ZeDong XuanJi: Di Wu Juan (The Collected Works of Mao Zedong: Volume 5)* (Beijing: Renmin Chubanshe).

Naughton, B. (1988) 'The Third Front. Defence Industrialization in the Chinese Interior' in *The China Quarterly* 115, pp. 351–86.

North, R. (1978) *The Foreign Relations of China* (3rd edition) (North Scituate, Mass.: Duxbury).

Radtke, K. (1990) *China's Relations with Japan, 1945–83* (Manchester: Manchester University Press).

Robinson, T. (1971) 'The Wuhan Incident: Local Strife and Provincial Rebellion During the Cultural Revolution' in *The China Quarterly* 47, pp. 413–38.

Rodzinski, W. (1979) *A History of China: Volume II* (Oxford and New York: Pergamon Press).

Ross, R. (1988) *The Indochina Tangle: China's Vietnam Policy, 1975–1979* (New York: Columbia University Press).

Salisbury, H. (1969) *The Coming War Between Russia and China* (London: Pan).

Schram, S. (ed.) *Mao Tse-tung Unrehearsed: Talks and Letters, 1956–71* (Harmondsworth: Penguin).

Schram, S. (1988) *The Thought of Mao Tse-tung* (Cambridge: Cambridge University Press).

Schwartz, B. (1960) 'The Legend of the "Legend of Maoism"' in *The China Quarterly* 2, pp. 35–42.

Selden, M. (1971) *The Yenan Way in Revolutionary China* (Cambridge, Mass.: Harvard University Press).

Shih, V. (1967) *The Taiping Ideology; Its Sources, Interpretations, and Influences* (Seattle: University of Washington Press).

Shum, K.K. (1988) *The Chinese Communists' Road to Power: The Anti-Japanese National United Front, 1935–1945* (Hong Kong and New York: Oxford University Press).

Snow, E. (1937) *Red Star Over China* (London: Gollancz).

Starr, J. (1986) '"Good Mao". "Bad Mao": Mao Studies and the Re-Evaluation of Mao's Political Thought' in *The Australian Journal of Chinese Affairs* 16, pp. 1–22.

Teiwes, F. (1972) 'Provincial Politics in China: Themes and Variations' in Lindbeck, J. (ed.) *China: Management of a Revolutionary Society* (London: Allen and Unwin) pp. 116–89.

Teiwes, F. (1993) 'The Establishment of the New Regime, 1949–1957' in MacFarquhar, R. (ed.) *The Politics of China 1949–1989* (Cambridge: Cambridge University Press) pp. 5–86.

Thaxton, R. (1983) *China Turned Rightside Up: Revolutionary Legitimacy in the Peasant World* (New Haven: Yale University Press).

Unger, J. (1982) *Education under Mao: Class and Competition in Canton Schools, 1960–1980* (New York: Columbia University Press).

Van Ness, P. (1970) *Revolution and Chinese Foreign Policy: Peking's Support for Wars of Liberation* (Berkeley: University of California Press).

Vogel, E. (1969) *Canton Under Communism* (Cambridge, Mass.: Harvard University Press).

White, G. (1976) *The Politics of Class and Class Origin: The Case of the Cultural Revolution* (Canberra: Contemporary China Centre Papers No 9).

White, S., Gardner, J., and Schopflin, G. (1982) *Communist Political Systems: An Introduction* (London: Macmillan).

Whiting, A. (1960) *China Crosses the Yalu: The Decision to Enter the Korean War* (New York: Macmillan).

Whitney, J. (1969) *China: Area, Administration and Nation Building* (Chicago: University of Chicago Press).

Whitson, W. (1969) 'The Field Army in Chinese Communist Military Politics' in *The China Quarterly* 37, pp. 1–30.

Whitson, W. (1972) 'Organizational Perspectives and Decision Making in the Chinese Communist High Command' in Scalapino, R. (ed.) *Elites in the People's Republic of China* (Seattle: University of Washington Press) pp. 381–415.

Whitson, W. and Huang, C. (1973) *The Chinese High Command: A History of Communist Military Politics, 1927–71* (New York: Praeger).

Wilson, R. (1979) *Mao, the People's Emperor* (London: Hutchinson).

Witke, R. (1977) *Comrade Chiang Ching* (Boston: Little, Brown).

Wright, M. (1957) *The Last Stand of Chinese Conservatism* (Stanford: Stanford University Press).

# MAPS

Map 1. Modern China.
Based on a map produced by the CIA, made available on the World Wide
Web by the University of Texas at Austen as part of the Perry–Castañeda
Map Collection (http://www.lib.utexas.edu/Libs/PCL/Map_collection).

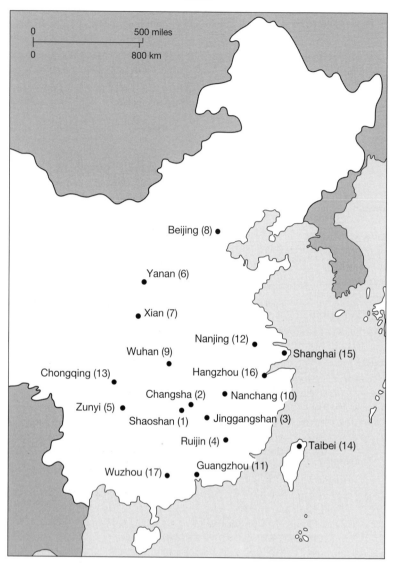

Map 2. Key locations for the history of Mao's China (for notes see facing page).

*Notes to map 2*

1. Shaoshan: Mao's birthplace.
2. Changsha: Where Mao went to school and later worked in the Changsha Normal School. Also the site of Mao's abortive 'Autumn Harvest' uprising.
3. Jinggangshan: The original safe haven in Jiangxi province that Mao and others fled to after the failed uprising of 1927.
4. Ruijin: The capital of the Jiangxi Soviet.
5. Zunyi: The site of the conference in 1935 where Mao became *de facto* head of the CCP.
6. Yanan: The communist headquarters after the Long March and throughout the war against Japan.
7. Xian: The site of Chiang Kai-shek's kidnapping by the northern warlords which led to the creation of the second United Front.
8. Beijing: China's capital before the collapse of the empire in 1911, and once again after the revolution.
9. Wuhan: Birthplace of the 1911 revolution and the site of intra-military conflict at the height of the cultural revolution. Also briefly twice China's capital under the Guomindang – first as they moved north before taking Nanjing, and later as the Guomindang fled Nanjing after the Japanese invasion.
10. Nanchang: Site of a doomed communist uprising in 1927.
11. Guangzhou (Canton): The Guomindang's headquarters after Yuan Shikai ignored the national election result in 1912. The scene of many and bitter battles during the 1920s. Also the site of a short-lived commune after the communist uprising in December 1927.
12. Nanjing: Capital of China after the 1911 revolution, and again after the Guomindang established a new national government after the Northern Expedition. Site of the 'Rape of Nanjing' after the Japanese invasion, and of the puppet regime of Wang Jingwei under Japanese control.
13. Chongqing: Became the Guomindang's base during the war against Japan.
14. Taibei (Taipei): The capital of the Guomindang's Republic of China from 1949 to the present day.
15. Shanghai: China's major commercial centre, and one of the centres of radicalism during the Cultural Revolution. The basis of the Gang of Four's power in the early 1960s.
16. Hangzhou: Another centre of radical leftism. Site of a number of important conferences and meetings at the outset of the Cultural Revolution.
17. Wuzhou: Scene of the intense fighting between rival groups during the Cultural Revolution.

# INDEX

Page references in **bold** refer to glossary entries.